True Stories

True Stories

*Guides for Writing
from Your Life*

Rebecca Rule & Susan Wheeler

HEINEMANN
PORTSMOUTH, NH

Heinemann
361 Hanover Street
Portsmouth, NH 03801–3912
www.heinemann.com

Offices and agents throughout the world

Library of Congress Cataloging-in-Publication Data
Rule, Rebecca.
    True stories : guides to writing from your life / Rebecca Rule and
Susan Wheeler.
        p.   cm.
    Includes bibliographical references (p.).
    ISBN 0-325-00046-8
    1. Authorship.   2. Journalism—Authorship.   I. Wheeler, Susan,
1936–   .   II. Title.
PN147.R76   2000
808'.02—dc21   99-41956
                                                            CIP

Editor: Tom Newkirk
Production: Renée Le Verrier
Cover design: Darci Mehall/Aureo Design
Manufacturing: Louise Richardson

Printed in the United States of America on acid-free paper
Docutech RRD 2008

To Adi Rule and Chris Cote
whose creativity inspires me every day.

For my brother Sandy
and as always, for Walker

CONTENTS

Contents

ACKNOWLEDGMENTS

THERE IS AN ENERGETIC EXCHANGE OF TEACHING IDEAS AND strategies in the composition department at U.N.H., and we have, as we did with our first book, swapped and stolen ideas from so many outstanding instructors that we can't remember now who invented or developed what. Their talent and dedication have nourished, prodded, and challenged our teaching and writing. We thank them as well as past instructors Elizabeth Chiseri-Strater, Mary Peterson, Bruce Ballenger, Barry Lane, and directors Pat Sullivan, Andy Merton, Sarah Sherman, and Les Fisher. We thank Don Murray who taught both of us in writing courses and later, during his years as director of composition. His influence is strong and obvious throughout the book. Pam Barksdale, Leslie Brown, Meredith Hall, and Barbara Tindall read parts of an early draft and made specific suggestions, many of which we adopted. We thank our student writers at U.N.H., at the New Hampshire Writers and Publishers seminars, as well as those writers in the Summer Studies Program at U.N.H., The Molasses Pond Summer Writers Retreat, and The Twin Farms Writers Workshop, sponsored by a wonderful couple, Dr. Gijs and Titia Bozuwa, in Wakefield, N.H.

We have been and are delighted with and grateful for Tom Newkirk who is the editor for this book. He has known when to let us work on our own and when to step in with advice; and his suggestions have been excellent. He has had a profound influence on our teaching for years as a former, and now again a current director of composition at U.N.H. We thank him as well as all the others at Heinemann who have helped enormously in pulling the book together.

Finally we thank our husbands for their wonderful support and encouragement.

ABOUT TRUE STORIES

What about we

ONE CHALLENGE WHEN COLLABORATING ON *True Stories* HAS BEEN what to call ourselves. We—Sue Wheeler and Becky Rule—have decided to call ourselves *we*. "We got our hair cut" doesn't mean we sat on top of one another in a swivel chair gossiping with the hairdresser. It means one of us is telling a story about getting a haircut, but it doesn't matter *who*, so we use the generic *we* instead.

Occasionally, when it seems to matter and especially when discussing our work, we call ourselves Becky or Sue.

What about truth

THIS IS NONFICTION, SO NO LYING ALLOWED—OSTENSIBLY. TELL the whole truth, the absolute truth, and nothing but the truth, as you perceive it. But that's the tricky part: perception. No two people perceive in exactly the same way; no two people will recall an event or a conversation in exactly the same way, even though they were standing side by side. You say the preacher wore white socks; your cousin says, no, they were lemon yellow. One of you is wrong; yet each of you is telling the truth.

Some writers, editors, and readers believe if you don't tell the truth exactly as you remember it, down to the color of the preacher's socks, you're not trustworthy. They say if you don't remember whether the socks were white or yellow, don't mention the color.

Some writers say, Who gives a damn. Our memories are often wrong anyway. If four people view a car accident, the police report will reflect four different, even conflicting, versions of the truth. The argument has been made that the truth doesn't exist or is unknowable. So why not lie a little, or a lot?

In Hillary Nelson's "Mildred's Snowdrops" (page 267) readers expect that the author really did, as she says, pick snowdrops in Canterbury, New Hampshire, the April after her mother-in-law died. Not daisies or wild roses but snowdrops. The reader believes the author picked those flowers, brought them home, and put them in "a sea-glass soft medicine bottle that Mildred had once dug up from deep in our garden." And that day, while the author was showing her daughter "the place where bright green hearts hide under a snowdrop's petals," her husband walked in and asked a pertinent question: "Where'd you get those?" And Hillary Nelson answered, "From your Mom," even though his mother had been dead a year.

On the other hand (and we're not suggesting Hillary Nelson employed this technique), what if when she brought the flowers home she put them in a canning jar, and only when writing did she think that she *could have* put them in the medicine bottle, and that if she had it would have provided a convenient way to get more of Mildred on her last page?

Or what if when the husband came in he didn't say "Where'd you get those?" right away? What if he complained that the mechanic charged them $260 for a tune-up? What if he then said, "Hey, those are pretty. What are they, snapdragons? Where'd you get them?"

Is it legitimate for Hillary to omit her husband's comment about the car and tweak the wording of his question? Maybe; maybe not. You must decide for yourself where to draw the line—and how much to stretch it in your own work.

Here's another kind of stretching that sometimes goes on in creative nonfiction. Some writers and teachers say, Who doesn't change events or even invent them? They believe it's fine to alter the objective truth about the acts and personalities of their subjects if these distortions are closer to the writer's emotional truth, or if such distortions make for a more artistic and powerful story. Some nonfiction writers even believe it's fine to invent people.

For us, these practices go too far. Here's why. First, when you change events, readers will know—eventually. Someone will point out that, in fact, there was no battle on this location on this date, so you couldn't have been wounded there. Whether readers see this as a deliberate distortion or a mistake, you lose their trust. Second, when you distort a person's acts or personality, that person—or someone close to him—may find out and be rightfully hurt or outraged. So many memoirs published in the last two decades reveal relatives, acquaintances, colleagues as sadistic, perverted, or eccentric that we've become cynical about how much truth there is in these books, and how much they exaggerate in quest of a bestseller.

Let's say your mother badly frightened you a couple of times when you were a child. She never hit you, but twice you feared she might. Once, in anger, she burst into your room after you'd gone to bed, turned on the light, and said that you'd dressed up in her clothes, ripped her favorite silk dress, smeared lipstick on her coat. Too frightened to defend yourself, you sat up in bed and watched, stunned, as she flung open your closet, yanked out an armful of your clothes, and threw them in a pile, shouting, "Now you know what it feels like to have someone invade your closet and ruin your things!"

An emotionally tough individual might experience this scene without being scarred by it, especially if, most of the time, mother was reasonable, friendly, warm, funny. But what if you were extremely sensitive? Let's say the incident *felt* much worse to you than it actually was, that it triggered a fear of violence that has escalated over time. When you write about the incident, the *factual* truth doesn't approach the horror of your *emotional* truth. Is it ethical, sensible, artistically defensible to say, "My mother cut one of my dresses with the kitchen shears"? Or to describe the shears, the sound they made as they sliced the fabric, and the look on your mother's face as she let the pieces fall to the floor as if it actually happened that way?

Let's say this narrative ends up in a desk drawer. After you die, your daughter finds it and shares it with other relatives. Suddenly, the woman-with-the-shears, who is named and known personally by many still-alive relatives and friends, and indirectly by even more, has been smeared. And all because you wanted to express *your* emotional truth. We've read creative nonfiction in which the writer presents his family as perhaps flawed but still economically successful, intelligent, decent. Nevertheless, the writer seems to think nothing of distorting, say, the character of a maid or a garbage man into an oaf or a thief for the sake of a good story. That's wrong. We don't like it.

If you want to explore the *emotional* truth by fictionalizing, write fiction. If you want to combine fiction and nonfiction, we urge you to tell readers exactly what you're doing. Consider explaining which people and incidents you've changed. In this way, you can be fair to your subjects and readers, as well as respectful of history.

Think carefully before you deviate from what you know or believe to be true. And if you have pressing reasons to opt for changes, minor or major, make those changes with integrity and a wise and generous heart.

Whenever possible, opt for accuracy, especially when the facts are known to others who might contradict you. If you're writing about baseball and you've got a guy playing outfield for San Francisco when he's actually the starting shortstop for the Orioles, somebody *will* call you a liar. Or, at the very least, misinformed. And readers won't be able to take your writing seriously.

Our guess is that Hillary Nelson may not recall *exactly* what her husband said when he got home from the garage and saw the snowdrops. Our guess is that she re-created the scene based on what she remembered about what he probably said. She told the truth as she truthfully perceived it. Which is all readers of nonfiction expect, all they demand.

To our readers

WHETHER YOU'RE A STUDENT TAKING A REQUIRED COURSE OR A retiree with time, at last, to write the family history or a parent with two preschoolers, twins on the way, a dog who has fits, and an idea for an article; whether you've been abused as a child and want to examine your experience on the page or you hiked the Appalachian Trail and would encourage others to try it; whether you're an occupational therapist or a psychologist or a teacher or a police officer or a commercial fisherman who wants to write—welcome.

You're in for a fascinating journey. When you write about your life and the lives around you, when you spell out your opinions and ideas, research special interests, record, describe, examine, analyze, and frame experience, you will discover insights. As these insights accumulate, you may change your opinions, ideas, and attitudes. Writing is a lens for seeing yourself and the world, a vehicle for re-seeing and reevaluating. It can change your life. It can become a way of life. We recommend it.

As you write regularly and seriously, you will learn the value of the process of getting an idea or an inkling, playing with it in your head, recording it, and revising to discover more and to do justice to your subject. For purposes of this book, your subject is yourself and your particular, evolving take on the world. Our emphasis is truth: writing true stories, seeking truth, insight, meaning. We use the word *story* not to mean fiction (short stories or novels) but to describe the this-really-happened stories of your life.

True stories emerge from activities, events, incidents, moments. They are set in places you know, places you once visited and never forgot, places so familiar you could walk around blindfolded and not bump the furniture. They concern family, friends, enemies, colleagues, mentors—people who affect you positively, negatively, or both. These stories are stimulated by what you read and what you think about what you read. They may be triggered by a television show, a movie, or a play. They are your visceral response to some political diatribe shaped into a scathing letter to the editor or speech at the city council meeting. True stories can be detailed accounts of what you do or think. When you express your opinions, your confusion, your memories, your convictions, your reactions, your passions and describe their evolution, that's a story. A true story is whatever you want and need and choose to express as nonfiction rather than poetry, fiction, song, drama, dance, or primal scream.

We believe in the value of expression and expressive writing. If you dash off a throw-away letter to a nasty boss or teacher, blasting him, you'll probably feel better afterwards. This book shows how to shape your feelings, ideas, and passions into something more targeted than blast. (Though we are not entirely opposed to blast.) Other books call these shapes by different names: essays, op-ed pieces, letters to the editor, critiques, arguments, comparison/contrasts, autobiography, memoir, analyses, sketches, narratives, articles, features, reviews, position papers, research projects. Different authors offer different definitions for these forms, which can be confusing.

We don't want to confuse you. Let's just say that for us names are less important than possibilities. We will encourage you to explore, shape, and reshape the material associated with a certain angle on a certain topic until the words on the page express what is in your head and heart. Here are four names we will use from time to time, mainly so we don't have to say "that thing you're working on whatever it turns out to be."

Essay

By this we mean trying out an idea to see where it goes. Often an essay will involve some personal experience, but at its heart is a concept. For example, Sandell Morse in "Canning Jars" (page 263) writes about an encounter at a secondhand shop, an experience.

But the concept the experience reveals and explores is prejudice and how one chooses to respond to it.

Argument

By this we mean an essay that attempts to persuade the reader to believe what the writer believes. Aren't all essays persuasive? Sure. But some are more blatant in their attempts to win readers over. Letters to the editor, op-ed pieces, position papers, political analyses—these are particular forms of argument. Our chapter "Passion on the Page" addresses the art of argument: how to drive home a point without sounding deranged.

Narrative

Here the balance shifts. If an essay is mostly *idea supported by story*, a narrative is mostly *story supporting an idea*. Is a narrative an essay? Yes. Is it an argument? Could be. Especially if your story is about the abortion you had when you were fifteen and how that decision continues to affect your political views. Pat Wilson in "Rabbit Doll" (page 281) spins a narrative about shopping at a crafts fair. She sees a doll. Buys it. Brings it home. Tosses it in the air. End of story.

Embedded in the narrative, however, is the narrator's ambivalence about her choice not to have children, and—between the lines—a commentary on what career women may be giving up when they make that choice.

A narrative may also contain comparisons and contrasts, especially when the writer compares what he once thought about an event to what he thinks about it *now* as he writes. Alan DeCosta in "Tracks" (page 248) focuses on a morning of cross-country skiing and, in recounting the events and his thoughts, addresses notions of independence, life-purpose, and loneliness—what skiing meant to him once is contrasted with what it means to him now.

Research project

We hesitate to say research *paper*. Papers are what teachers assign you—and some of you may not be in school, so we prefer *project*. We think an excellent research project resembles a feature you might read in *Smithsonian* or *Harpers*, including information, anecdotes, quotes from experts, and a personal connection between the author and the subject, perhaps a recounting of personal experience.

Becky wrote about an ocean-side campground in Maine. She read what others had written; interviewed owners, workers, campers; spent time on site observing; and included childhood memories of camping. She published the article in *Yankee*. Had she written the same thing for a college writing class, it would have qualified as a research project.

Techniques suggested throughout this book, from time stretches to flash-forwards and dialogue, can be used to make information-dense writing more lively—with your teacher's or editor's permission, of course. Some teachers or editors will forbid the use of I. Some will tell you not to offer your opinion or quote directly. Some will list rules on everything from margin width to number of sources. These rules can be helpful; they let you know the boundaries so you can work within them. And if you want a good grade or publication in that magazine, you better darn well follow them.

We won't give you a long list of rules; you will set your own boundaries. But we will detail ways to meld and mold information, experience, and opinion. If the finished product mixes personal experience and opinion with facts, statistics, and quotations from interviews or books, we call that a research project.

Piece

When we don't know what to call something, or want to suggest that it could be *anything*, we call it a "piece." The truth is, what you call your writing is less important than fully engaging with your subject, trying different forms, mixing and matching. You will see that a strong narrative not only uses the persuasive techniques of argument but *is* persuasive. You will discover that as a nonfiction writer you can borrow techniques from fiction writers and poets and playwrights, just as they borrow from other genres. In other words, forms and genres blur.

True Stories is, in itself, a long narrative-argument-essay-research project-review on the topic of writing nonfiction. We discuss craft and process—the techniques and skills writers need. We quote from fiction and nonfiction stories because we want to illustrate our points with the best examples we can find, whatever the form. We discuss ethics. We present ways to approximate other points of view without appropriating them. We encourage you to read widely and attentively, adopting techniques from writers you admire. And we expect that as you write and read, you'll resee, reevaluate, and learn more about your experiences, your life. You'll go through your days with sharper eyes and ears. You'll become more tuned to your senses. You'll speculate about people, places, events, ideas. You'll become, as artists and photographers do, a keen observer. And your life will be enriched.

To teachers

WE ENCOURAGE STUDENTS TO WRITE FROM WHAT CHURNS THEM up intellectually and emotionally. Usually this means stories— their true stories and the stories of people they know. We don't view these stories or narratives as baby steps to be followed, in time, by more important, intellectual, and difficult tasks like writing argument, analysis, or exposition. To us, writing is writing is expression. Form matters because it allows expression. Mastering a certain form is not the goal; expression is. A book-length argument on a philosophical or scientific theory is no more difficult or advanced than a novel or a memoir. All forms are demanding. All build on insights and ideas. All are persuasive and contain comparisons and analyses. All are important. But what's even more important is to hone skills on material that matters to the writer. We learn faster and write with greater meaning when we are fascinated by our subjects as opposed to being merely interested in them.

Although we appreciate the fact that forms merge, we are not cavalier about them. Writers who study different forms and understand their usefulness will develop a repertoire of approaches to subjects and audiences. Anthologies organized by form show a range of choices and how one piece fits several categories. Reading from anthologies leads writers to subjects and may help them see new ways to express themselves. You'll find some of our favorites in "Recommended Reading," page 283.

We have discovered that after students write what they want for most of a semester, which is almost always personal and in the form of stories, skills carry over into research projects, reading responses, reviews, and arguments. These forms can be addressed directly as in-class exercises and revised at home or assigned. Our students consistently say it is easier to write literature papers and research projects than narratives that have shape and meaning. Personal essays, narratives, true stories—call them what you like —seem easy only if students haven't learned the craft, haven't learned to delve beneath the surface to seek and express meaning.

Which is why we wrote *True Stories*: to teach them how.

GETTING STARTED

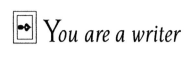 # You are a writer

IF YOU'VE KEPT A DIARY, RECORDED YOUR TRAVELS IN A DAYBOOK, filed away ideas for the memoir you might write some day when you have time, you are a writer. If you're an e-mail junkie; if you've written letters, memos, reports, press releases, speeches, or articles for the company newsletter; if you've worked on essay exams, term papers, or poems, you are a writer.

Perhaps this startles or embarrasses you. For some, the word writer is in caps: WRITER. Writers publish. Young. Probably six or eight or twenty books. They win prizes. They have MFAs. They appear on TV. They speak in complete sentences. They've read everything.

This may be true of some writers, but not many. And to fantasize that these attributes define writers is wrong-headed and counter-productive.

Of course, you admire some published writers and wish you could write with their skills. But they were writers even at the beginnings of their careers. They wrote a lot. They improved. They sent out their best work, which was rejected again and again. Kept writing. One day, an editor bought something. They went back to their computers and wrote some more. Got rejected again. Sold another piece or two. And kept writing.

Writing is a lifelong apprenticeship, like many others—painting, teaching, engineering, fixing automobiles, acting, designing buildings. You never stop learning. There is no magical moment when the apprentice transforms from writer to WRITER. The real writer works away at her desk; she hasn't time to think about whether she's capitalized or not.

On the other hand, wanting to be a writer, saying you're going to write, imagining that you *could* write or you *will* write, doesn't get words on the page. If you want to play clarinet with an orchestra, you don't just buy an instrument and show up for a few rehearsals. To become an accomplished clarinetist, you must put your heart and talent and lips and ear and dexterity and focus and time into the task. You are not waiting for the day when you become a MUSICIAN. You are a musician all along, learning your craft.

Some dedicated and serious writers compose poetry or essays or stories in their journals and never show them. Some belong to workshop groups and share drafts regularly. In our town, once a month writers come from all over to read their original works aloud at a series called "Writers Among Us." We never know who will show up or what they will read, but we applaud their efforts. And we notice that those who keep writing over a year or two get much better at it. Writers in school share with classmates and the teacher, who, in turn, may be writing each summer and sharing work with other teachers, writer friends, or editors. We know an eighty-six-year-old woman who writes down her most interesting encounters and thoughts each day. She's been doing this for more than ten years. A group of retirees took a class with us fifteen years ago. They decided to keep meeting after the class ended. Members came and went. The group continues to meet monthly. They critique work, and publish a small magazine to showcase their best. Several of these dedicated writers have published elsewhere, too, in bigger magazines, even books.

These people are writers. Your stories don't have to be available in hardcover at the local bookstore or printed in the paper for you to think like a writer, act like a writer, be a writer. If you take your work seriously and work hard, steadily, as time allows, you are a member of the community of writers.

It is an energizing, supportive, creative community.

Welcome.

◫ Dare to take yourself seriously

YOU MUST BELIEVE THIS: YOU ARE IMPORTANT. YOU AND YOUR experiences, your questions, your opinions, your ideas and feelings are important and interesting. The things and people you notice, and what you think and feel and say about what you notice, are important and interesting. Your spiritual quests, your loves, your hates, your jealousies, your competitions, your drives for excellence, your fears and angers, your failures, your triumphs, your losses and griefs and joys are important and interesting. They matter. Write about them.

You must trust your world and way of seeing and write the stories only you can write. Don't try to sound like other writers. Tell your truths as you experience them. Sound like yourself. Your favorite writers were true to their visions.

If you had Mrs. Bascomb in Grade 7, you were told not to use the word I in an essay. She said that because she thought you were young and not terribly well read, your ideas were likely invalid, or at least they were not very important. But we are here to tell you this:

MRS. BASCOMB WAS WRONG.

Some of our students have said, "Who cares about my life in a small Kansas town?" or "How dull to be middle-class and middle-aged." Whether you're a farmer, a nuclear physicist, a mother, or a doctor; whether you live in a penthouse in New York City, a bungalow in East Iowa Falls, or a yurt in Alaska; whether you're eighty years old or eighteen: Trust that your way of seeing and thinking and feeling and knowing are worth writing about.

They are. Write about them.

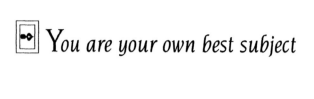
You are your own best subject

SOME PEOPLE BELIEVE—YOU MAY EVEN HAVE BEEN TAUGHT—THAT it isn't nice to talk about yourself. If you do talk about yourself, these people say, be brief, be discrete. These are the same people who say politics should never be discussed at a dinner party.

Why not?

Diners might get fired up? Passionate? Raise voices? Friends might try to persuade one another to change their minds or see a new angle?

That's the essence of essay—trying out ideas.

A woman at a cookout started to talk about a fall down Tuckerman's Ravine. After only four or five minutes, she broke off her harrowing narrative: "Oh, I've really talked too much. It's someone else's turn."

Was she kidding? A fall down Tuckerman's Ravine, that enormous crevasse between the biggest mountains east of the Mississippi? Who wouldn't want to hear more? We missed out on a good story that might have got us thinking, gasping, wondering, imagining, all because the speaker didn't trust that her story mattered, that her listeners would care about it and her.

In an Introduction to Art History course in college, we encountered a professor who said, "When you talk with me or when you write papers for this course, don't say whether you like or dislike a painting; at this point you don't know enough to have an opinion worth discussing."

Well, we didn't know much, but had we been able to air our developing opinions, then studied and learned more, we could have revised, revisited, revamped, and re-created our initial impressions. We would have had something to build on and with.

When you dare to express an opinion on the page, you can examine it more carefully than if you just think it, or worse, stop yourself from thinking it at all because you have been brainwashed to believe your thoughts aren't worth much.

Everyone holds back sometimes. We doubt ourselves and our opinions, even our intelligence. Sometimes our confidence leaves us, cowers in a corner, and we can't find it anywhere. Of course, if you're asked in an essay exam to compare the east and west pediments of the Parthenon, you will not gush over your favorite figure. That's not the point of the question. For a statistical report on the fat content of ten processed foods, you won't begin with a story about the time your brother stole your Twinkie. But for writing inspired by your life and experience, true stories are central, because your fundamental subject is how you see your life and the lives of others.

To write well you must have confidence. You must believe in the importance of ME, because ME is also YOU and US. The more particular you are—the more you reveal the specifics of your situation—the more universal your points will be. To understand politics, don't try to write the history of the United Nations, unless you have five or ten years to devote to the subject. Examine instead a heated exchange at your recent town meeting between two selectmen on opposite sides of the Barking Dog Ordinance. And it would help if you own a dog who barks.

Writers need to believe that readers care about barking dogs and the quirks of law enforcement in small towns or big cities. Writers need to know that understanding the complications surrounding the Barking Dog Ordinance can lead to an understanding of complications on a global scale.

Writers need egos—and we need to keep them well fed, at least when we are at our desks. We may be insecure in some situations, but when we write, we must forget our insecurities. We must push them away and focus on our subjects. We must allow ourselves to be fascinated. We must believe our ideas and our experiences count, our slants on life are original and valid. Not when we grow up. Not when we've taken more classes. Not when we've passed through menopause or gone bald or made our first million on a bestseller.

Now, dammit. Now.

# Ways writers write

YOU WILL DEVELOP YOUR OWN WAY OF WORKING. NO TWO WRITERS, probably, work in exactly the same way. But all serious writers have this in common: We write many drafts.

Writing can be all of the following: fascinating, playful, fun, exciting, gut-grindingly slow, surprising, frustrating, infuriating, misery-making, therapeutic, amusing, joyous. When you've finished a piece that matters to you, and done the subject justice, writing can be profoundly satisfying.

First comes the idea or a whisper of it. You're intrigued; you sense you're on to something. You may feel a tingle of excitement. You may feel exhilarated. You may feel drawn to your desk, anxious to begin. Don't talk about your idea; it may drift away or burn itself out. Get to work on it—in your head, in your journal, in a first draft.

Some writers play with ideas in their heads for an hour or a day or even, in some cases, for months or years. At this stage, you are a child—open to possibilities. The critic in your head is banished. Just as a child at the beach sifts sand through her fingers, wondering if she'll make a castle or dig a hole or sculpt a dragon, writers take notes, make lists, consider their inkling of an idea uncritically.

Some writers advise, "Don't attempt a first draft until your thoughts reach the boiling point and threaten to blow off the top of your head." Others say, "If I waited that long, I'd be dead." Some plunge into first drafts on hunches, feeling that if they did any pre-writing or pre-thinking, the hunch would go stale. Some take notes in journals. Many nurture ideas before drafting. They know how an idea can crystallize in the shower, on a bus, during a party, while washing dishes. Try different methods and see what works for you.

After gestation comes the birthing process: Draft 1. For some, words come in a rush—scenes, facts, and details spill out so fast the writers leave blanks on their pages. They know they'll need to come back and expand, but for now they are too bombarded with forward-moving thoughts and images to stop.

For others, words come slowly and first drafts can be agony. One writer we know has to perfect each word in a sentence before he goes on to the next sentence. He asks, "How can you possibly skip ahead?"

Often slow writers are plagued by nasty critics in their heads. (See "Bypassing Writer's Block," page 231.) These writers must work hard to muffle the critics if they are to get any work done at all. Such a writer might elude her critic with bursts of several paragraphs or pages, but then the critic catches up. She stares at the screen, pulls on her ear until her hearing aid beeps. During lulls, she's happy when her coffee mug is empty so she can leave her desk and fill it. In a few minutes—or an hour, or more—the next idea, example, detail, or scene will sneak by the critic and she's off again.

After the first draft, many writers let the work cool for a few days in order to gain objectivity and let the critic have her say. You'll find revision can be a pleasure when you know a first draft is good, and when you want to make it even better. In revision you distance yourself from the passion or agony or euphoria of the first draft. Now you evaluate what's effective and what isn't and determine how to move on. This distance will grow draft by draft. By the time you reach a final draft, you will see your work coldly, analytically, clearly.

Even after the "final" draft, it is wise to put the piece away for days or weeks. Start something new or revisit something old. Then pull out that "final" draft once more. Often, you'll see improvements you'll want to make.

How do you know when a piece is truly done? When you've put it aside; reworked it; had it critiqued by fellow writers, teachers, editors; when you've looked at it coldly and said, "I can do no more."

Try this

1. Read interviews with published writers who talk about the excitement, drudgery, and occasional urge to leap off a bridge or become an accountant. It can be instructive, inspiring, and comforting

to read what they have to say. Your librarian can point you to collections of interviews, including Donald M. Murray's *Shoptalk: Learning to Write with Writers* and *Writers at Work: The Paris Interviews*. Tapes, CDs, and videos are also available.

2. Go to readings at colleges, bookstores, libraries. Hear writers' written words in their own voices. Often, after the reading, writers will take questions or discuss their work.

Jot down random ideas

YOU'RE WALKING DOWN THE AISLE OF A SUPERMARKET OR WATCHing a baseball game from the bleachers or waiting in a restaurant for a friend. If an idea strikes you, jot it down. Maybe it's an ending to a half-written essay. Maybe the perfect title hits you as you're waiting for a bus. You think you'll remember it, but you might not, so carry a pen or pencil at all times. Carry a notebook in your pocket or a folded piece of blank paper.

The act of recording ideas, impressions, feelings, memories, encounters, words, and phrases sharpens the mind. It makes you more susceptible, open to possibilities, fascinated by oddities. Throw your jottings into a shoe box. During a dry spell, open it. Often, you'll find several subjects worth writing about.

◧ Finding good subjects

TO FIND YOUR BEST SUBJECTS, ALWAYS LOOK WITHIN YOURSELF first. Do you have a strong conflict with someone or has something dramatic happened in your life that you want to write about? Do you need to make a critically important decision? If so, you don't need to list several possible dramatic subjects or try mapping or any of the strategies we suggest here. Just start writing now.

You may find that occasionally, as many of us do, you'll be stumped and need a nudge or jolt to find a good subject. We've listed ways we and other writers have found ideas and we believe many of them will work for you. Most of these strategies can be found in exercises throughout our book, but we have gathered a number of them here in case you need a head start.

1. List your train wrecks. These are big, obvious experiences you've had that you know are worth revisiting. Start with emotional, dramatic, perhaps traumatic experiences: a divorce; living with a mentally ill sibling; braving a hurricane; experiencing the death of a friend or an enemy; flunking out of school; getting fired; winning a championship game; adjusting to retirement, school, a new roommate, a new community, physical changes or limitations; being diagnosed with cancer; working as a pit mechanic; living with an abusive parent; trying to get rid of (or get close to) a lover or friend; suffering a crisis of faith; being rejected by a club or group; being labeled, publicly ridiculed, an object of prejudice.

If you discover a gold mine experience that demands to be excavated, start writing now. Write what you remember, in detail and in general. Write what you felt, thought, did, didn't do. Write what you feel, think, wish you had done, hadn't done. Write it all.

2. List conflicts, past and present. These conflicts can be external —a street gang is after you; you were caught in a blizzard and went off the road; your credit is bad. The conflicts can be internal—you want to stop drinking or gaining weight or shoplifting. Conflicts can also be simultaneously internal and external—you've been diagnosed with a chronic illness and are struggling to stay positive; you need to improve your grades, but you're working and have no time to study; you want to free yourself from a sour relationship, but fear being alone; you want to win the skating championship but you clutch in competition; you want to move into an apartment of your own, but your parents' home provides financial and emotional security; your Visa is maxed out but you must have those fabulous shoes to wear to the dance.

When you write, state the central conflict in the first paragraph to hook yourself and readers. It will provide energy, focus, direction, and momentum.

3. List the following emotionally and experientially loaded words on two or three sheets of paper. Leave lots of room between words. Then go back and fill in the name of someone or something associated with each, perhaps a phrase or two to remind you of an experience or idea.

love	jealousy	procrastination	grief
joy	failure	success	anger
humor	fear	distractions	hope
goals	dreams	humiliation	hate
loss	greed	courage	discipline
beliefs	faith	competition	wish
want	injustice	embarrassment	revelation
disgust	respect	inspiration	panic
karma	loser	excellence	luck
despair	winner	obsession	enemy
friend			

Do this exercise quickly. Some words will not resonate for you. Fine. Leave them blank. If one word appears in several places—if *mother* is listed under love, hate, fear, injustice, friend, and enemy—you've got a loaded subject.

4. List by mapping. Mapping is nonlinear listing. More visual than other forms of brainstorming, maps allow us to associate up, down, around, and sideways. Place a word that's emotionally or intellectually charged for you in the center of a page. Circle it. Then draw lines out from the center, adding words or phrases you associate with the central word. You may find yourself circling out and out and out. Work quickly. Some words will lead nowhere. That's fine. Go with the ones that lead somewhere—a word to a phrase to a memory to a name to a notion to a word to a feeling. The object is to get thoughts flowing, to map the territory, to see if a subject reveals itself (please see the example on page 29).

5. List questions. Begin with something you want or need to figure out.

- Should I major in engineering to please my parents, or sociology, which I love?
- Should I take this job even though it means uprooting my family and leaving friends?
- What are my immediate and long-term personal goals?
- What are my dreams?
- How can I cope with my neighbor who calls every day to complain about our boundary line, his arthritis, our dog, his cat, the president, the local laundry that scorched his white shirt?
- Should I have children?
- Should I quit my job to become a full-time poet?
- Should I stay in my own house, move to an apartment, or move into a retirement-to-grave home?
- Should I end this relationship?
- How can I reconcile with my brother after five years of estrangement?
- Why is it so hard for me to take risks?
- Why do I lie?
- Do I want to change religions?

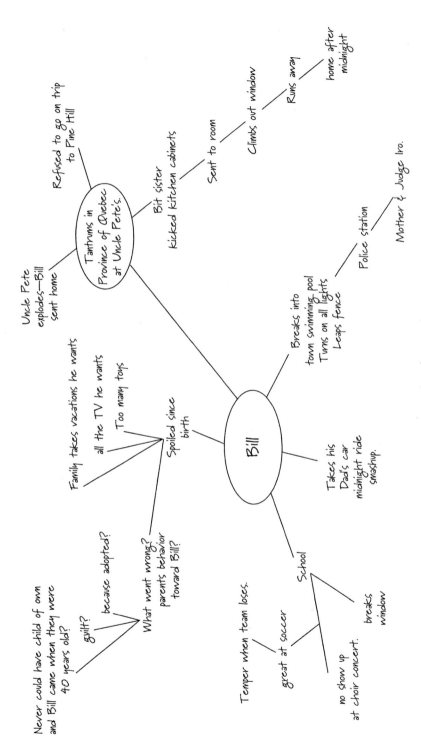

An example of mapping.

Choose one question to write from and about. If the question seems too big, you may want to break it down into smaller questions in hopes that one of those will provide a break-in point. For example, Why do I lie? might lead to When do I lie? When was the last time I lied? To whom? What did the lie accomplish? Do I lie to myself? Am I too much like my father, a notorious liar? Do people realize I lie? Aren't they really just "white lies" that don't hurt anyone? What is a white lie? Has my lying ever led to serious problems? Should I go into therapy? Doesn't everybody lie? When is it good to lie? Can a person become addicted to lying? Am I?

Grab a thread that seems to lead somewhere. You may find that the question with which you began is not the one you're most interested in exploring. That's fine. Write to answer the question that interests. Don't worry if you can't actually answer it. What matters is the attempt, the exploration of an idea, the possibilities revealed. The best questions do not lend themselves to easy answers; in fact, the more you think about them, the more complicated and unanswerable they seem.

6. List your flaws. Brainstorm flaws that cause you trouble: taking on too many projects; procrastinating; losing your temper; sloppiness; being gloomy or selfish or manic; making impulsive decisions without thinking them through; showing insensitivity; being overly sensitive; drinking or eating or exercising or working or watching television too much; overspending; being underconfident or bossy or whiny.

Start by stating the flaw briefly. Then explore how it creates problems for you and others. This exploration will probably take the form of a story or a series of anecdotes. As you write, you will see the effect of the flaw on you or others. You may want to speculate on how this flaw came to be and why, and on how you might overcome it. You may decide it's not so bad after all, resolve to live with it, or even embrace it.

This kind of essay has tension from the start. You're motivated to keep writing because you want clarification and understanding.

7. List smalls. For auction-goers smalls are the little objects you might collect or bid on—salt-and-pepper shakers, spoons, knick-

knacks, buttons, cups and saucers, hand tools, rickrack. For writers, smalls are bits and pieces of experience that may not seem like much at first but can lead you in, lead you on, lead you to ideas, evoke response.

Many writers note smalls in their journals—an ongoing list that might include overheard bits of conversation, the smell of garlic on the breath of a man beside you on the bus, a woman in the street with a parrot on her shoulder, grass growing from a crack in the sidewalk, the luminescence of fish in a tank, a line from a song, an unusual name, a striking scientific fact, the shape of a stain on your bedroom ceiling, the sound of an oboe from the apartment above, your friend's annoying habit of saying "essentially" to begin every other sentence.

These observations of moments, images, sounds, smells, words stay in your mind long enough for you to recall them and write them down. You're not sure why or if they're important, so you write to find out. You carefully describe what you've observed and see what emerges. How do these smalls connect to other parts of your life?

If your momentum fades after a paragraph, fine. Put the piece in your shoe box or paste it in your journal. Let it marinate. Some day you may come back to it.

8. List issues and ideas you want to know more about. Here are a few examples:

- Sexism, racism, ageism in your school, college, community
- Cloning or genetic engineering
- Eating disorders
- Adult children of alcoholics
- Grading, testing, evaluation
- Education
- Tax structure
- Censorship, pornography, rating systems
- Drug abuse
- Legalization of drugs, medical use of marijuana

- Homosexuality
- Media
- Volunteerism
- School sports, professional sports, money, coaching styles
- Dress codes
- Civility (or lack of it), manners, etiquette
- Fashion
- Health
- The latest medical fad

Research the issue so you have a lot of facts. Explore the territory to find a specific area of interest or controversy. Use the Internet. Go to the library. Telephone friends, experts, organizations to gather opinions and materials. Do one-on-one interviews with key people. You will be amazed how often people will talk with you. We all love to share our knowledge and opinions, especially with someone who listens carefully.

9. List what you do. List even ordinary things to get yourself going. For example:

get out of bed	answer e-mail	floss
brush teeth	water plants	run
park the car	sit in calculus class	eat
repair bicycles	fight with professor,	dress
drive to school	supervisor, spouse,	walk dog
or work	roommate	

There. Now. You see "fight with roommate" and you have something. The minute you do, start brainstorming, like this:

> fight with my roommate—a slob, yesterday's spaghetti stuck to sides of sink, her books, clothes, hairdryer and last night's five beers all over living room. Her feet smell. So do her socks and shoes. Friends here at least three days a week until two or three in the morning, loud music, stupid talk. Time she tried to steal my boyfriend. Owes me $45 for phone bill.

Keep up this free association as long as it has momentum. When it wears out, return to the original "What I Do" list until you find another strong word or phrase. At least one of these lists will yield a good subject.

In all of these exercises, we stress *you* at the center of the subject. *Your* strongest interests. *Your* most important experiences, thoughts, feelings. Enhance the *you* with conflict, tension, something off, out-of-whack, at stake, at risk. When these elements combine, you'll have an essay.

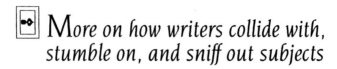# More on how writers collide with, stumble on, and sniff out subjects

BE FASCINATED, SUSCEPTIBLE, CURIOUS, PLAYFUL, AND RESPON-sible. Assume that if you don't write it, no one will.

Some subjects you collide with: the illness of a loved one, the loss of a dream, how you tried to save a friend from drowning. Other subjects excite you: a cliff you scaled; a bizarre taxi ride; a play in which you starred. Some anger you: the way a policeman harassed a teenager; a friend's disloyalty; a politician's self-serving position. Any person or event or idea that churns you up emotionally and/or intellectually can yield gold.

What is it that you can't stop thinking about?

This is your first, best subject.

But there are others, and here are a few ways to find them.

Recognize the subjects growing in your life

Some subjects insinuate themselves gradually. You wonder what to do about a friend who's struggling in her marriage. She calls you once or twice a week, late at night, to talk, sometimes for an hour and a half. You try to help by listening. This goes on for months, until the day she appears at your door with a suitcase. You didn't see this coming at all. Why not? What is the best way to help? Can you help? Why is her dependency so disturbing?

You write to find out, maybe starting with a question: What is going on with Sylvia? You list thoughts. You toss around the question in your mind and on paper. You begin to remember comments that seemed unimportant at the time, but they speak to how this move parallels others in her life and yours. You begin to see a pattern to your confusion and involvement. You write to make sense of it.

Accept gifts

Some subjects are gifts. For example, last winter we drove by an old woman gripping a walker and jerking along through the snow and slush on the street. Later, we saw her in the market. We asked: "Why weren't you walking on the sidewalk? Aren't you afraid of getting hit by a car?"

The sidewalks, she said, weren't sanded, so they were more slippery than the road. She was damned if she'd be housebound. "Besides, I'm eighty-nine," she said. "So what if I get bumped off? Probably a good thing." She laughed.

Not everyone will be moved to write about this plucky woman's actions and attitude, but maybe the subject of aging or independence resonates for you. You might see the woman as someone whose bravery you'd like to emulate. Or maybe you think her walk in the street was foolhardy.

Whatever your connection, the woman has walked into your consciousness, perhaps into your heart, and from time to time for the next few days or weeks or years, you picture her in her red hat and black overcoat, leaning on her walker, lifting the walker over the slush and bringing it down hard as cars shoosh by.

You may not know why the image stays with you, but you respect your instincts and jot down impressions. This may not become a true story right away, but it wants to be one. And if you play with the idea as it resurfaces in your journal, some day it might be.

Some subjects emerge when an incident in the present triggers a memory. For example, you meet a woman whose husband had been unemployed for six months. The woman tries to be positive, saying this "hiatus" is an opportunity to reassess and grow. But you sense the anxiety behind brave words and recall your own dread and anger when—years earlier—your husband quit his job in a fit of temper and the bills kept coming. From this connection, two stories merge, insights rise, and writing proceeds.

Be susceptible to smalls

Smalls are snatches of conversation, glimpses, fleeting observations, moments that come and go so fast you hardly have time to notice—but, because you are a writer, you do.

A five-year-old with a new sweater, bulky with red and green stripes across the chest and over the upper arms, believes the sweater makes him look bigger and stronger. He says, "I'll wear this to school tomorrow and Carlos won't dare hit me." A college student complains that her roommate's feet smell. She says, "She leaves her stinking socks on the floor. Every night I have to pick them up and put them in the laundry basket." A parent of a Little Leaguer hears the coach say, "There's three kids crying in the dugout." The wind blowing up the lake makes a kind of melancholy music, almost choral. Aunt Betty always has a jigsaw puzzle going in the parlor. Is it the same one she's had out for the last thirty years, or does it just seem the same?

Each of these observations contains a subject, perhaps several. A writer not only notices, but wonders why he notices, and is willing to try to figure it out through mapping, brainstorming, free writing, drafting, and revising.

Know your themes and respect them

We all have themes that run through our lives, or periods of our lives. For several years, Becky wrote about growing up in a country environment among avid hunters, trappers, fishermen—and feeling ambivalent about the lifestyle. Now she's writing more about ghosts, heritage, spirituality, mortality—not *instead* of earlier themes but in addition to them. She doesn't consciously choose her themes (may not even be fully aware of them except in retrospect), but they arise from her life as it evolves, and she embraces them.

The theme of loss or abandonment reverberates for Sue. When she was four and living in New Hampshire, her father moved to Montreal for a winter, trying to find a job. Sue, her mother, and her brother moved into her grandfather's house. Finally they did join her father, but that fear of loss or worse, an actual loss of almost any kind—the death of a relative, the end of a friendship—triggers the memory of that first lost. These feelings are frightening, but they're clear signposts guiding her to strong subjects. Another theme for her is courage, because she's had close-up views of friends and family who have shown remarkable determination and courage in their lives.

Be alert to your life themes. If you have an encounter or hear a story or remember an incident that takes on unexpected significance, it could well be because it resonates with one of your life themes. Respect these resonances; let them lead you to subjects.

Steal ideas

Writers steal from published stories, essays, novels, poems, songs, plays, cereal boxes, speeches, articles. Not the words but the inspiration—and sometimes the form or an approximation of it. Reading Susan Minot's serial short story "Lust," in which she lists, matter-of-factly, several love encounters between her main character and various young men, might help you write a piece on sexism at your workplace. Adapting Minot's form, you list several anecdotes about sexist incidents without much explanation or commentary. Like Minot, you let the images speak for themselves.

If you read about a mountain climb in India and you're learning to rock climb in Montana, the India article might give you confidence that your training is worth writing about.

If you're enjoying a play about a family of whacky characters from the hills of Kentucky, you may think about how different they are from your earnest, conservative family from Pittsburgh. Consider writing about your family. As you describe your father or mother or Uncle Joe, you may begin to wonder: What makes them the way they are?

For every subject, there are hundreds of approaches. If one person writes about a camping trip where he sees his brother in a new, more compassionate way, you too can write about a camping trip where you saw yourself, your spouse, your brother in a new way. This doesn't make you a copycat. Even if all the members of your writing group or class were to write this same story, each would be unique—because the writers, their experiences, and especially their perspectives are unique. Each writer would have a different relationship with his or her brother. Each trip would involve a different lake, canoe, tent, weather, scenery. Different details emerge because what *you* notice is different from what anyone else would notice.

We urge you always to be looking for subjects. Observe your world carefully: the garage mechanic with two missing fingers; the student who drinks two glasses of water before every meal; the doctor who, delivering the bad news, maintains an impassive facial expression, but clenches and unclenches his fists.

Be susceptible. Respect those incidents that strike you as intriguing, funny, irritating, sad, peculiar. Take notes. Revisit your notes—wonder, play, connect.

That college student who always drinks two glasses of water before meals: What does this mean? A kidney infection? A pagan ritual? Maybe her mother sent her off to school every day with the mantra: "Don't forget to drink two glasses of water with each meal and always floss after."

You find out that the student flosses often and quotes her mother even more often. Does she always do what Mummy says? You investigate further and notice the student, who happens to be your lab partner and sorority sister, makes harsh, judgmental statements and speaks with exclamation points: "That's stupid!" "Betty's room is so tacky!" "I can't believe you said that!"

She continuously criticizes others, yet she slavishly follows Mummy's rules—a puzzling combination. Perhaps she's mimicking her mother. Perhaps she's afraid? Of what? You become a psychological detective, and as you speculate a narrative emerges that leads you to deeper understanding of this woman's motives, fears, demons—and maybe some of your own.

Try this

1. Promise yourself that for two weeks you'll keep a small notebook in your pocket. Jot down ideas and observations, quotes, descriptions. Keep the notebook beside your bed at night. Every two or three days, look over your notes. Select one and, for ten minutes, write from it. This is brainstorming. Don't worry about how you write. Free associate. If the writing goes nowhere, fine. At least you've practiced the fine art of playing with an idea.

When you record your observations, you'll become more observant and curious. Your eye will grow keener, and your life more interesting.

2. Free write. If you can do this first thing in the morning before you talk to anyone, that's best. In any case, for five minutes a day over two weeks, sit at a desk and write as fast as you can about whatever

comes into your head. If nothing much occurs, write exactly that: "I can't think of a thing. This is stupid. I ought to come out with something. And here it is . . . drivel drivel drivel . . ."

Forget logic, commas, grammar, spelling. No one will see these scribbles. Exercise your writing muscles. After a few days of free writing, you will stumble into meaningful subjects. You will find an issue or generate a question that makes you curious to know more. You will be flung head-on into subjects that make you angry, fearful, proud, sad, joyful—all wonderful stimuli for writing.

3. Think of an object you feel strongly about: your father's blackened pipe; a wart on your chin; the guitar in the closet you haven't touched for a year; a favorite fishing rod; the grinning gorilla on the coffee mug your snide coworker uses.

Describe the object carefully. Then loop out and make a connection between the object and why it's important to you. If this loop ends abruptly, return to describing the object, then loop out again and again. See what happens.

4. Think of an argument you've had with someone in a specific place. You should feel strongly about the person and the issue. First, describe the place. Then write the scene using dialogue. Include body language and facial expression. How did you feel when he said, "I can't stand it when you get jealous of other women at parties when they talk to me." What did you think? Say? Keep going. Write about the argument and why it mattered, what it meant.

5. Think of a short incident—maybe one to six minutes—that seemed to last a long, long time: watching a loved one wheeled into an operating room; being in a car accident; taking a foul shot in a basketball game; receiving bad news. Now replay the incident in your head in slow motion. Be specific. Write down everything you saw, heard, smelled, touched, tasted. Write down everything that went through your head. Capture the moment and its significance on the page.

6. List your major conflicts, present and past. Pick the one that resonates most strongly for you now. Write about it.

7. Describe how you live now. Be specific and honest about the facts of your life: what your home looks like inside and out; what's in

your bedside table drawer; what you wear, eat, read; what music you listen to; people you associate with (or would like to); people you avoid; how much you work, study, play, worry, obsess. What do you do when you're alone? What delights you? What troubles you?

You may be pleased or proud of some of the ways you live now; you may be ashamed or disturbed by others. Once the details of your life are on the page, the next step is to evaluate them—and your life. "I am hung over every Monday morning," or "I get to the office half an hour before everybody else to get a head start," or "When I eat I always watch TV," or "The funny pages are the only part of the paper I really pay attention to." An accumulation of specifics like these will reveal you to yourself in surprising ways.

This exercise takes courage, but it can produce wonderful writing.

8. List the pressing concerns of your life: health, money, love, aging, passing history, having sex, being popular, boyfriend/girlfriend/spouse, job, drinking, sports, getting a promotion, balding. Write a sentence or two about each concern. Star the one that seems most pressing right now as you sit down to write. Write the concern at the top of a page and free write. Keep your pen moving and see what you come up with.

9. Think of someone you can't stand, or better, someone you both hate and love. Start with a fact or observation that most interests you now. Keep writing.

10. List your life-changing events: being adopted, going to college, learning how to handle a bully, joining a church. Choose the one you think you have the most to say about right now. Explore how you were changed and why the changes are significant.

11. Think of an incident that shifted your perception of yourself or someone else. Maybe you'd always seen yourself as physically timid until you saved a person from drowning. Or you always admired your older sister until you found out she cheated on exams and turned in plagiarized papers to keep her grades up. Write about the incident in detail. Explore the before and after to show the impact on your life. As you write, you will likely have even more insights. Get these on your pages, too.

# Hot topics

WRITE FROM THE CENTER OF WHO YOU ARE. WRITE ABOUT YOUR deepest concerns, fears, joys, loves, hates, griefs, triumphs, failures, hopes, and dreams. Write on subjects that are critically important in your mind, in your heart, in your gut. Write from the hot zone.

The more you care, the harder you'll work, the more your readers will care, and the faster you'll improve. If you're writing for a teacher and your material is private, mark the paper "confidential." Teachers honor this, but if you're worried, ask ahead of time if she'll keep your paper to herself.

Writing is hard work. Writing about material that bores you is much harder than writing about material that matters. Professionals know this; they seek material that stirs them intellectually, emotionally. They don't diddle around with half-baked subjects and neither should you. This doesn't mean all good work springs from emotionally devastating subjects—abuse, divorce, death, illness, loss—though your readers will have experienced such pain in one form or another so the appeal is universal. Suki Casanave's fascination with tree houses earned her a feature in *Smithsonian* magazine. Artist and naturalist David Carroll's love of turtles led him to write and illustrate *The Year of the Turtle: A Natural History*. Denise Grady's specialty is science and scientific breakthroughs; she's written hundreds of articles for magazines like *Discover* and newspapers like *The New York Times*. Even readers who don't think they care about tree houses or turtles or science will be drawn into these subjects by the passion of the writers. Whether your passion is medicine or witchcraft, football or religion, crossword puzzles or hang gliding, it will focus and energize your writing. What a pleasure it is to read the work of a writer whose subject is also his obsession. Such a writer pulls us into the center of his true story, his life. We can hear his heart beat.

Try this

List the three most memorable experiences of your life: your parents' divorce, being picked on in school, the death of a relative, catching a big fish, learning to cope with a handicap.

List the two most pressing concerns of your life right now. What am I going to do about the problems with my lover, father, child? How can I stop dieting to the point of starvation? Should I change jobs? Go back to school? Keep trying to get pregnant or consider adoption? Should I carry a knife in school for protection from others who carry them?

List your long-term conflicts, your ongoing problems with a painful history: an alcoholic parent; a schizophrenic sibling; worry about money, grades, career; dilemmas regarding your sexual orientation; pressures from parents, peers, bosses, the media.

As you look over your list, you'll see many possibilities for writing. Items that appear more than once or seem to connect are especially promising. Circle them and draw lines between them. That plane crash may be related to your reluctance to take a new job that requires travel, which connects with your money problems and pressure from your spouse to buy a house. What seems at first to be four subjects may be one, a rich one.

Any subject that seems too hot, too complex, too personal, too revealing is probably worth exploring.

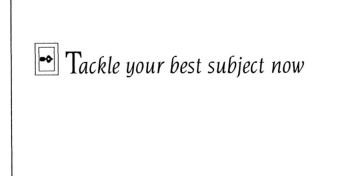

Tackle your best subject now

YOU MAY FEEL YOU SHOULD SAVE YOUR BEST FOR LATER. MAYBE A subject seems too big, too important to take on now. Maybe later you'll be a better writer, better able to do this subject justice.

We believe that if you tackle your best subject at once, you'll learn more and write more skillfully than if you play around with subjects that are not as compelling. Wrestling with one critical subject will expose others. As you write you'll come up with ideas for the next piece and the next. Trust this process. It works. The more you write, the more you have to write about.

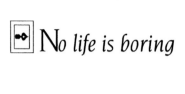# No life is boring

"MY LIFE IS SO BORING," A WOMAN TOLD US. "NOTHING HAPPENS." We were stunned. She is brainy & interesting. She has a thirty-year-old daughter with multiple sclerosis. One of her daughters ran away from home for a year when she was seventeen and now, six years later, still won't say where she went and what she did. This woman works as the treasurer of a large investment firm. She leads groups to Europe every year, has traveled to China, Africa, Europe, and South America. If she started to write honestly about her life, she would discover troves of material. Some discoveries might frighten her, or make her sad, angry, confused, regretful. Perhaps this is why it's easier to label the whole thing "boring" and dismiss it. Here are a few subjects she might take on:

- Is there something in the way I raised my daughter that caused her to bolt for a year? Why does she still refuse to tell me what happened while she was gone?

- What have I learned during one of my trips? Have I seen one country in a new way? Or myself or someone else in a new way? What intellectual and emotional impact has one specific travel experience had on me, one bowl of minestrone soup consumed at a back-alley restaurant in Venice? What was my best trip? Worst? Why? What have I learned about being a leader that I can pass on to other leaders?

- What does it mean to have a daughter affected by multiple sclerosis? How does the disease impact her life? And mine?

Compare the writing possibilities for this woman to those of Betty, one of our students who was not bored by her life. Betty grew up in Newmarket, New Hampshire, a small factory town, once prosperous. By the time she was seventeen, Betty had driven twice to Boston, a ninety-minute trip. She had visited Maine several times. But that was it.

Yet she wrote insightful reminiscences of growing up, including an essay called "Bea's Cut and Curl Hair Salon," in which she described listening, over the years, to her mother gossiping with other patrons as Betty had her hair cut. The result was a sharp look at a small town through the writer's clear perspective.

Your life is interesting. Write to find out why.

Try this

1. List possibilities and then talk them over with a friend, or better yet, another writer or teacher. Ask this person to help you brainstorm about each subject, perhaps by asking questions. Begin your draft with a line or phrase that jolts or interests you.

2. Write the story of your hypothetical best or worst day. Poet, essayist, children's book author Donald Hall, in his memoir *Life Work*, writes twenty pages describing his best day, and all the things he would do from waking to sleeping—what he would read, what he would write, who he would see, what he would do, how and with whom he would make love, whose words of wisdom he would recall, how he would feel, what he would accomplish. This hypothetical *best* illuminates his life and attitudes.

3. Comment on the passing scene. For two weeks, take notes on your life, whatever you notice, whatever penetrates your consciousness: a girl crying in the next room; a couple kissing in a subway station; a street fight; a chickadee at the feeder; the smell of much-needed rain; a dog trying to get at something in the bottom of a trash can; a long talk with a friend. Note whatever strikes you. Rely on facts, anecdotes, details. Record what you see, hear, taste, smell, touch. Write how you regard these observations—why you think you noticed, what meaning the moment might have. Chances are you'll end up with a series of snapshots or short takes that reveal the passing scene and, more important, reveal *you*. Revise these and rearrange them into a collage of impressions.

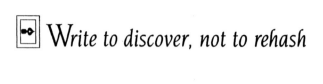

Write to discover, not to rehash

MANY PEOPLE BELIEVE PROFESSIONAL WRITERS KNOW EVERYTHING there is to know about their subjects before they write, and from this knowledge words flow. This might be true for some, especially when writing in a familiar form like a friendly letter, a press release, a brief report. But with personal stories, essays, arguments, reviews, analyses, and in-depth responses, not so.

Writers write from what they know in order to understand something new, or to see something familiar in a new way. Or to articulate something they may have sensed or vaguely considered but have never thought through clearly, fully. They write to shine a high beam on a subject they want or need to know more about.

If you merely rehash what you know—that time you skipped school and, with friends, roamed the San Francisco waterfront— you may write gracefully and specifically; the piece might not be awful, but it's apt to be bland.

But if on that outing a conversation between you and a friend disturbed you, if you noticed behavior that seemed out of character or did something you regret, and if you don't yet fully understand the meaning of what you experienced, then you can write to discover more.

Of course you know a lot about, say, your father. And if you write all you know about him, that's fine. Better though, to write with the purpose of seeing him more clearly, of probing the dynamics of your relationship. Write the images, memories, snatches of conversation that come to mind. You need specifics on the page to use as trampolines to your next level of understanding. Ah yes, Dad was always busy Saturdays. He worked on his brother's roof or his friend's Mustang, or he tended his weedless garden, but he didn't go to my Little League games. The hope is you will be led to a side of him you never considered before, a new perspective.

Writing to discover infuses purpose and energy on every page.

Discoveries vary. Some will astound you. In a piece called "The Fish," student Lori Tomsic discovered that her fascination with the dying fish in her tank was bred of her strong feelings about her dying grandmother. She had no idea why she was so upset about those dying fish until she got to the last word in the last two paragraphs. Her piece began as an in-class assignment to "write about an object you feel strongly about":

The fish eyes stare at me . . . wet, full blisters. Dull, stationary. I want the eyes to move. Jerky motion to indicate life. Like this, the eyes look dead.

The tank is on the kitchen counter halfway between the stove and sink. The fish is black, bulbous. It flips its tail once and turns abruptly to face me. The face looks smashed, as if it had run into the glass wall, pushing the skin up in large folds near the eyes and around the mouth. The mouth drops open, gulps, and snaps shut. It's large enough to eat a baby bird, I think. Obscene.

The fish is large as a mouse. That's the trouble with this fish. It's too big to kill. I can't step on this fish. A mouse trap would not work and a gun would blast it to hell. I did read in *Mother Earth News* that a bowl of baking soda and a bowl of water can be set down for cockroaches and the roaches will eat the baking soda, get thirsty and drink the water, get gaseous from both, not have any way to release it, and explode. Maybe this works with fish?

I want to stick a pin in its eye.

. . . It's Tuesday and the fish is still dying. Has been since Friday. First it was the tail I noticed. Ragged. As if the goldfish in the bowl with it had tugged and ripped at the edge of it with its tiny teeth. Chewed at Blackie while he was sleeping; carefully so as not to wake him. On Friday the tail had been erect and black, a fine fin; stiff enough to hold back the water while pushing the body forty degrees in one whack. Today, Tuesday, the bastard can hardly turn forty degrees in four or five whacks with that tail.

. . . The fish is getting old. Gray hair, gray scales, old age. . . .

. . . It does not stare at me today. It can't. One eye is completely covered with a milky slime, a cataract. The goddamn thing has cataracts. Silver scales, with cataracts and all I can do is just sit here and watch it die. Like my grandmother.

It's not the fact of the dead fish that bothers me. Or even the fact of the live fish now. It's that in-between stage that is haunting . . . humiliating to both forms. Not able to breathe or even to clean itself right, not gutsy enough to die. Like my grandmother in the St. Francis Nursing Home with tubes up her nose and out her bowels; pumping it in and out and she won't stop breathing. It's the waiting for the fish to die. When will I see its belly sticking out of the water? Going out of this world as it came into: exposed. How long will the fish be able to float and gasp in mid-water? How long will my grandmother's lungs choked by emphysema still bring in and push out the air? The in-between stage. I want the fish to be either alive and to do it, or to die. I want the fish to come to a decision.

Note the care with which Lori describes the fish. Those details, developed over several drafts, allow her to *see*, to discover the link between the fish and her grandmother.

Writing to discover succeeds when you write specifically, precisely, and honestly. If you are vague, if you cover up or distort for fear of what readers might think of you, you won't discover much. It took courage for Lori to write "I want to stick a pin in its eye." A scientist can't discover much when her microscope is out of focus either—or when she looks into it with half-closed eyes.

Judy O'Donoghue gained insight into her attitude toward aging in the last paragraph of "The Nursing Home" (page 272). After comparing the physical traits of her grandmother and her father, she realized that as a child she had sensed in her father the signs of aging she saw in her grandmother—double chin, wrinkles, sagging skin under his eyes. She realized she'd been afraid he would "catch" old age from Grandmother and die. This piece started as an in-class exercise and, like Lori, Judy had no idea where it would go. She was surprised and delighted by the final insight, which came after she'd reworked her first draft through many drafts over several weeks.

One student—after writing about the brutality of football, the abuse of his body, the stereotypes he suffered as the "dumb jock" even though he was a good student—decided to give up his football scholarship, leave the university, and go to college in another state to become a high school teacher. Now that, by God, was a discovery draft.

Other students have written to explore their sexual orientations, religious experiences, relationships. A poet wrote about a woman he'd been seeing for several months. By the time he finished the poem, he'd discovered he was in love, gave her the poem, and proposed marriage. In an essay called "Puppy Biscuits and One Brass Key," Sue discovered she needed, in her late thirties, to go back to college.

Some discoveries scare us. Some delight us. A discovery doesn't have to be big and dramatic to matter. Insights come when a writer sees a little more clearly, not necessarily in a whole new way. Stephen Small compared growing up gay in Newmarket, New Hampshire, to what two published writers said of their own experiences. Stephen knew how hard it had been to be gay in his town, but as he read and wrote he noticed similarities and differences not only in the experiences of the two writers but in how they chose to write about it. He discovered, through many revisions, effective ways to help readers understand his—and other gay people's—predicaments. His discoveries emerged as he chose passages to quote and examples from his life to illustrate his points.

He had a strong need not only to write on this subject but to discuss it with his writing class. The effect was immediate. The class discussed the paper and asked Stephen questions for an hour and a half. One young woman later said she had let go of some of her earlier prejudices about gays as a result of Stephen's presentation.

Another kind of discovery in writing is the satisfaction of finding an appropriate form or innovative way to approach a subject. Most writers enjoy crafting a sentence, finding the perfect phrase or word. Esther Pank wrote about a vacuum cleaner. Before she wrote she knew she resented the machine. For her, the surprises came in the language. You'll see from the first sentence how much fun she had crafting "The Dragon of Marlon Lane."

> For our anniversary my husband gave me the deluxe, new, super, hi tech, razzle-dazzle, time-saving, space-saving, easy-as-pie, handy-dandy, no-house-should-be-without-it, if-you-love-the-little-woman-make-her-life-easier, Sears vacuum cleaner. Complete with twenty-five attachments, carrying case, three hoses of differing lengths, wands, brushes, scrapers, squeegees and nozzles of every kind.

I hate this monster with its glowing golden-lighted eye dead center in its square forehead, its four little black wheel feet, its distended brown body.

It lives in my front hall closet, concealed behind the folding chairs, under boots and shoes, its limbs buried beneath bats, balls, rackets, and roller skates.

At any time of day—morning, noon or afternoon, daddy-is-home-from-the-office time, company-for-dinner time, where-is-my-coat-I-have-to-rush time, my dragon tries to escape from his den. Open the door and out writhes its mushroom-pale tentacle, slipping, slithering, and falling out onto the red tile floor, tripping everyone within its six foot reach.

Its purpose is to help me provide our family with an unblemished life. Now I am to clean crevices, cushions and corners. I can reach high moldings with Wand A and low baseboards with Brush B. Clean radiators, closets, drapes, walls, picture frames and bed frames; eliminate the last mote of dust from inside lampshades, outside light fixtures, underneath refrigerators and atop door frames. I can scrape, wax, burnish door knobs, polish light bulbs, buff banisters. No fissure, surface or plane is safe. Dirt is banished. Pestilence kept at bay.

I insert wand O into slot X, adjust, calibrate, snap, twist and plug the cord into its feeding supply. It clings. I push. It bolts. I tug. It darts up behind me, hits me mid-calf. I reach up, it whacks me on the shins. I stretch its cord, it balks, grips corners, comes un-plugged, refuses to budge.

It is sabotaging my life.

If I follow its grand scheme there will be no time to play the clarinet, dream of hiking in Nepal, imagine the sunrise from the bottom of the Grand Canyon, read Dostoevsky and Morrison and Poe. I will have no time to understand congressional resolutions and body counts, or argue for peace. There will be no time to dream my babies' dreams, or teach my four-year-old son to swim.

If I attack all the crevices and surfaces now within my reach, the stories that come unbidden at night will remain unwritten. There will be no days for me to cogitate, agitate and organize; no time to find my place as a peacemaker. There will be no time to wonder . . . Why this gift?

If your story feels flat, stop. Ask yourself if you stand to gain anything by writing this. What can you learn? If there are no surprises along the way—insights large or small, surprises in language—choose another subject or angle.

 Try this

1. Think of an object you feel strongly about: a squeaky door; your boss's purple coffee mug; a wheelchair; your motorcycle; a favorite fishing pole or bracelet or book; a snuggly winter coat or one that is ill-fitting and frayed; a birthmark; a double chin; a waterfall; a tombstone; a painting; a spot on the ceiling; a train that rockets past, shaking your apartment.

Describe the object using as much detail as Lori Tomsic and Esther Pank used in their descriptions. Then branch out and see if you can connect the object with meaning. How did the object come to you? Why is it significant? What does it represent? What does it remind you of? Forget grammar, punctuation. Forget logic. Don't worry about transitions. Fool around. Be playful and explore. After you describe the object loop out into your associations with it. Or describe it in a different way. Loop out again. Loop from a loop. See where the details lead.

If you make a substantial discovery and generate five pages, terrific. If you make an intriguing connection and produce two focused pages, terrific. If you have fun playing with different ways to describe your objects, as did Esther Pank, terrific. If your object refuses to yield meaning, at least you've practiced describing something accurately. After all, not all hard-hit baseballs go over the fence.

2. Read Richard Selzer's much-anthologized essay, "The Knife." In it, he describes his surgeon's knife, how he uses it and what it means to him:

> Mostly you are a traveler in a dangerous country, advancing into the moist and jungly cleft your hands have made. . . . Oh, there is risk everywhere. One goes lightly. The spleen. No! No! Do not touch the spleen . . .

He moves from description of the knife and its use to a memory of being taken to a hospital as a child by his doctor father. He tells stories about his work. He explores the mysteries of his profession from several angles.

3. Pose a question you want answered or at least illuminated: What will I do with my life when I graduate? Am I wasting my talents, time, life at this job? Is there a God? And if so, what does he or she think of me? How do you know if you're in love? Why do I feel tired all the time? What are my strengths and weaknesses? What do I want out of life versus what I've been told I ought to want? What do I hope to contribute to the world? Why am I so jealous of this person? Who am I? What makes me happy?

Write from a compelling question.

◧ The no-critics-allowed notebook

WE FOUND THIS IDEA IN *Writing Down the Bones* BY NATALIE GOLDBERG. She recommends you keep a notebook in which you can write anything you want in any way you want. No critic enters here. No critic says, "How could you be so shallow, mean, boring, or whiny." Or "You never did learn grammar." Or "Why don't you quit and become a dental hygienist?"

In your notebook you can experiment with exercises. Take risks and fail. Brainstorm subjects. Try three different approaches. Admit you're stuck and brainstorm solutions.

You can write a long description of a bag lady you saw at the corner of Madison and 33rd Street. Or a short one about paddling a canoe at six in the morning on the Merrimack River. You can write about the horrors of Dad's birthday dinner, the waitress at Jack's Diner who always says, "Hello, Honey, I feel lucky to serve you today." You can draw, make lists, write key words to remind you of events. You can respond to books, essays, articles. You can compare the tight prose of one writer to the leisurely descriptions of another. You can list the reasons you can't stand your boss or teacher or former friend. You can rant, rave, complain, and snivel. You can be unjust. You can be funny, serious, angry, sad, goofy. You can examine your conscience, confess. You can write about your hopes, fears, dreams, joys, heartaches, failures, and triumphs.

You can write one hard-to-admit truth about yourself or someone you love. If you do this regularly, you'll uncover subjects to write about. May Sarton said in *Journal of A Solitude*, "At some point . . . one has to stop holding back for fear of alienating some imaginary reader or real relative or friend, and come out with personal truth."

Joan Didion keeps a journal "to find out what I'm thinking, what I'm looking at, what it means." Most of us are taught by parents, the media, and peers how we ought to feel and think about many subjects. We are taught socially acceptable ways of thinking and talking about our parents, going to college, money, a run-down trailer park, teachers, hitchhiking alone across the country, sex. A private notebook helps us find out how we actually feel and think. And as you see what you think and who you are more clearly, you'll learn to trust your voice.

Alexandra Johnson in *The Hidden Writer: Diaries and the Creative Life* says people who write in journals yearn "for a coherent narrative of inner life, a continuous sense of identity."

Some writers write every day in their notebooks. Some write every day for a few weeks, abandon the book for a month or two, and when they've finished a writing project or face life pressures, begin to write again. Some write for posterity in journals, but many of us feel inhibited by the thought of keeping a journal for the public. The No-Critics-Allowed Notebook frees us.

HOW-TO TECHNIQUES

⊡ Why learn craft

LEARNING CRAFT MEANS MASTERING BASIC SKILLS AND TECH-
niques so thoroughly you don't need to stop a rush of words to pon-
der questions like these: How do I get the reader to understand my
fear as I fell from that window? How can I explain my long and complicated friendship with Peter without writing ten pages? How can I
make this dialogue sound real?

Writers learn craft to make ideas and images more accessible
and vibrant. They learn craft so they can explore their subjects with
agility, care, and depth.

Craft rescues you from mere emotion and inchoate thought. It allows you to give these emotions and ideas a form you can stand
back from and look at and evaluate carefully. Let's say you want to
write about arriving home from school to find your father, recover-
ing from an operation and on medication, running through the
house in his underwear, waving his arms and yelling for help. You
were alone with him. You were stunned.

If you don't understand the importance of details and the elements of scene, you're likely to try an opening like this: "I looked at
Dad. He was running about and yelling. Finally I lost it, too, and began yelling back." This does not do the moment justice. You must,
instead, record what your father said, where he was standing as he
said it, where you stood, what you thought, and felt, and noticed,
and said. Then you and your readers will be able to grasp what happened. You and they will envision the scene fully and clearly. And
because you can examine the scene, you can come to insight and
write with meaning.

If you don't know how to summarize your relationship with your father in a meaningful way, you may not be able to express some of the complexities and intricacies of that relationship or write your way to an understanding of his behavior (and your reaction to it) in this instance. An accurate summary allows you to push into your subject.

Just as the carpenter needs to learn basic carpentry skills such as how to hold the hammer and hit the nail, how to push and pull the saw through the wood, and how to build the frame before erecting the walls, so a writer needs to know basics:

- How and when to use specific information
- How to engage readers with the five senses, especially sight
- How to work dialogue, action, reaction, and commentary into scenes
- How to summarize a long period of time
- How to expand a short period of time to a page or more of writing
- What to include in leads and endings
- How to move in and out of flashbacks
- How to shape sentences

We learn craft by writing. And studying the techniques professional writers use. And writing. And developing the ability to look at our own work as though it were written by someone else and assess its effectiveness. Craft allows us to step back after a few drafts and say: What do I have here? What am I actually saying? How can I say it better?

Some people believe techniques like flashbacks are too difficult for new writers. And that weaving narrative into a scene within those flashbacks or writing a summary or time expansion is even more difficult. But that is simply not true.

Once you have scrutinized and understood the construction of a well-written scene or flashback or summary or expansion, you will start using them right away. That's why we discuss specific skills in the chapters that follow. As you learn these skills, your writing will improve dramatically.

Leads

"START WITH THE GOOD STUFF," AUTHOR ANDREW MERTON HAS SAID. Start at a point of intense interest to you right now as you sit down to write. This may not turn out to be the lead of your final draft, but it's enough to get you going. You'll be motivated to stick with your subject as one sentence leads to another. Start with the material that made you want to write in the first place. You can always add background later. If you start with somewhat dull background information, by the time you get to "the good stuff" you'll be tired and your writing will be, too.

Each of the following leads begins in the middle of something—an affair, an argument, a relationship, a crisis, a revelation—a point of intense interest.

Today I met the woman my husband is in love with. The meeting was not an accident; I arranged it.

Beryl Donovan, student, "The Other Woman"

At just about the hour when my father died, soon after dawn one February morning when ice coated the windows like cataracts, I banged my thumb with a hammer. Naturally I swore at the reckless thing, and in the moment of swearing I thought of what my father would say: "If you'd try hitting the nail, it would go in a whole lot faster."

Scott Russell Sanders, "The Inheritance of Tools," *Best American Essays*, College Edition

Speedy is in a wheelchair. He swings his heavy head around in the direction of his friend. His eyebrows rise and his forehead, abnormally long, wrinkles up. He's excited because someone is paying attention to him, not because of his handicap but because they have something to tell him. Even though he has a thick, wiry beard and a hairy back, there's the anxious look of a little boy who never got to play dodge ball during recess or share perverted locker room stories after soccer practice with the boys. Speedy wants to be one of the guys but it's a little too obvious and that's what sets him further apart from people. This compels me to talk to him a lot and, perhaps, laugh more than I normally would whenever he says anything humorous.

Jenn Rowland, student, "Speedy"

"People don't live more than three years with a heart as damaged as yours," he says, looking right at me. He's handsome, Irish, reminds me of a boy I used to date from Notre Dame more than thirty years ago.

Joan Mikulka Albert, "Counting on the Heart," from *Surviving Crisis*

There was an angel in my grandfather's obituary.

Michael Lowenthal, "Saying Kaddish for Peter" (page 259)

A lead lifts the roof on a house full of activity and drops you into the middle of it. A lead opens the door to a room with secrets in every corner and surprises among the shadows. You and your readers are immediately involved, intrigued. In Joan Mikulka Albert's essay, quoted here, the scene continues in the doctor's office for a few paragraphs. Then, after a space break, she switches to background on what has led to this shocking revelation about her health. She anticipates questions and answers them.

Thoroughly ground readers in the present action of a story before you shift to background information or another scene, before you flash back or forward. Let readers know where they are. Give them time and space, perhaps a paragraph or several, to absorb whatever you are showing or telling them.

Beware of grabbing the reader with an enticing line or two and then flashing back too soon. If you begin with "The canoe tipped, and we were thrown into the river where the current dragged us toward the rocks" and then you flash back to how you came to be in the canoe that day, you'll disorient your readers. They'll wonder: *Did some people drown? Are they out of the river now? Is this the same day?* Readers need a chance to visualize that canoe and who was in it and whether the river is ten or twenty-five feet wide. Stay with that first action before you move on to something new.

Beware, too, of leading with too much background information before introducing conflict. You risk boring readers and yourself. Here is our boring version of Gabriel Garcia Marquez's lead to *Chronicle of a Death Foretold*:

> Santiago Nasar was born into a large family in South America and went to a Catholic school run by Jesuits where he obtained a solid, classical education. In high school, he was captain of the soccer team and one of the top three students in every grade. He particularly liked history, and in his senior year . . .

Readers yawn. They must sense a purpose, a compelling reason to keep reading.

Here is Garcia Marquez's actual first sentence:

> On the day they were going to kill him, Santiago Nasar got up at five-thirty in the morning to wait for the boat the bishop was coming on.

John McPhee says a good lead is like a beam of light that shines into the heart of your subject. It tells readers where they'll be going. In your lead, you commit to a subject and an approach. Be true to that commitment. Don't imply you and your family were nearly murdered and then, on page four, reveal that a stranger climbed through your basement window and slept on the washing machine.

One of our students wrote at length about his desire to see a deer while hunting. He wrote about the hike with his father in the woods. He described their outfits, their guns. For six pages, readers anticipated a deer. Then in a single phrase the much-anticipated deer leapt from a bush, crossed a small clearing, and disappeared.

That writer had promised us a deer. He had focused on becoming a hunter and seeing, perhaps killing, his first deer. We expected a deer. We deserved a deer. He owed us a deer.

After a conference, he decided to use the technique of time expansion (see page 108). He slowed his glimpse of that leaping deer by expanding the moment to half a page. He kept the promise of his lead.

Some advice on leads

Put a hook in your lead. Catch readers in the first paragraph and don't let them go.

Don't waste a reader's time. Picture your reader in a doctor's waiting room, impatient, perhaps in pain. The doctor is running half an hour late. The reader wonders if she'll make it back to her job at City Hall by 4:00 P.M. She picks up a magazine, reads first paragraphs, flipping pages rapidly. Sometimes she glances at only the first sentence or two. Your lead needs to be compelling enough for this woman to read beyond the first paragraph, to look up, surprised, when the receptionist calls out her name.

Start with conflict, tension, or a pressing question that needs to be explored.

Establish your voice. Use your lead like the beginning of a good piece of music. Show readers something of your attitude toward your subject. You're angry or reflective, irreverent, sarcastic, outraged, worried, grateful.

Use your lead to set the style. Can the reader expect short, snappy sentences or long, complex ones? Will you use the casual I or the more formal one? Will details abound? Abstractions? Questions? Assertions? Will this be easy to read or require rereading because of its density? Should the reader have a dictionary close by? Will it be funny? Serious? Can we expect to be surprised? Enlightened? Horrified? Seduced?

Consider that a good lead might make a good ending and vice versa. Leads and endings are similar. Both tend to be focused, intense, and full of meaning—distillations of the most important aspects of the piece. Maybe what you think is the lead would work better as the ending. Maybe the ending you imagine would make a perfect lead.

Don't tease readers by withholding basic information, hoping to lure them in. Don't be like the writer who detailed his lust for firm breasts, supple, golden skin, and a tender heart only to reveal, three pages later, that his subject was roast chicken.

Here's another example of a confusing lead: "There I was teetering on the edge and if I fell, I would plunge to my death." In the next sentence the writer describes how her body aches from the strain of hanging on. Then she starts a new paragraph with the sound of the alarm waking her that morning. She told us she chose the lead to make the reader wonder what she was on the edge of. A cliff or a mountain in Utah? A rooftop of a skyscraper in Dallas?

The trouble is, if readers don't know what's going on, they may stop reading. Manipulations like these irritate us. Some writers do withhold information in a first paragraph on purpose, to tantalize. But it's a risky, gimmicky technique that can backfire. It's better to assume that your reader is intelligent enough to be caught by a scene or an idea or a snatch of dialogue or a question that is genuinely—even profoundly—interesting.

Avoid vague beginnings. Don't say, "It was the most exciting experience of my life, something so important that it changed me forever." What does that mean? What is *it*? Readers can't see, smell, taste, touch, hear, or even imagine *exciting* or *experience* or *something* or *important* or *change* or *way*. The sentence is vague. It means virtually nothing and packs about as much clout as the fist of a flea.

Instead, load your lead with specifics. Emulate the impressive density of specifics combined with humor and an unusual perspective in this lead to Nancy Mairs' essay "On Being a Cripple."

> The other day I was thinking of writing an essay on being a cripple. I was thinking hard in one of the stalls of the women's room in my office building, as I was shoving my shirt into my jeans and tugging up my zipper. Preoccupied, I flushed, picked up my book bag, took my cane down from the hook, and unlatched the door. So many movements unbalanced me, and as I pulled the door open I fell over backward, landing fully clothed on the toilet seat, with my legs splayed in front of me; the old beetle-on-its-back routine. Saturday afternoon the building was deserted, I was free to laugh aloud as I wriggled back to my feet . . . I decided it was high time to write the essay.

Flannery O'Connor's classic short story "Everything That Rises Must Converge" also relies on specifics, humor, and an unusual perspective—this time belonging to her main character, Julian, as opposed to the author herself.

> Her doctor had told Julian's mother that she must lose twenty pounds on account of her blood pressure, so on Wednesday nights Julian had to take her downtown on the bus for a reducing class at the Y. The reducing class was designed for working girls over fifty, who weighed from 165 to 200 pounds. His mother was one of the slimmer ones, but she said ladies did not tell their age or weight. She would not ride the buses by herself at night since they had been integrated, and because the reducing class was one of her few pleasures, necessary for her health, and FREE, she said Julian could at least put himself out to take her, considering all she did for him. Julian did not like to consider all she did for him, but every Wednesday night he braced himself and took her.

Because of her *blood pressure*, Julian's mother must lose *twenty pounds*, not just weight. He must take her on the *bus* to *reducing class* at the Y, not just escort her. The people in the class aren't just vaguely heavy; they weigh *between 165 and 200 pounds*. Whether you're writing fiction or nonfiction, readers will trust you and believe in the truth of your writing, if you persuade them to trust and believe with accurate, irrefutable detail.

The next lead comes from Emily Jacob's research project in which she shares personal information about her experiences with an eating disorder and combines these with physiological and medical facts.

> Come with me, if you will, into a dimly lit bedroom in a house in a neighborhood in a quiet suburb in middle-class America. There is a young girl—perhaps thirteen or fourteen years old—lying motionless underneath a soft, flowered comforter. You see that her eyes are open, and she is looking at the ceiling. If you could read her thoughts, you would find that she is dreaming of food, systematically walking through a grocery store and fantasizing about picking up different foods, chewing them, tasting them, swallowing them. If you could see her body underneath her blankets, you would find it emaciated. If you could feel her pain, you would ache as her coccyx hits the mattress if she lies on her back, and as her hipbones become bruised as she lies on her stomach. Just steps down the hall are cupboards full of food, and parents who can't sleep. Their daughter is starving herself, and they can't seem to do a thing about it.
>
> I want to introduce you to this girl. This girl is me seven years ago.

Some leads hook readers instantly. Others are more leisurely, like Emily Jacob's slow, careful crafting of her opening image.

After you finish a first draft, you will likely have learned something about your subject that you didn't know when you sat down to write. Since you see your subject differently, your second draft may require a different lead. Maybe you'll find that lead on page two and move it up, or decide on a whole new approach. Don't fuss too long over leads in your early drafts—they may not stay. Use them to engage yourself; worry about readers later. Trust that, through drafting, a lead will evolve to draw your readers in.

⊶ Try This:

1. Type three of your favorite leads so you can see exactly how they work. If you are in a writing group, all of you might type your favorites, read them aloud, and discuss them.

2. Rewrite the lead to a piece that you think needs work. Show the original and the revision to someone in your class or writing group, without revealing which is which. Ask, "Based on this lead, what do you expect will follow?" Then, "Based on this other lead, what do you expect?" How do the two set up different expectations? Which lead seems to more accurately introduce the piece you want to write?

3. Look through a draft of an essay you're working on that needs a better lead, possibly a tighter focus. (Often if a lead's not working it's because the focus is not yet clear.) Choose a lively paragraph from the middle of the essay and try that as a new lead. Go from there. This may not prove to be *the* lead, but this experiment may suggest a different focus or direction.

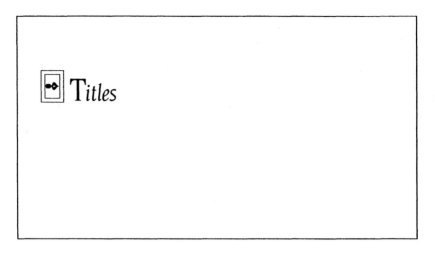

Titles

SOME WRITERS LIKE TO HAVE A WORKING TITLE BEFORE THEY BEGIN drafting. Often a title evolves with the piece. Brainstorming titles can lead you to an early, tentative, focus. Some writers won't use any title at all until the final draft. How can they tell readers what the piece is about until they are absolutely sure?

A good title is a lead to your lead, and serves a similar purpose. It directs readers to your subject. It can suggest tone, angle, voice. "Exploring the Universals of the Human Spirit in Poetry and Prose: A Linguistic Pilgrimage" suggests a substantially different approach than "What Lies Beyond?" or "Chaos: You Gotta Love It," though the subjects may overlap. A title can be thematic, as in Sue's story "Grieving." It can have an internal tension, as in Becky's essay "Rocks Rising." (Do rocks rise? Like balloons? How?) It can be broad and encompassing, as in John Irving's *The World According to Garp*. Specific and intriguing, as in Charles Simic's *Return to a Place Lit by a Glass of Milk*. Poetic and enigmatic as in Maya Angelou's *I Know Why the Caged Bird Sings*. Technical, as in Sebastian Junger's *The Perfect Storm*. It can be the name of a person or place: Jane Austen's *Emma*, Thomas Williams' *Leah, New Hampshire*. It can refer to a particular time and place: Robert McCloskey's *One Morning in Maine*.

If a title entices you to read the first paragraph and, at the same time, suggests the writer's approach, then it has done its job.

Below are some titles and leads that we think work well together. They are accurate and illuminating. They jump-start these pieces; set them humming.

SIXTY

When I woke up that morning I sat bolt upright in bed staring straight ahead. *Kiddo, you're sixty*, I said to myself. It was hard to believe.

Florence Epstein, from *Surviving Crisis*

ROOMMATE BLUES

I spent the first semester of my freshman year fighting with my roommate, Mel. We were in a forced triple and, although it was bigger than most forced triples, it was too small for Mel, Jess, and me to live in peacefully, but so is Texas.

Sarah Hamilton, student

DIAMONDS, DYKES, AND DOUBLE PLAYS

I've known I was queer since I was about twelve years old.

Pat Griffin, from *A Whole Other Ball Game: Women's Literature on Women's Sport*, edited by Joli Sandoz

And, finally (just for fun), one of our favorite titles and first lines from James Patrick Kelly's sci-fi novella, winner of the Hugo Award for 1997:

THINK LIKE A DINOSAUR

Kamala Shastri came back to this world as she had left it—naked.

James Patrick Kelly, from *Think Like a Dinosaur and Other Stories*

 # Try this

1. Read titles and first paragraphs of ten published essays or short stories, one after another. Which is your favorite, and why? What are the best title and lead you've ever written? Why? How are your title and lead similar to your favorites among the published ones?

2. Read all the titles on the contents page of an anthology or two. Check the ones that make you want to turn to that piece and read. What do your checked titles have in common? If you're in a class or writing group, compare your favorites with those selected by the

others. Do any preference patterns emerge? This might lead to a discussion of how certain titles appeal more to certain kinds of readers than others.

3. Be alert for good titles or leads in conversation. And when you hear one, record it in your journal.

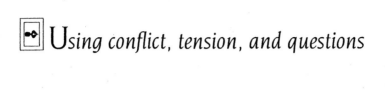

Using conflict, tension, and questions

WRITING THRIVES ON CONFLICT. START YOUR STORY WITH CONFLICT and keep it going all through. Conflict will hold readers in its prickly arms. It will keep you, the writer, focused and motivated to learn how deep the trouble goes, what's behind it, what it means, and how it can be resolved. Writing *is* a form of therapy.

Conflict can be external: "The breaks on the van got spongy, then at the top of the hill, they failed altogether." It can be internal: "I have a drinking problem." It can be both: "I hate losing my temper with Bill, but his 'who cares' attitude drives me crazy."

Some subjects may not have an explicit, in-your-face conflict, but they have its twin: tension. Often this takes the form of a question.

- Should I confront the soccer coach about favoring Jack and Saul?

- How will I stay busy and fulfilled if I take early retirement?

- Should we adopt a three-year-old?

- Should I see a holistic doctor about my pain?

- Why did I buy that doll at the craft fair?

Get quickly to the problem or question and explore from there. As you explore, your interest and your readers' will mount. Something will happen: you'll decide to confront the soccer coach; you'll join A.A.; you'll write about your friends who adopted an older child and had a terrible time living with the child's behavioral problems; you'll see that the doll represents children, childhood, and speaks to your doubts about your decision not to have children as Pat Wilson does in "Rabbit Doll" (page 281).

Strong writing often springs from negatives: the things you didn't do, the things you wish you hadn't, difficult decisions and relationships, painful experiences. To make a reader care about your well-behaved, affectionate dog is a mountainous challenge. On the other hand, if your dog has bitten your neighbor and the police are about to drag Pokey to the pound to be gassed, the reader will be interested in how you react, what you think, feel, do, learn. Even those of you whose lives are blessedly free of conflict can seek angles that explore small and large tensions: "I lived a storybook childhood in a storybook house in a storybook neighborhood. Sometimes I wonder what I missed." Or, "Most actors run a gauntlet of rejection before getting their big break. I got a leading role in an award-winning film the first time I auditioned. And yet . . ." Yet what? Yet you don't feel you've paid your dues? Yet you think you'd have done a better job had you had more training? Yet you haven't found a second director willing to take a chance on you?

Another reason strong writing springs from the negative is that we may be more inclined to write in depth about our troubles than to speak of them. With friends, family, and at work, we usually share positive or mildly annoying, maybe humorous, experiences. We don't want to pull our friends into the ditch with endless Oh God stories: Oh God, my cat died, my grandmother's sick, I spilled coffee on my expensive white couch and my husband's in a rage, Dad's cut me out of the will again, my ingrown toenails have developed infections and they're killing me, I hate my roommate, I flunked French, I owe $10,000 to MasterCard. If we do tell these stories, we try not to dwell on them.

Writing is dwelling. We hoard what affects us deeply and can't be explained over coffee or even a long drive in the country. These stories, experiences, feelings, almost-insights build up steam. When we let them out, energy pours onto the page.

Pat Wilson's story "Rabbit Doll" begins with an image:

I found her at the Stratham Memorial School Craft Fair last Saturday. Around one booth huddled children and parents touching an array of doll-size dresses in blues, greens, reds and yellows, plaids and prints. Amid the array of dresses sat cotton rabbit dolls. There I knelt, a 43-year-old single career woman with no children, looking for a doll I did not need.

The tension in this paragraph takes a couple of forms. First, "I found her" raises questions: Who is speaking? If this *who* found the doll, does that mean she'd been searching for it? Is this a story about loss, as in lost and found?

Two sentences later—after orienting the reader with details about the fair—Wilson lays out a more explicit conflict. She is "a 43-year-old single career woman with no children." Common sense says her biological clock is ticking, loudly. And, of all the ways Wilson could describe herself, why does she choose the negative, "no children"? Is this a problem for her? The last few words of that sentence reinforce the conflict. She's looking for "a doll I did not need." But the implication seems to be that the doll—a child's toy—is something she desires. Does she desire a child as well?

In subsequent passages she describes the dolls specifically and her reactions intimately. She picks up each one and replaces her "as though she would remember my hands." The more she describes the dolls and her interaction with them, the more human they seem. She loves one for her dangling legs, bright eyes, content expression, her smell of "clean, fresh cotton"—using details of touch, sight, and smell. She even uses sound when she muses aloud, "What will I do with you?" and "I guess you are for me."

Wilson skillfully mixes feelings about the doll with feelings about having children—an immediate conflict merging with a long-term conflict. She does this through comments like "There was no answer. There was no putting her back either." And "I did not want to put her away when I arrived home."

Every word of the last paragraph seems thematic, especially when she tosses the doll into the air, "momentarily suspended as images of children washed through me. . . . None of them my own. None would be mine." Instead of articulating doubts, Wilson lets action reflect them. "Though I know the decision was the right one, and though largely at peace, tears blurred my sight. I caught the rabbit doll in a lavender dress. I held her close, and let myself dream of the daughter I would not have."

Wilson wrings poignancy and depth from detail by connecting what her character (who may or may not be Wilson herself) does in this moment (buying the doll) with what she has chosen not to do (have children). She may not have recognized that connection when she began drafting, but she undoubtedly started with conflict, tension, a question: Why did I buy this doll? She explored the question in detail. She exposed the nature of a woman's personal resolve to readers who, perhaps, gain insight into decisions with which they are not quite at peace either.

Try this

1. Draw a life line from your birth to the present. Mark the times you experienced strong conflicts or difficult choices. Write the year, your age, and a word or two below each mark to remind yourself of the incident. You may find you have several significant conflicts. Choose the one that seems most urgent. Write from it and about it.

2. Think of a time you behaved in a way that surprised and puzzled you. Choose a behavior that in retrospect seems related to an ongoing conflict. This might be the time you began to cry when the repairman said your washing machine could not be fixed. Maybe this was the last straw in a series of money problems. Or the time your husband put too much sugar in your tea and you decided to leave him immediately after breakfast. Clearly, the sugar didn't cause the rift, but the tea was a turning point. Or when you "forgot" your mammogram appointment three times in a row; your mother was your age when she died of breast cancer. Or the time you punched your best friend in the stomach and knocked him to the ground. And all he did was make fun of your haircut.

Begin by writing about what happened. Stick with the moment. Try to recall all the precipitating details. As you write you may begin to see what you were really reacting to and why—how the short-term conflict illuminates the long-term. Your readers will see it, too.

3. List self-descriptors—names you could call yourself or others might call you. Try for those with tension, negatives. Sometimes what you are not is more interesting than what you are.

- a someday professional basketball player
- Franz's dorky little brother
- an unpublished writer
- my music teacher's worst nightmare
- the former "Miss Alabama"
- a straight-A engineering student who wants to be a poet
- the rebellious daughter

List ten to twenty descriptors. One or more of them should suggest enough conflict to get you writing.

Finding an angle into your subject

YOU DECIDE TO WRITE ABOUT HIGH SCHOOL. THAT'S A FOREST OF material so broad and deep you could get lost in it. You could write a book. If you try to write about all your high school experiences in, say, five to ten pages, you'll be forced to use meaningless generalities like "I mostly hung out with five friends who were athletic and we had lots of exciting times together." Or, you might try skipping around, from soccer championship to the agony of French verbs to the prom to the teacher with bad breath. Either way, you come off sounding scattered, shallow, unintelligent.

You need to find an angle that excites you and gives you a chance to expound, discover, and reveal. You need to narrow your subject. Enthusiasm and energy are critical. Pick an angle that appeals to you *now*. You may decide to shift later, but you've got to start somewhere, so start at the point of your particular interest at this particular time. Here are some angles a writer might choose on the subject of high school:

• How students behave at freshman dances

Or even better, because it's narrower, more focused:

• How students behaved at your first school dance

Or:

• Being a fat kid

• Being a member of a clique or not being a member

• The trip to Chicago with your school band when Peter walked on the ledge, from your hotel room to the girls' room, risking his life

- The pressure to get good grades: be popular; make the team; have a boyfriend or girlfriend; wear the right clothes

- The time your parents had to meet you at the principal's office along with the guidance counselor and three of your teachers because of poor grades

- A secret you kept even from your best friend

- An attitude you're ashamed of; an act or a failure to act or speak up; a time you wish you hadn't spoken up

- An event that seemed insignificant at the time, but you still remember it and why; looking back you begin to understand the significance

Sometimes a writer determines her focus before she begins. Sometimes she'll stumble into it after a few drafts that seem to be going nowhere but are actually leading the way. Karen Otash, one of our students, worked as a waitress every summer and on weekends during the school year. She had no idea how to write about this. At first she tried chronological order, describing each job, starting with the first. The draft wandered from restaurant to restaurant without purpose. Reading this draft, Sue was impressed by Karen's descriptions, but wondered: Why are we being told these things? What's the point? Karen was the one to say, "It's boring."

She needed a path into this material. An approach. An organizing principal. An angle. She considered comparing bosses or describing the traumas and temper tantrums of the kitchen. For some writers either of these approaches would have yielded good work, but they didn't stimulate Karen, and she wisely abandoned them. Finally, she found an angle that grabbed her: She'd write about her worst customers. This approach would provide direction as well as tension. Writing about these customers was fun. She could vent.

She called the paper "Why I Quit Waitressing." Here's her lead:

Then there was the time the woman waved her liver in my face. It wasn't her own God-given liver of course. It came from the kitchen. But she ordered it, and I wrote it on her check, and I feel justified in calling it her liver. On to the story. This customer snatched her liver from the plate, shoved it under my nose, and while twisting it into loops and spirals, castigated its every feature. She pronounced it inedible and dropped it into her dish.

Karen continued with descriptions of characters such as the Manhattan Lady and the Sole Lady. Finally, one customer accused her of cheating on the bill and Karen quit.

She produced a delightful, light-hearted paper that works because of her sharp angle and ability to describe whacky characters vividly. An aside: In this paper, she was not writing to discover deep insights. Her discoveries came through the language: "Then there was the time the lady waved her liver in my face."

Some writers will list many possible angles before trying one in a first draft. Some brainstormed angles may seem ridiculous, but we try to withhold judgment. We're getting thoughts on paper, trusting that workable ideas will emerge.

Another way to find an angle (or let one find you) is to stare out the window a long time and think: What most interests me now? That *now* is important; what mattered to you a year or a week ago might not matter as much now or a month from now. Turn different approaches over in your mind. Allow yourself mulling time. Develop the habit of quiet reflection.

For some subjects, you'll recognize the angle almost instantly. A writer in Sue's class, Jacob Swain, often hunted deer with his father. For weeks they hunted without even seeing a deer. Then one Saturday, the father wounded a doe. He and Jacob followed the trail of blood until the father shot again and killed it. Jacob had been told that deer don't feel pain, but he knew better. When it was time to write, he didn't have to grope for an angle into the subject of hunting. It was obvious he would write about this one hunting trip and the impact it had on him.

Plunging in without knowing the angle can work, too. Use this approach if an angle isn't apparent or forthcoming; if you sense your subject is complex and has deeply affected you, such as the relationship between Pat Parnell and her mother and grandmother in "Visitation" (page 275); if you are writing to understand more about a critically important event in your life that has somehow changed you, as Sandell Morse did in "Canning Jars" (page 263). You'll want to think about your subject, yes, but resist too much preplanning. Start with a detail, scene, line of dialogue, or metaphor. Start at a point in time that fascinates you. Chances are you'll discover the angle as you write.

It takes faith to write this way—faith in yourself and faith in your subject.

 ## Try this

1. Think of a trip you've taken. Pretend you'll write about it. What are some angles you could choose? List them. If one appeals far more than the others, try writing from it.

2. Look at a favorite published essay or story. Articulate in one sentence the angle the writer chose. Now list four other approaches to that same subject.

3. If you have a subject but are uncertain about what angle to use, write a page or two from one that seems promising. Stop. Write another page or two from another angle. Which feels best, and why? Which allows you to write what you know in order to discover more? Does either feel like a dead end? Does either feel like it wants to go on? It's that feeling of more-to-come that keeps you writing and lets you know this approach might be the right one.

4. Try the "What I Did This Summer" subject you were probably assigned in grammar school. Of course, this is a difficult subject because it's too big. Find an angle that allows you to write in depth and with meaning what you *really* did this summer—what you did that mattered; what you did that distinguishes this summer from all the other summers of your life. You may narrow the subject to the hour your baby brother was lost and you'd been left in charge. You found him, finally, crawling out of an empty garbage pail lying on its side in the garage.

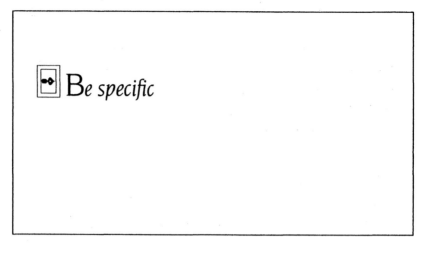

Be specific

"SPECIFICS ARE TO THE WRITER WHAT HAMMER AND NAILS ARE to the carpenter." Donald Murray said this, and we pass it along to you. When you rely on facts and details, you write with authority. Avoid vagueness:

> My family just got together for a big reunion. Everyone came. The food was spread out all over the place. Everything you can imagine. Afterwards we played games. It was wonderful fun.

What does "big reunion" mean? Some families consider ten people in the living room big; others would say it's seventy or a hundred in a rented hall. A gathering of a clan of Scots drew over a thousand people. They filled two hotels. "Big reunion" means different things to different readers, who will be distracted, wondering: ten? thirty? a hundred and fifty?

Another problem: "The food was spread out all over the place."

"All over the place"? What does that mean? On rented folding tables in the yard? Is the setting a small apartment with food on every flat surface including bedside tables, bureaus, and the ironing board? Or is it a mansion where caterers have arranged canapés on a twenty-foot banquet table under a chandelier in the ballroom?

By now readers are more than distracted; they're confused. Then the writer makes things worse by saying, "The food consisted of everything you can imagine." Are we talking hot dogs, caviar, octopus, monkey brains, macaroni and cheese? And what about the "games" they played at this reunion: Chess? Touch football? Did they shoot bunny rabbits?

Vague writing irritates, confuses, and bores readers. Specific writing snaps with authority and life.

Vague: The weather was dreadful for much of the year in the place where I grew up in Ireland and it caused poor health in the people who lived there. Different remedies were tried to cure us when we got sick but, frankly, the atmosphere of the whole place was, to say the least, hardly inspiring.

Specific: Out in the Atlantic Ocean great sheets of rain gathered to drift slowly up the River Shannon and settle forever in Limerick. The rain dampened the city from the Feast of the Circumcision to New Year's Eve. It created a cacophony of hacking coughs, bronchial rattles, asthmatic wheezes, consumptive croaks. It turned noses into fountains, lungs into bacterial sponges. It provoked cures galore; to ease the catarrh you boiled onions in milk blackened with pepper; for the congested passages you made a paste of boiled flour and nettles, wrapped it in a rag, and slapped it, sizzling, on the chest.

From October to April the walls of Limerick glistened with the damp. Clothes never dried: tweed and woolen coats housed living things, sometimes sprouted mysterious vegetations. In pubs, steam rose from damp bodies and garments to be inhaled with cigarette and pipe smoke laced with the stale fumes of spilled stout and whiskey and tinged with the odor of piss wafting in from the outdoor jakes where many a man puked up his week's wages.

From *Angela's Ashes* by Frank McCourt

Vague: I have a lot of material possessions, enough so that you might say that I have indulged myself, am perhaps even somewhat spoiled, but oddly enough, those objects I possess have not brought me the amount of pleasure and spiritual rewards I anticipated.

Specific: I live in a house with an outdoor Jacuzzi. I owned, until an embarrassing little accident, a pair of roller skates. I still own a volleyball, Frisbee, tennis racket, backpack, hiking boots, running shoes, a Mercedes 240 Diesel and a home burglar alarm system. But I cannot say that I am satisfied.

From "Real Property" by Sara Davidson

Vague: I find a turtle. It is an interesting creature.

Specific: I reach down, finger into the mud, and pull out a spotted turtle.

The turtle, an adult female, withdraws into her shell. I can feel the familiar form of her bottom shell, the orange and black plastron, resting in the palm of my hand. Her wet top shell glistens in the April sun, deep blue-black, with scatterings of lemon-yellow spots in arrangements that suggest constellations in a star-studded sky.

From *The Year of the Turtle: A Natural History* by David M. Carroll

Name your world specifically. Name people, towns, streets, rivers. Tell us the baby eats canned apricots. Let us know if a hat is purple or beige, made of fox fur or hemp, shaped like a bowl or a stovepipe. Use lists to pack in details as Sara Davidson does with "volleyball, frisbee, tennis racket, backpack, hiking boots, running shoes, a Mercedes 240 Diesel, and a home burglar alarm system."

Look for details that distinguish each person, place, and situation. Don't say, "He is tall with brown hair and eyes." That describes half the men at the party. Say instead that his eyebrows are so bushy they nearly meet over his nose. Mention his blue tie with the small sailboats, the crumbs on his sweater.

Each person, each place is unique. Find the details that express that uniqueness. Don't tell your readers the fourth-grade classroom was large and square with cutouts of pumpkins on the windows. You may want to mention the pumpkins, but focus on the torn one, flapping in the breeze of an open window. That one pumpkin makes the others believable. Mention the student in a wheelchair or one with a three-inch strip of masking tape on his forehead, or the one twisting in his seat, waving an arm to catch the teacher's attention, clearly in need of a trip to the bathroom. Look for a light that's not working, or the five-foot stuffed giraffe with about forty construction-paper rings around its neck.

Develop the habit of noting unusual details. As you walk down the street, scrutinize the woman walking toward you. What details distinguish her? Do the same with family and friends. Next time you're in a restaurant, pretend you will describe it in a story. How is this restaurant different from every other restaurant in the world?

Flaubert told Guy de Maupassant: Look at a line of cab drivers sitting in their vehicles on the edge of the street. Choose the driver and cab unlike any other and write about them. If you have shown them as unique, you will have captured the essence of cab driver.

Ironically, if you describe a cab driver as "typical," you won't capture the essence, and your reader won't respond viscerally.

When your family and friends tell stories, who speaks most specifically? We bet those who tell the most interesting stories are specific. Instead of saying, "I wouldn't trust Cousin Ham with heavy machinery," the good storyteller predicts, "If Ham had a chipper-shredder, it wouldn't be long before he was squirted out the other end."

We had heard of the relentless gambling in Las Vegas, but it came alive for us when a friend said, "I counted seventy-three one-armed bandits in the lobby of the Bigham Hotel where I spent the night. There were one-armed bandits in the elevators and, on the second floor where my room was, on either side of the elevator doors in the hall." We begin to understand the pervasiveness of the gambling when we hear about the seventy-three one-armed bandits in the lobby of a specific hotel and the gambling machines in and around the elevators.

Try this

1. Select a page from a favorite piece of writing. Bastardize it. Make it embarrassingly vague. Type your version. Then leave a space and type the original. You'll get the idea.

2. If you don't think you use enough distinctive details, revise a page of your writing to make the details memorable. Then revise another. And another. Revise it all.

3. We stole this idea from Dan Halliday, who revised several horoscopes for THE *North American Review.* Of course, all horoscopes are vague, but Halliday made them specific and outrageous and funny.

Clip some horoscopes from a newspaper. Revise a couple. Our students worked on this exercise in pairs. Here's one example of what they came up with.

> *Newspaper horoscope:* Situations that have hemmed you in will be somewhat alleviated today. On a modest basis you'll be able to lessen pressures and call your own shots.

> *Student revision:* When your VW doesn't respond to your prayers this morning and you miss the 7:45, your boss will call to inform you that Harvey, his son-in-law, has been promoted to your position as Assistant Vice President in Charge of Interplanetary Diplomacy.

Despair not! Aunt Bertha Mae has fallen into the gin vat and dis-
tillery in Critter Creek. Kentucky is all yours.

4. Write a letter to an advice columnist like Dear Abby asking for
help with an imaginary but specific problem. Give it to a friend.
Have your friend answer, specifically.

⟨⊷⟩ Create an experience for your reader

READERS LONG TO LIVE OTHER LIVES, UNDERSTAND HOW OTHER people feel and think, act and react. They want you to create an experience for them on the page so they can be transported.

One way to provide this is to show more than tell. Rely on the five senses so readers see, hear, touch, taste, and smell, just as you did at the time an important encounter took place. Most important: Readers must see. We cannot stress enough the importance of SEEING.

Novelist John Yount creates an experience for the reader by showing what occurred when a boy jumped into a swimming hole filled with cottonmouth moccasins. What if Yount had merely written: "A boy jumped into a pool of snakes, which, of course, killed him. It was horrifying, terrifying, revolting, and the friends watching were unable to move." That is a detached account. It needs details to bring it to life. Now read Yount's passage from his novel *Trapper's Last Shot*. He doesn't need emotional descriptors like *terror, pain, horror*. Why? Because he shows the specifics of what happened so we experience it, too.

> The next day five boys started out to go swimming in the south fork of the Harpeth river. Except for a thin crust like a pastry shell over the pink dust, there was no evidence of the rain. As they walked toward the river, the heat droned and shimmered in the fields, and locusts sprang up before them to chitter away and drop down and then spring up again as they came on. When they got among the trees on the river bank, the oldest of them, who was fourteen, shucked quickly out of his britches and ran down the bank and out on a low sycamore limb and, without breaking stride, tucked up his legs and did a cannonball

into the water. The surface all around, even to the farthest edge, roiled when he hit as if the pool were alive, but they didn't see the snakes at first. The boy's face was white as bleached bone when he came up. "God," he said to them, "don't come in!" And though it was no more than a whisper, they all heard. He seemed to struggle and wallow and make pitifully small headway though he was a strong swimmer. When he got in waist deep water, they could see the snakes hanging on him, dozens of them, biting and holding on. He was already staggering and crying in a thin, wheezy voice and he brushed and slapped at the snakes trying to knock them off. He got almost to the bank before he fell, and though they wanted to help him, they couldn't keep from backing away. But he didn't need help then. He tried only a little while to get up before the movement of his arms and legs lost purpose, and he began to shudder and then to stiffen and settle out. One moccasin, pinned under his chest, struck his cheek again and again, but they could see he didn't know it for there was only the unresponsive bounce of flesh.

According to the coroner who saw the body, the boy had been bitten close to two hundred times.

Try this

1. Think of a dramatic encounter you witnessed or experienced. Write it with details that create an experience for readers.

2. Reread this snakes passage aloud, preferably to a friend so you can watch the friend's reactions and see and hear the power of Yount's prose. Say to yourself, "What if the writer had been vague and relied on words like 'terrifying' to communicate emotion and create the scene?"

◼→ When to show and when to tell

WHEN YOU SHOW, YOU RENDER A MOMENT SPECIFICALLY, sensuously, so readers see, touch, taste, hear, smell; so they feel they are in that moment. But to rely only on showing limits you and your subject. Let's say you want to give background on years of enduring your brother's temper tantrums, or write about your mentor's remarkable solo trips to National Forests to study lichen. You can't show thirty-five tantrums. Nor can you show each path, tree, species of lichen. Not unless you write a book, or two. So you *tell* the reader much of this information.

In her reflection "Backstroke" (page 257), Donna Kuethe *tells* her history of learning to swim—years of Red Cross swimming instruction at Camp Indian Run, later going on to become an instructor herself. She *tells* us that she still swims often, at her condominium and the health club. She *tells* us she never sees anyone doing the elementary backstroke.

Then she *shows* her elementary backstroke, at a specific time in a specific place, complete with precise physical movement and the moon:

> So one evening alone in a pool . . . , after I did a couple of laps of freestyle (we learned it as the crawl at Camp Indian Run) and breaststroke and the real backstroke, I brought my thumbs to my armpits and shot straight out with my arms in perfect coordination with my legs and the "whip" kick. I snapped it all together and glided 1-2-3.
>
> I looked at a royal blue evening sky; an orange full moon. My arms pushed against the warm water. Glide.

When to tell and when to show? You *tell* when you have important information that will substantially enrich your reader's appreciation of the event or person or idea on which you are focusing. You *tell* when that information is too complex, or lengthy, or just not worth the space of showing. You *tell* insights and comments. Kuethe, for example, comments that she was swimming alone, despite the fact that she had been well taught by her Red Cross instructors never to swim alone. Later, she comes to this insight:

> Maybe we need to learn more things like the elementary backstroke. More things that don't lead to something bigger, better and faster. Things with a glide. More things you can perfect at ten years old at Camp Indian Run and know you learned it. Something you can still enjoy some thirty years later in the quiet solitude of a pool.

On the other hand, you want to *show* when it's important to pull readers into an important moment through their senses, through details.

Try this

1. Tell (in writing) about what you did once when you were ill, in bed or confined for a few days or weeks. Now take a piece of what you told, and show it. For example, if you told how you knit a scarf seven feet long, now show the activity; describe how the knitting needles fit into your hands, how the growing scarf curled around you on the bed and eventually trailed onto the floor, where the cat set to work unraveling all your work.

2. Tell (in writing) how your attitude toward someone in your life changed from, say, not liking him very much to feeling close. Comment about the meaning of this change and why you think it came about as well as how. Comment on the importance of the relationship. Now write a scene between the two of you, showing your closeness or your initial dislike.

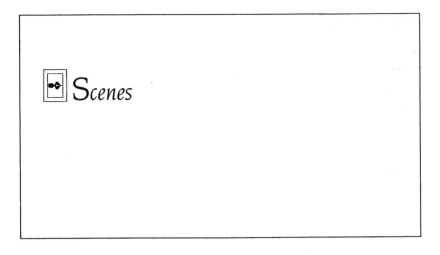

Scenes

SCENES SAY TO READERS: PAY ATTENTION. SOMETHING DRAMATIC IS happening here. They stress critical moments and confrontations. Scenes employ strong sensuous details along with compelling dialogue, a clear setting, thoughts, feelings, the characters' physical actions and reactions, and insightful commentary. They pull the reader into the world you're creating on the page, immediately and vigorously. Most writers love to write them. They energize the writers as well as the readers.

Some scenes use little dialogue; others are almost entirely dialogue. In some, the setting is precisely described; in others it's sparsely sketched. As you study different writers, you'll notice how scenes work in different ways; you'll pick up techniques to create certain effects.

Setting the stage

Think like an acting director. Gather your characters and essential props: the people, furniture, and set. Just as a director doesn't heap the stage with unnecessary furniture, so you shouldn't heap on unnecessary details. However, you must provide enough detail for readers to see. If they don't see, they will lose interest just as they would at a movie if the screen went blank. Even more important, if you don't do the groundwork of fully imagining and describing the setting, *you* won't be transported into the scene. To transport readers, you must first transport yourself to that window booth with the red leather seats at Goldie's Deli, a Swedish ivy hanging overhead, one leaf dropping into your soup as you bite into a hot pastrami on rye. If you smell the pickles say so. If you remember sitting opposite Josh, who had a dollop of mustard on his black mustache, say so. Record who said what when and who reacted how, as if you'd had a video recorder going. You may, at first, include too many details. Not a problem; cut later. For example, in the deli scene you may show Carla with loose bootlaces, and as she walks toward your booth she trips over them, bumping a square, Formica-topped table, jostling the salt shaker. Then you may decide, in another draft, the bootlaces are irrelevant. And so are the table and the salt shaker.

Place affects behavior and events. If you have an argument in the desert, you might stomp around, sneakers filling with sand, turn to your companion, raise your fists to the sky, shout. But if you're having tea and scones at the Ritz with an impeccably dressed couple whispering at a nearby table, that same argument might be subdued, even mimed. The emphasis will come from hissed s's and crisp t's and d's. Perhaps you place one hand firmly on the table and accidentally pull the cloth so tea spills into your saucer. A waiter offers more tea, a new saucer, thus decimating your clearly articulated logic. The fight will be different in each setting. And the outcome will be partly, perhaps hugely, affected by where you are.

Let readers see place influencing your scene.

A scene can be pages long or only a few lines. The more important the scene, the more important it is to show place vividly. In *Catcher in the Rye*, J. D. Salinger's character Holden Caulfield has just been kicked out of prep school. He goes to his history teacher's house to say good-bye. We learn that the teacher sits in a leather chair in his bedroom, wrapped in a Navajo blanket. Salinger writes: "The minute I went in, I was sort of sorry I'd come. He was reading the *Atlantic Monthly*, and there were pills and medicine all over the place and everything smelled like Vicks Nose Drops."

Salinger inserts those nose drops close to the beginning of the scene—a wise choice, because we smell them throughout.

When you've established the people and the place, play out the scene using dialogue, action, and reaction. You may also want to express your thoughts and feelings at the time the scene occurred and now, as you write.

Dialogue

Use essential dialogue only: meaningful exchanges that reveal the characters, their motives, their wants, their conflicts. Cut the *hellos, good-byes, how-great-to-see-yous,* and I-*ran-into-Uncle-Fred-yesterdays,* unless these add to the tension, purpose, forward motion of your piece. Writer Nancy Hale may have said this first, so she gets credit for this excellent definition: Dialogue is what people *do* to each other. The following lines of dialogue *do*:

- I love you.
- I'd like to wring your neck.
- What a brilliant solution you've come up with.
- Stupid idea!
- How could you?
- I want to understand, but I'm not sure I've got the stomach for your new set of excuses.

Study Hemingway for hard-working dialogue. His short story "Ten Indians" sets Nick and his father in a kitchen. The father has seen Nick's girlfriend with another boy and feels he has to tell his son. We're told the father sits in a chair beside the table covered with oilcloth, watching Nick drink milk. Then he cuts a piece of huckleberry pie and says:

> "I saw your friend, Prudie."
>
> "Where was she?"
>
> "She was in the woods with Frank Washburn. I ran onto them. They were having quite a time."
>
> His father was not looking at him.
>
> "What were they doing?"
>
> "I didn't stay to find out."
>
> "Tell me what they were doing."
>
> "I don't know," his father said. "I just heard them threshing around."

In "Ten Indians," Hemingway first sets the scenes visually. Then the dialogue plays out with almost no action, no description, and no commentary. After a while he lets readers see place again and shows the action. Then, once more, several lines of nearly uninterrupted dialogue.

Do not use dialogue to sneak in background facts. For example: "Dahlia, how great to see you, my dear niece who lives so far away in Syracuse. Why, you must be sixteen years old by now. And that blue dress compliments your eyes, as blue as your mother's, my sister, whom I haven't seen since the time we went to that crazy concert and Paul got busted for marijuana." This is ridiculous. If you must include this background, put it in your narration or commentary. For example:

"Dahlia, is that blood? God, that's blood on your dress."

I took my niece's hand. It was cold. She was my only sister's only child—just sixteen years old and, now, in serious trouble.

Never use dialogue to set the scene or feed the reader facts. Here's a grotesque example:

Annette, behind your right shoulder is a window. There are three chairs you'll have to push aside to get to the window, but I wish you'd open it as it is eighty-five degrees in our Introduction to Asian Geography classroom at Burke College in downtown Columbus, Ohio, this early May afternoon and, due to the high humidity, very stuffy.

No one speaks like this. Instead, say it was eighty-five degrees and humid in Columbus, Ohio. In the Introduction to Asian Geography class at Burke College, the teacher asked Annette to open the window. Then mention Annette pushing aside the chairs and opening the window. Or, if need be, say it was eighty-five degrees and stuffy in the class and the teacher asked Annette to open the window. Indirect dialogue is sometimes a better choice than direct, quoted dialogue. In indirect dialogue you refer to what was said but don't deliver it word for word.

Direct: "I can't open the window. My wrist is sprained."

Indirect: Annette said she couldn't open the window because she'd just sprained her wrist, so the teacher asked Lisa.

Sue uses almost 100 percent indirect dialogue in this section of her story "Hangin' on the Wall" that appeared in *The North American Review*. Ned is the father, Stacey the mother. Ned's job was threatened for three years. He was laid off for seven months. In the previous scene, Stacey insulted a woman named Anne.

> Amy, aged six, came crying from the porch. Brother Sam had called her mud fort "dumb" and flattened it with a spatula. Sam said he had started the fort first and Amy and Candace had taken over. Ned wondered why they were taking kitchen spatulas outside in the first place. He had spent a fortune on sand shovels and pails for them. Stacey said she'd given them the spatula as well as a rolling pin and colander and furthermore she would continue to do so. They could have the kitchen sink if they wanted and she wished to God they would take it. Ned said he didn't want them playing with expensive stainless steel kitchen . . . ah . . . ah . . . tools. "Utensils," Stacey said. The word he groped for was "utensils." If he used them occasionally, as even Jack the Jock did, he might remember the correct term. And as for perceiving he wasn't made of money, he could be absolutely certain she understood. In fact, now that he mentioned it, she wanted him to know that for three years and seven months he had nagged. Relentlessly. So that she was unable at the grocery store to decide whether to buy medium or king-sized eggs and . . . "Extra large," Ned said. The words she groped for were "extra large."

This dialogue goes on for another full page.

Often people speak in fragments. They repeat words, stumble. The particulars of their speech reveal character. In Salinger's *Catcher in the Rye*, Spencer, the history teacher, says to Holden: "Why aren't you down at the game? I thought this was the day of the big game." And Holden says: "It is. I was. Only, I just got back from New York with the fencing team."

How much dialogue to use? It depends on who said what and how much it mattered. In scenes with little or no dialogue, the focus may be on action and reaction, thoughts and feelings, or the writer's comments about meaning or background.

Warning: Don't let one person talk too long unless he is emotionally overcharged. Readers won't believe you could remember such a lengthy blast, and you probably can't. But you may be able to truthfully re-create the dialogue from what you recall, filling in what was likely said and how. If you want to give the impression that a speaker went on and on, use a mix of direct and indirect dialogue. Quote a few lines, then report what was said next, dipping back to quote pithy or significant phrases. In "Saying Kaddish for Peter" (page 259), Michael Lowenthal describes a long, recorded monologue. He could, of course, have transcribed the whole thing and written it out verbatim—he has the tape. Instead, he summarizes, interspersing direct and indirect quotes with his own actions and thoughts.

Some writers believe using direct quotations in nonfiction is a mistake, unless you have the words on tape or took copious notes. Direct quotations that seem made up may suggest that you aren't being exact, because who can remember conversations *exactly*?

You have a choice. Use quotations, re-create dialogue as best you can, and assume readers know that you can't remember every single word but will go along with your re-creation. Or, use no quotations at all except when your memory or notes or transcription is a hundred percent accurate.

In the nonfiction bestseller *The Perfect Storm*, Sebastian Junger uses indirect dialogue much of the time and quotations only when he is positive a person said exactly what is quoted. He explains this system to readers in the book's introduction.

Another technique is to quote without using quotation marks. For instance:

> Do you want to go, I said.
>
> He looked puzzled. Maybe I do, he said. But maybe not. Depends on the weather.
>
> Look, I said. You've got to make up your mind.

For attribution, use *he said* or *she said* 99 percent of the time. *Said* is the least interesting word in your sentence. It is nearly as invisible as punctuation, clarifying without calling attention to itself. Don't embellish with words like *replied, responded, retorted, asked, answered, acknowledged, cajoled, begged, growled, howled, groaned, complained, grunted, squealed, intoned*. Well, rarely, maybe once every twenty pages, when it's essential to your meaning. You can use *said* line after line and readers will glide right over it, but they may stumble over those other words.

Instead of

"I just won the sweepstakes," she squeaked.

Say:

"I just won the sweepstakes," she said, and her voice was high and squeaky.

Or, even better:

"I just won the sweepstakes." Her voice was high and squeaky.

Unless she's a door or a mouse, she probably doesn't squeak, and to say so would be inaccurate.

Yes, of course you can throw in an *answered* or a *replied* once in a while for sound and rhythm, but strong dialogue does not need to be explained. You don't need to comment on *how* the line was delivered if the line speaks for itself. "You ass. You stupid, self-centered, ignorant ass." Clearly this is not murmured, whispered, or cooed. The dialogue itself implies a tone and a manner of delivery.

Avoid adverbs 98 percent of the time when attributing quotations. Readers will groan if you write "*I just won the sweepstakes!" she exclaimed excitedly.* Obviously she exclaimed. Obviously she was excited.

Don't say *"You did not win the sweepstakes," she snorted.*

She did not snort words. We challenge you to snort that entire sentence. She said those words, then she snorted. So write *"You did not win the sweepstakes," she said and snorted.* Or you may write *"You did not win the sweepstakes." She snorted.*

Even a small inaccuracy will disconcert readers. They'll sense you're careless, therefore untrustworthy.

Physical action and reaction

Be sure readers can see. Having lived a life among people, you already know a lot about body language. How a person looks on the outside, how he moves, holds his arms, twists his face, places his feet, twitches—all this reveals what's going on inside. For instance, Ann says:

"It makes me furious when you forget my birthday!"

Sam stood, smiling. He nodded thoughtfully, pleasantly, and began to hum.

Sam's reaction tells readers as much—perhaps more—about his attitude toward Ann and her birthdays than anything he might have said. Include physical actions and reactions. They reinforce your dialogue, develop a sense of what the people in the scene are like, suggest conflict, and let readers know what's going on.

One last technical point: Each speaker in a scene is entitled to a new paragraph for her words, direct or indirect, and her actions. This simple technique prevents readers from attributing words, actions, or thoughts to the wrong person, then having to go back and sort it out.

Pay close attention to how actions and reactions fit the words of people you talk with. Notice how they move or do not move in conversation and, especially, in confrontation. Writers observe partly because they can't help themselves, but also to make scenes true to life.

Thoughts, feelings, and comments

Sometimes a scene is so dramatic, the dialogue so strong, you don't want to interrupt it with your thoughts or assessments—your commentary—about the scene. The excerpt from Hemingway's "Ten Indians" (page 89) is an example of a scene that needs no narration. Often, though, including thoughts, feelings, and your interpretation adds meaning. You can also contrast your thoughts *then*, when the scene took place, with your thoughts *now* as you write. Such contrast adds perspective, depth, and meaning. It shows an intellectual or emotional ripening.

In the essay "Canning Jars" (page 263), Author Sandell Morse describes a visit to a thrift shop where she bargained over some jars. The shopkeeper asked for $20. She offered $18. As you read the end of this scene, excerpted below, pay attention to the actions and reactions of the writer, the shopkeeper, and his wife. Notice also Morse's comments about what happened.

> The man lifts his chin and looks at his wife who no longer sits in back of the store. She stands now, behind a counter, leaning an elbow on an old cash register. "Up to you," she says to her husband. "A bird in the hand . . ."
>
> "What's the tax?" the man says.

The woman holds a small calculator and punches numbers. "Eighty-one cents," she says.

"Make it nineteen," the man says.

I smile. "Nineteen."

He looks at me, and I expect that he'll smile, too. After all, he's saved face. Nineteen. Less than the twenty, but more than the eighteen I'd offered, originally, so I'm not prepared for what he says, can't believe I'm hearing correctly. I lean in. His words slur. Understanding seeps, slowly, so slowly that he must repeat. "I hate a woman Jew," he says.

The blow is swift, rushing quickly into my stomach where revulsion and fear swirl in a vortex. I'm stunned; my friend is too, and in that instant when our glances meet, I see her wince. She feels the blow as keenly as I do, for we are women; we are Jews. We know the same icy fear, bred into us for centuries—flee, but not too swiftly. She walks slowly toward the door, moving backwards. I want to move, but I can't. I feel rooted, rooted and mute, and I wonder: Does he see a telltale sign? Smell an odor?

Morse, as she writes now, resees, reexamines, and re-creates her experience then in the shop, her fear, her wanting to ". . . flee, but not too swiftly." As she writes, her response to what happened ripens and matures. Now she can move beyond that first gut reaction of "flee" to the wisdom in the last lines of the essay: "In fertile soil, misunderstanding takes root, grows and flowers into hate. Best to dig up those roots and dry them out in the glittering sunlight of a nearly perfect autumn day."

Read this entire essay, page 263. Not only is it beautifully written, it will teach you a lot: about writing scenes and including background information, about writing with depth and insight, and about prejudice.

Below, we include a paper by our student Maria Roache who writes a wonderful scene about a confrontation with her mother. Imagine if she had just set the stage visually and used only dialogue. It would be a pale scene. We need Maria Roache's comments, now as she writes, about her own and her mother's backgrounds, we need Maria's thoughts as the scene occurred. We also need the indirect dialogue she uses.

Strong impression of mother. Wonderful first sentence. →

Setting established. We see. We hear. We care.

Now the tension builds. This dialogue shows what mother does to daughter.

Maria's reaction. What she thinks, feels, and says.

Maria now as she looks back, commenting on what happened then.

Strong dialogue; strong reactions.

MOTHER

Mom reclined on her fainting couch with her eyes half closed, sipping wine. On the other side of the room, I huddled in a dusty old chair, and slurped Diet Pepsi. A Bach Cantata blared from the speakers at my side, and I glanced longingly at the pile of rock and roll albums in the corner. It took a while for her voice to register in my mind, and even longer for me to react. She wasn't even facing my direction when she murmured, "Why don't you get your hair cut? It looks like a mop?"

The moment I realized she wasn't directing her comment to the cat, who was out of sight, I took offense. My intent was to calmly tell her I liked my long hair, but the moment I opened my mouth to speak, I screamed "You'd love me to get it cut wouldn't you, because you know damned well I'd look like a dog, and that's what you want, isn't it?"

I still wonder which one of us was more shocked. I spent the next few minutes contemplating the possibility of breaking into a loud laugh, as if I were testing her sense of humor, but I had waited too long; the moment had passed, and the damage was done. I glanced at my mom, who had her blue eyes fixed on me, as if waiting for me to fall on the floor and throw a fit. Finally, she broke the silence. Sounding out each syllable, she calmly said, "Do you really think that was necessary young lady?" She had succeeded in making me feel five years old again. The little hairs on the back of my neck stood up with the "young lady," but this time I checked my temper. "Sorry mom," I mumbled, "that was my insecurity speaking."

What mother says and what Maria thinks about it.

"What do you have to be insecure about?" she asked me. Mothers were supposed to understand the deep, tortured psyche of their children; I was determined to make her understand.

I started with my thick ankles, and ended with my turned up nose. Between the ankles and my nose, I focused on every lump, bump, bulge and scar. Her only response was to roll her eyes, flash me a disgusted look, and tell me that if I was that hung up about what I looked like, she didn't have much sympathy for me. Although it hurt, I knew she was right.

Indirect dialogue

Direct dialogue for an important line.

I took a deep breath and asked her to let me explain. "It's not my thick ankles that bother me, mom; it's my thick ankles having to compete with your perfect ones." Mom is tall, slender, dark haired, and was voted "most beautiful" in her high school. I am short, plump, have "mop-like" blond hair, and was voted "most shy" in high school. I hated the puzzled looks mom's friends flashed me when she introduced her "little girl."

Maria interrupts the scene to give important background information.

No unnecessary veers into the past, though.

It wasn't only the contrast in physical appearance that bothered me. Mom was a talented singer. Regardless of how many people assured me that my voice would be just as fine as my mom's, my voice refused to cooperate. I can remember mom drilling me at the piano bench since I was five years old. We'd start with "do-re-me-fa-so . . . ," then, when mom realized I was hopeless on scales, she'd work on enunciation with "ma-may-me-mo, fa-fe-fey . . . ," but to no avail. I knew mom and her "fan club" were all waiting for my "sweet little voice" to develop into mom's rich, controlled alto. I could have told them not to hold their breath.

Back to the original scene with cue of the wine glass, so we know where we are in place and time.

Specifies show mother's reaction through her body language.

Of course mother's cat would be elegant. A great detail that reveals character. We see that cat chasing the fly. Maria lets us see all through this piece.

Again, Maria comments.

Background information

Skillful transition

Maria forces a hard truth on the page.

Mom was now studying her burgundy; gazing into her glass as if it were a crystal ball that had all the answers. "Mom," I asked her, "why didn't you listen to me when I told you we were both wasting our time at that piano bench? I could accept my voice with all its imperfections, if you, and the rest of the world, would stop waiting for it to transform into a booming alto."

Mom was chewing on her lip and fiddling with her wedding ring, like she always did when she was trying to stop herself from speaking out. She sensed that I had not yet relieved myself of my burden, and she tactfully waited for me to continue. I gazed out of the window. The cat, mom's elegant angora beauty, chased a fly around the yard. When I spoke again I had relaxed and my voice reflected the change. It was easier to spill my guts facing a window, than to confront her stern expression. "Mom, I didn't mean to make you sound like the bad guy. I know you haven't been plotting all my life to make me look bad."

In fact, I always had her support. She never did, or said, anything to make me feel inferior. I knew there was an undercurrent of disappointment that I didn't "follow in her footsteps," but there was also continual respect for my individuality. When I worked over the summer on a farm, her initial reaction was "well, if you need money that badly I could loan it to you," but then I'd hear her boasting to her friends about her "tough little kid, what a fighter she is."

I was the one who always did the heavy comparing. Always my own worst critic. And her biggest fan. I'd always wanted her to know how much I admire her, but I'd never been able to tell her. I was afraid that I'd be admitting that she was "better." It wasn't easy for me to choke out, "Mom, I've

A fast summary of what was probably a lengthy tirade.

Indirect dialogue turns into direct dialogue.

Strong physical reaction, description. Maria's comments reveal both women.

We need Maria's comments here. Imagine this story told with dialogue and almost no commentary. We'd miss most of the meaning.

always wanted to be outgoing. I've never been able to make friends as easily as you."

Mom had waited patiently while I sniveled, bitched, moaned, and groaned. Now she willed me, through her silence, to face her. When I finally turned around she told me never to let the world get me down. "I'm just as jealous of you as you are of me. I'm sure much more so now." She told me, "I've always wanted to be little. I've always wanted to be able to dance, and I've always wanted to be able to wear frilly blouses without looking foolish. All those friends you tell me I have are hardly friends. They're acquaintances, admirers. They may like me or admire me, but they could never get too close to me, nor I to them. You're lucky to have real friends. You're close to them, you love them, you need them, and when they aren't around you miss them. I don't miss any of my "friends.""

Mom was now slumped back on the couch, as if someone had just kicked her in the stomach, and she was too weak to fight back. She studied her ankle, moving it around and exploring it with her eyes, as if it were a fine artwork in a room full of junk. When she spoke, her voice was quiet and monotone, out of character for her. "I'd love to have that 'mop' on your head, because it's thick and blond. It's not thinning," she paused grasping for the words, "and it's not streaked with gray. You have your youth, count your blessings."

I knew it hurt her to admit age mattered. The years were catching up to her. Her dark skin now sagged at the jowls, and the wrinkles could no longer be covered with makeup. It seemed as if, when she turned fifty, every sag, crease, and bulge that she had so successfully disguised before came

Time summary followed by a short scene

comment

out of hiding. She rationalized that the extra ten pounds she carried now would keep her warm in the winter. She said the wrinkles that surrounded her eyes and were creeping toward her mouth gave her face character with a bottle of foundation. A few weeks before I had watched as she carried out her morning ritual. She flicked on the brightest lights in the bathroom, leaned over the sink toward the glaring mirror, then grabbed the nearby bottle of "Cover Girl." When she finished, she pushed the makeup aside, took a last look at her reflection, tried to smooth away another line, and finally dropped her hands and walked dejectedly out of the room. It had been a long time since I'd seen her look satisfied with the results.

Maria stands back and comments further.

But in a way, I was relieved she was finally showing her age. I was rarely compared to her anymore. It was nice to know that the average dirty old man watching mom and me walk down the street would most likely be checking me out if he were looking in our direction.

Back to the scene; again we know where we are in time and place. That wine glass is present throughout. If you get good details going early in your piece, some will reappear, unifying the text.

Mom wrapped an afghan around her shoulders, stood up, and walked slowly to the kitchen to refill her empty wine glass. She had been drinking too much lately. She was slumped over like an old lady, and I wondered whether this was a reflection of her mood. Perhaps I had simply never noticed she had bad posture. When her face relaxed, her jowls sagged and made her look angry. I knew they hadn't appeared overnight, but I couldn't recall seeing those jowls before. She left the room and I heard her rattling around in the kitchen.

I had yelled at her for telling me to cut my hair, and accused her of trying to make me look like a "dog." I was still competing with her, and I knew it was time to stop. I

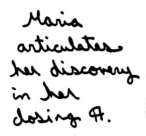

Maria articulates her discovery in her closing ¶.

had not realized, until that day, that the competition was over. I had youth on my side; she was right. I needed to count my blessings and stop rubbing it in her face. I had forced her to remember that her days of beauty—the days when she had a fan club—had passed. No, she still had a fan club. I was her biggest fan, forever.

Student, Maria Roache

Obviously there is no formula for writing scenes. The demands of your material, your attitude toward it, and your temperament will guide you toward deciding how much dialogue or physical description or commentary is needed.

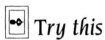 Try this

1. Think of an argument you had with someone. Feel strongly about the person and the argument. Write, and set up the scene so readers see the people and the place. Try to use at least three of the five senses, including smell. Then play out the scene in writing. When you revise, you may want to add more of your thoughts and feelings at the time the scene occurred, and, perhaps, your revised thoughts, now as you look back. You may want to add some background information. Or you may decide the dialogue's so forceful, the conflict so clear that comments are unnecessary.

2. Read the work of several writers you admire. Find scenes with lots of dialogue or almost none, with long descriptions or short ones, etc. Mark where scenes begin and end, then study how the elements intertwine.

3. When you find a scene you love, type or handwrite it, slowly, admiring how the writer chose the perfect detail or wove in a revealing physical reaction as well as feelings and thoughts. This is like taking a chair apart and putting it back together to see how the parts fit. If you're planning on building a chair or writing a scene, the experience will be invaluable.

4. Visit a café where the tables are so close together you can eavesdrop. Bring a notebook and write down what you hear. Record how

people speak, hesitate, repeat themselves. Try to catch the rhythms of their speech, the colloquialisms, the punctuation of laughter or silence. If you were to include the conversation in a scene, what direct dialogue would you use? Indirect? What would you cut altogether?

Write out the dialogue, re-creating the scene using some of the techniques discussed in this chapter. This may turn into fiction—especially if you guess at the speaker's thoughts. On the other hand, thoughts may be preceded by phrases like "She must have been trying to get a rise out of her friend when she said . . ." Or "He seemed to be thinking . . ." Or "Maybe she thought . . ." Such speculation will deepen the reader's understanding of what was going on between the speakers without stepping over the line between nonfiction and fiction. (See "Stretching the Boundaries of Nonfiction," page 221.)

5. Think of a confrontation you had with one person where at the time you felt and thought one way (perhaps angry or stunned or embarrassed or afraid), then later you felt and thought about the experience another way (angrier or amused or worried or reconciled). Write the scene as it happened. Add background, including how you thought and felt at the time, as Maria Roache does in "Mother." Add how you thought and felt later, as Sandell Morse does at the end of "Canning Jars" (page 263). The process may take two or three drafts, but eventually you'll have an essay with richness and meaning.

Playing with time, or the day grammaw died

WRITERS CAN CONTROL TIME ON THE PAGE. IT'S A POWER AND A privilege and we should take advantage of it.

In life, time sometimes controls people. You see the optometrist at 9:00 A.M., go for a job interview at 11:30, and catch a train for New York by 3:00. You rush to and through appointments, wishing you could have stretched the final minutes of the interview. You didn't explain all your qualifications because your prospective employer was standing, waving you toward the door. As the door closed, you walked away thinking: If only she had given me another ten minutes I could have proved I was right for the job.

In your daily life time ticks on, but on the page you can manipulate it. You can stretch a critically important two or three minutes into a page or more of prose. You can describe the last two minutes of your interview for three pages, showing exactly who said what, how the interviewer shuffled papers as you spoke, and at one point leaned forward as if pleased, even excited by what you said, then cleared her throat, sat up straight, raised her shoulders, then lowered them as if something had been decided. And frowned. By slowing time, including detail, you say to readers, "Pay attention, now; I'm allowing this moment to fill three pages because it's central and full of meaning."

You can also compress or summarize time. You can sum up five years of jobs you've hated in a specific, dynamic paragraph or two. Or in a list. You can dismiss a decade in a phrase: "After ten years of living in Atlanta, I moved to Detroit." In "Saying Kaddish for Peter" (page 259), Michael Lowenthal summarizes four years in a sentence: "Since my parents' divorce four years earlier I had been living with my mother and sister, a life nearly devoid of older male figures." Summarizing allows you to emphasize the significance of a period of time.

One way to look at structure is to note where the writer moves quickly through time and where she slows time, where she skims years and where she hovers over a moment. So how do you decide which periods of time to stress and stretch, and which to skim and condense?

Let's say you're getting dressed one morning, not rushing, not dawdling. At 7:30 the telephone rings. It's the person you love most in the world calling from across the ocean, to ask, "Will you marry me?" or to admit, "Our beloved parakeet is dead and I killed it. You'll find his little body in a Tupperware box at the back of the freezer."

Those three minutes on the telephone are far more important than the twenty minutes it took to shower and get dressed. Who cares whether you brushed your teeth before or after you shaved? As writers, we're freed of such trivia. We can write pages about that phone call. We can do justice to its emotional import by carefully examining those few minutes that changed your life.

One pit to avoid: giving every episode equal weight, equal space. Let's say we are writing a story called "The Day Grammaw Died." Say we don't know how to control time on the page. Whenever there's a change in scenery, we start a new paragraph, because that's what we learned from Mrs. Bascomb in seventh grade—a shift means make a new paragraph. We make each paragraph about the same length. This is what happens.

PARAGRAPH 1—THE WAKING UP SCENE

We wake to our digital alarm clock with the small red numbers and smell the coffee and bacon downstairs, swing our feet over the edge of the bed to the floor, which is gritty and dusty. We get dressed, go downstairs.

PARAGRAPH 2—THE MAKING OF THE SANDWICHES

Grammaw is making bologna sandwiches with mustard and wrapping them in wax paper. She is whistling, "Rock Around the Clock," "Rock-a-Bye Baby," and "Rock of Ages," a good sign. She seems okay to us.

PARAGRAPH 3—THE EATING OF THE BREAKFAST

Billy knocks over his glass of milk again. Grammaw says she'll clean it. Mother says, "No, sit down. I'll do it." Grammaw frowns. She sits down.

Paragraphs 4 through 7 detail, in similar fashion, Getting Into the Car, The Fighting of the Kids in the Car and Grammaw's face going red, The Arrival at the Beach where Grammaw tries to carry the cooler and Mother won't let her, Settling Down on the Beach. Then:

PARAGRAPH 8—THE EATING OF THE BOLOGNA SANDWICHES

They eat the bologna sandwiches. Sean spills grape juice on the blanket. Billy calls Sean a slob. Sean says he's not a slob. Billy says he's a baby. Mother says they're being impossible. Grammaw stares at the water, her face pinched as though in pain, and says nothing.

PARAGRAPH 9—THE DYING OF GRAMMAW

Grammaw stands, saying she wants to take a little walk by herself. She walks toward the water. At the edge of the water she stands for several moments, her back to the family. She seems to be looking at the ocean. Then with no warning, no cry, not even a gasp, she falls down, dead.

Obviously no one would write the story this way. Every element is given equal emphasis—from the bologna sandwiches to Grammaw falling down dead. Readers don't know what to make of this story. What is the focus? Where is the meaning? What is it about?

Judging from the title, Grammaw is the focus. Perhaps it's about whether the family is to blame for Grammaw's death. Or maybe it's about Grammaw's health. In future drafts, the significance of Grammaw's death will become more apparent. But for now, with Grammaw as a general focus, we can begin to decide what parts to cut, what to slim down, what to fatten up.

Why not cut the first paragraph? Who cares if the narrator awoke to a digital clock or a windup clock unless Grammaw gave it to her last week? Who cares if the floor is gritty unless Grammaw, after sweeping up sand into a dustpan yesterday, emptied it by the bed because she got confused and believed the floor was the garbage can? And later, who cares that Grammaw wraps bologna sandwiches in wax paper or a Ziplock bag unless at the beach she drops her sandwich out of the Ziplock bag and, leaning over to pick it up, nearly passes out because the blood has rushed to her head?

If it upsets Grammaw that Billy spills his milk, we'll describe the moment, her expression. Maybe the car scene where the kids slug it out agitates Grammaw. If so, we'll show more of the fight. We'll show Grammaw's back and neck stiffen. Show her turning around, looking worried, shaking her head unhappily as Sean cries.

Readers need to know: Was she sitting between Mother and Father? Or by the window? Was her face flushed throughout the trip or for only a little while? How red was her face? What was the set of her head, her shoulders at key moments during the ride? Did she tap the side window with her fingertips? And later, at the beach with the cooler, was she warned about carrying the cooler because she recently had a triple bypass? Here is a chance to summarize Grammaw's history with heart trouble in a short paragraph or two. Also, here or elsewhere, we can enrich the piece with background on Grammaw's spirit, her independence, how much she likes to contribute. We'll want to include comments on Grammaw. Do we share or admire these qualities?

When Grammaw got up during that last fight on the beach blanket, how did she look? What was her expression? How did she sound? These next three to five minutes were the last time we saw her alive. We'll stretch those moments. Was it difficult for her to get out of the chair? Did she wobble? What did her footprints look like in the sand? Did she walk quickly or slowly, steadily or tentatively, toward the water? Did she appear composed? Confused? Sad? We could write a page or more about that last scene on the beach with Grammaw standing and walking away.

To control time on the page, we must first establish focus. Sometimes this takes several drafts, but once we have a good idea what the piece is about, we'll know what's central and worthy of emphasis. We'll also know what is peripheral, trivial, disposable.

In the next two chapters we'll show how to stretch a short, important period of time and how to summarize a long period.

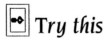 ## Try this

1. Tell yourself or another writer a story from your life. It should have a beginning, middle, and end. You should care about the story.

First, massacre your story as we did with "The Day Grammaw Died." Give everything equal weight and emphasis. Then decide what your story is really about. What is the focus or purpose? What will you eliminate? What will you emphasize? Summarize? What background information will you include?

Now, tell the story again—with emphasis, focus, and feeling.

If you're working with a partner, she should also tell you her story both ways: flat and then with emphasis.

2. Listen to a good storyteller. Pay attention to how the teller slows important moments with details that make you feel part of the scene.

3. Examine the time structure of one of your drafts. Then change the structure to make the focus clearer and put the emphasis where you want it to be.

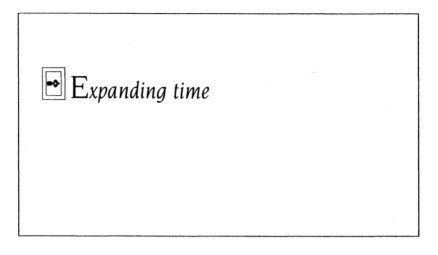

Expanding time

A TIME EXPANSION, LIKE A DRAMATIC SCENE, IS ONE OF YOUR BEST ways to emphasize a critically important moment. Expansions say to your reader, "I've been moving quickly through this story but now I'm going to hover, scrutinize. This moment matters."

To stretch a very short incident to a page or more, first, recall those few minutes in detail. Replay them in slow motion. You've likely seen an Olympic runner on TV finish a race. Probably you noticed only a few details until the finish was replayed in slow motion. Then you saw much more: every movement; grimace; even the position of the runner relative to his closest competitors. It's fascinating to watch a slowed replay on TV. It's fascinating to read of a slowed event on the page.

First you'll need to set the scene so readers see place. Try to use at least three of the five senses. As you recollect what happened, you'll be flooded with details. Let's say you're describing how your dog got hit by a car. It happened fast. He escaped from the house at 6:00 A.M., ran down the steps onto the sidewalk, and started across 32nd Street toward Harry's Market where the cashier would sometimes slip him food. You shouted at the dog. Several cars whizzed by on green lights. You glimpsed the yellow cab. Brakes screeched, someone screamed, the dog was hit, rolled toward the sidewalk. From somewhere a child was crying. An old man ranted: "It's the devil in that car! The devil!" One of the dog's eyes was wide open and crazed.

Although in life much of this happened almost simultaneously, in writing you can present only one detail or fact after another in a linear way. It may help to think of time expansion architecturally: The details are bricks you place one on top of another until you have created the impression of everything happening fast and even at once. Until you have created an experience.

If you record events precisely, using the five senses, you'll be drawn back into that moment and you'll remember even more. Often, you'll discover meaning in these details. This happened to our student Judy O'Donoghue, whose time expansion turned into an essay which we include on the following pages.

Judy described visiting her grandmother in a nursing home when she was ten years old. For Judy the walk down that nursing home hall with old people staring at her took . . . how long? One minute? Two? But the sensations were chiseled into her mind and the experience disturbed her then and as she wrote about it years later. In an early draft she wrote generalities such as "The old women lining the hall were strange and grotesque. They were smelly and they frightened me." Later she revised, specified, and re-created her experience on the page.

The Nursing Home
JUDY O'DONOGHUE

MY FATHER PULLED OPEN THE HEAVY GLASS DOOR OF THE NURSING Home. Each Saturday he came to visit my grandmother. The time had come for me to see her. The air was stale and warm. He guided me with his hand on the back of my neck into the black tiled hall. I was ten, and ever since I could remember, I hated how he led me around by my neck.

The hall was wide and long. Light came through the windows but didn't reflect off the dirty floor. A flickering overhead light stretched down the center of the ceiling. It reminded me of a school corridor with rows of windows on either side. Some windows were open, some were shut. The shades were pulled halfway and were stained with large brown rings.

Old women lined both sides of the walls. They slumped in their wheelchairs or sat in chestnut rocking chairs. A silent television rolled its picture in a corner. One old woman stretched from her wheelchair and stroked the screen with bent fingers.

They smelled of urine and soiled clothing. Their clothes were wrinkled and fit loosely about their figures. Gingham dresses were faded, and old sweaters stained and crusty. They wore black leather slippers and orthopedic shoes. In one corner, an old black woman clawed through a hamper stamped in red, "Dihnan Memorial for the Elderly."

My father's hand fell from my neck and I followed him, almost stepping on the backs of his shoes. I kept my eyes on the floor, and counted the number of tiles that my father stepped in. His pace grew faster and each stride covered more tiles. I moved beside him and glanced up to his face. His eyes were fixed on the far wall.

The halls were so wide and the old women seemed so small. One woman sat in a large chair with gray stuffing hanging from the torn seams. She looked like a squirrel, peering from her hole in the tree. Her eyes seemed too large and round for her face. Her chin was drawn into a bony point. Strands of frizzy hair curled over her ears like tufts of fur, while the rest was pulled tightly into a knot on top of her head.

She startled me with a tug on my skirt. I tried to pull away. Her hand quivered under the hem of my skirt and her fingers gently touched the fabric. Her hand was thin and had brown spots connected by ribbons of blue veins. Her blouse hung loosely off one bony shoulder and gathered at the waist by the elastic band of her blue stretch pants. She mouthed silent words through yellow-chapped lips, like a fish gasping for water. Father tugged my nylon windbreaker and I stumbled back beside him.

The old women stared at us with bulging faded eyeballs and gaping mouths. They seemed like spectators at a circus parade. Except they were the freaks and we were the normal ones.

Their shapes were distorted as they leaned on the arms of their chairs. A few slowly shuffled by us, bending their elbows and clutching their hands tightly against their stomachs to hold themselves up. Some twitched and squirmed, pulling on the white cloth strap that restricted them. Bones poked through flabby skin. A slanted mouth smiled at me with one gray tooth, and a pair of eyes slid under gunk filled lids. I looked away.

An old woman rocked slowly back and forth ahead of us. Her chair creaked with each tilt forward. Her eyes were familiar. They looked like my father's, only his were a darker blue. It was Grandma. I swallowed the dry lunp that had tightened in my throat.

Pulling a chair next to her, I picked up a knitted afghan that was tangled about her thin ankles.

I put my hand over hers. It was so soft. It reminded me of chicken bones surrounded by overcooked skin. The nails were rounded and yellowed, her fingertips dry. I warmed her hand between both of mine and looked up to her face. The skin around her mouth wrinkled into tiny folds and she smiled.

Father sat with his legs crossed so that his narrow-cuffed pants pointed upward above his ankle. He crossed his arms and rested them on his stomach, and looked toward me.

His conversation was light, the weather and what my mother had made for dinner just an hour before. He laughed as he teased her about an old joke that had once embarrassed her.

Grandma didn't understand him, and she stared at the television as he talked. Glancing toward him occasionally, she'd stare blankly at his neck-tie.

Father nudged her gently and patted her on the hand. She scratched at the nick in the arm of the chair. Sometimes, she'd tilt her head when he raised his voice to laugh or tell a joke. Father sat back in his chair, uncrossed his legs and stretched them out in front of him. He crossed his ankles, sighed and touched his hand to her knee. She looked to the floor and began to hum.

I wanted to cry and shake her out of her daze. I wanted my father to do the same. I hated how we pretended that she knew us and was still the same. She wasn't. Her clothes were messy and stained. Her nose was crusty and her eyes were puffy from sleep. The nurses kept her dentures out because she would bite her lower lip and bruise it.

One black slipper with a hole in the toe was half-way off her foot. Her heel was chapped and wrinkled with purple and blue swollen veins. I bent down and slipped her shoe over her bare foot. She leaned, straining over the white cloth belt that tied in a double knot behind her, and fingered the toe of the slipper.

Grandmother's nose was long and it curved down into a slight hook. Father's formed the same shape but was broader at the nostrils. Under his eyes, the skin had begun to collect in crescent-shaped bags as my grandmother's had already done. Her cheeks hung down like saddle-bags but Father's still remained firm.

The longer I looked, the more and more they looked alike. Grandma's face had fallen and Father's was beginning to pull from his cheekbones. His chin hung down like a hammock attached to his neck.

I shifted in my chair and looked up to the clock above the exit light. I wanted to leave. I wanted my father to go away so he wouldn't catch it.

I moved my hand to his and he squeezed hard. It was still tight with muscle. I smiled at his strength and I let his large fingers spread mine apart. I wanted to tell him that I loved him and wished he'd never get old.

* * *

"The Nursing Home" is a good piece to study: It slows time. Many details are outstanding: for example, one woman strokes the rolling TV screen with bent fingers. Judy includes the sense of smell early in the piece so it stays with us throughout the scene. Often she places the strongest sentence with the best details either at the beginning or the end of a paragraph which is a trick writers use to emphasize their best facts, details, sentences.

When Judy first wrote this, she knew only that the old women disturbed her. As she revised, she recalled how she had, as a child, noticed that her father resembled her grandmother. As she wrote, she realized why the encounter had so profoundly affected her: She had been afraid her father would "catch" old age from the grandmother. It was Judy's first awareness of aging, of impending death.

Many time stretches rely mostly on describing the external world, but we include one that has many of the author's thoughts and feelings on page 278. It was written by Dr. Stephen Schultz, who had been one of our students. As a resident in a Rochester, New York hospital, he had about a five-minute encounter with a neurologically damaged baby and his two young parents that so affected him, he rushed from the room and wept. The essay was published in a medical journal. In the essay, Stephen imagines the father of the damaged son thinking these specific thoughts: "Will he live? Will he breast-feed again? Oh Sweet Jesus, please, what has happened to my son." It will be helpful for you to compare Judy's greater emphasis on external details with Stephen's combination of similarly precise external details along with specific reflections.

Try this

1. Select an incident that took only a few minutes but is imprinted in your brain so you can replay it in slow motion on the page: being told by someone you love that he doesn't want to see you anymore; receiving an award; running from a mugger; watching someone you care about make a fool of himself; surviving an accident; meeting a moose on a hiking trail; anticipating the results of a medical test.

Identify your task. Title it: for instance, "The three minutes after I opened the kitchen door and found my mother unconscious." Then plunge in with a key detail, fact, or observation. When you've run out of momentum on this first draft, try again. Build the details. Check to see if you've engaged at least three of the five senses. Be sure readers can see. Look for openings, opportunities between sentences, to expand even further. Better to put in too much than too little; you can cut all but the best later.

After several drafts, the time stretch may stand on its own, serve as a dramatic lead, or be embedded in a longer piece.

2. In your reading, notice how writers slow time. Take time yourself to reread a slowed passage. Read aloud. Underline striking details and note where they are placed in paragraphs. How many of the five senses are used? What is the mix of physical detail and thought or speculation?

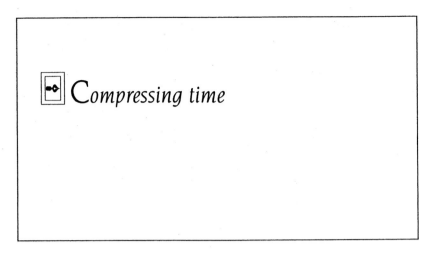

Compressing time

YOU CAN SUMMARIZE SEVERAL DAYS, WEEKS, YEARS, OR DECADES IN a specific dynamic paragraph. This will add depth, meaning, scope, and efficiency to your writing. Before you write a time summary, think purpose. What do you want to show? What is the nature of this period? What is the dominant impression you want to create? It helps to let readers know the length of time you're summarizing. Words like *often, frequently, always, usually, again and again, sometimes, occasionally, from time to time, now and then,* and especially *would* suggest actions were repeated. If your summary fills several paragraphs or pages, you can stop using *would* after you feel readers understand the repetition; then you can switch to past tense. For example, start with "Joe would often take his dog on hikes in the White Mountains." Continue with the *woulds* for a few sentences. "They would bring lunch— a Snickers for Joe, Milk Bones for the dog." Then shift to simple past. "Joe liked to push himself until his heart pounded, his knees ached, and sweat soaked through his clothes; the dog just liked to run."

In "Bluestown," Geoffrey Becker tells of a boy who takes off with his father for a weekend without first informing the mother. The parents are divorced. The father, a failed musician, is charming, irresponsible, impetuous, and, in most ways, less mature than his son. Becker chooses to show how the boy and his father spent time together mostly talking about and listening to the music his father liked—dominant impression. We also see how the father backs away from family responsibilities even though he loves his son— purpose and meaning.

The story opens with the father taking the boy out of class, pretending his son has a doctor's appointment. After he gets the boy in the car, the father says it's too nice a day to be in school and the boy ought to be "sprung."

Becker could then have merely recounted how, as they drive toward Canada, adventure turns to misfortune. But he adds meaning by revealing the history of the father-son relationship. What comes after reverberates with the knowledge of a big chunk of life expressed briefly but with detail and power, as Becker tells us the father lives in an apartment over Angelo's Pizza and Calzone. Notice that he names this place, Angelo's; he's not satisfied with the generic "pizza house." The boy *usually* goes to the apartment after school even though the father's supposed to see him only once a week. The time summary begins:

> He loved to break the rules—it was one of the things I liked best about him. . . . [We] hung around listening to albums or playing cards. . . . We'd sit up there in his cluttered apartment, albums and cassette tapes strewn over the floor, the smell of pizza wafting up through the floorboards, and he'd tell me how he was never really cut out to be a family man.

The reader learns that possessions:

> . . . made him nervous, even things like his stereo and television, but even so, whenever he got some money he'd spend it on a new toy— a phase-shifter or a compressor or maybe a graphic EQ . . .
>
> He played me albums too, everything from Robert Johnson and Lightnin' Hopkins to Jimi Hendrix and Duane Allman.

Notice the smell of pizza. And how Becker names names, not musical equipment in general but a phase-shifter, a compressor, a graphic EQ. He names recording artists, too: Robert Johnson, Lightnin' Hopkins, Jimi Hendrix. Even if you do not recognize those names, they add authority.

Go through the paragraphs again, noting shifts from *we would* or *we'd* to the simple past tense as Becker leads readers to understand the nature of these visits.

How many *woulds* to use? Trust your common sense. After two or three or four sentences, ask yourself: Is it obvious that these incidents happened again and again? If so, use past tense for a while, returning to *would* or *too* or *often* from time to time to remind readers the summary continues. Don't worry too much about *woulds* in the first draft. Get the details down; refine the structure in revision.

Becker's time summary showed up in the ninth paragraph of his piece. He hooked us into the tension of current time, then delivered this condensed background.

Many papers, essays, articles are launched by time summaries. In "My Month in the Cascades," our student Ross Robinson summarized a month of camping in his lead, then detailed a particular experience.

> Every morning we would wake up with the sun. All month we had fooled ourselves by changing the time on our watches. We would rise at first light when our watches said seven a.m., when actually it was five. After a few days we forgot we were fooling ourselves.
>
> Every day (with the exception of a handful) we would pack our Sierra Designs Dome tents and expedition gear into our packs, then set out. . . . It was usually a place on the map where the contour lines were widely spaced and water source was close by. . . . There were so many things I loved about being up high: the crisp air that bit at your face, the winds that howled in strange directions, and views of high mountains, glaciers. . . . We could see the weather rolling in sometimes days before it reached us.

To transition from a time summary to a specific incident, use cues like *once* or *that Tuesday in December*. Ross writes, "There was one day of hiking in the trees that . . ." and he's off.

When you first try a time compression, don't worry about choosing brilliant examples to illustrate, say, your awful two weeks on an Outward Bound sailboat. Don't choose at all. Jot details and incidents as they come to mind—the forty-mile-an-hour winds; rain for three days; the pitch of the boat; throwing up; listening to Bill whine about his sore knee, cramps, cold feet; wondering why you ever signed up for this damned trip anyway. In a later draft, you can add or substitute more precise or revealing details: the waves cresting at fifteen feet; the soggy oatmeal bread and even soggier Fig Newtons; somebody else's vomit in the bilge.

How do you know when to use this technique? Let's say you are writing to understand more about your complex relationship with your father. You start with the argument about your not filling up the gas tank after you'd used his car. He called you irresponsible, immature, and proceeded to verbally attack your room, your grades, your attitude, even your friends. This fight was particularly hard to take because, though your father has always been critical, you've lived away from him for two months and felt free of him. But now he's undermined your newfound confidence. Had he been a supportive parent, this fight might have been an aberration, and therefore not essential to who you are today. But he has never been supportive, and it's important for the reader to understand that history and the nature of his criticisms. Did he criticize the way you spread butter on your toast when you were five? The way you made your bed? The dust on the top shelf of your closet? The size of your ears?

A time summary following the opening fight scene will provide the reader with this background. Or maybe the summary should come first and lead into the fight. Use time summaries when you feel the reader's understanding of your subject will be enriched by the backdrop that makes this particular experience resonate for you.

Try this

1. Think of a long period of time you feel strongly about: your first marriage, the three months Grandmother lived upstairs, a decade of competitive skating, a year with a terrible landlord, a decade of trying to learn to play the piano, two weeks at the lake, the six months before your parents separated. Now tap into your strongest impression of that period. For instance, the six months before your parents separated were hell. Or the four years of competitive skating were a roller coaster of highs and lows.

With this time period and your impression of it firmly in your mind—you may want to give it a few hours or days to incubate—label a page: Three Months of Grandmother in the Spare Bedroom. What are your associations with that time? Generate as many specifics as fast as you can. In the next draft you can choose among them or add to them. Warning: As you write these details you may find your impression changing. That's OK. Start again with your new perspective.

2. Recognize and appreciate time summaries in your reading. Which facts, details, and incidents reveal the most? Which are the least effective? Imagine what the piece would be like without the time summary. What would be lost? Say to yourself, "Good grief, the author just covered fifty years in six sentences. How did she do that? Read the sentences again to find out.

Use and misuse of chronology

GOOD STORIES MAY BEGIN AT THE BEGINNING AND END AT THE END.
If the experience is dramatic with a clear sequence of events, you'll
need little or no commentary or explanation. Just tell the story, or
let the story tell itself: This happened, then this and this.

Let's say you want to write about your week-long climb in the
mountains with your older brother and his friends. He had not
wanted you along: You were too young, not strong enough, and socially, you'd be "out of it." You begged; he relented. On the second
day you ran into a freak snowstorm with winds of sixty miles per
hour. Everyone was cold and exhausted. The next morning your
brother said if you wanted to turn back, he'd go with you. Although
you were aching and frightened, you said no. As you describe this
trip from beginning to end, with your final triumph of returning to
base camp with the others, the coming-of-age message can't help
but emerge. You passed a test. You joined the adult world of men.
In this case, chronology *is* the story, and the meaning is inherent
and obvious.

For other stories, strict adherence to chronology will not be effective. Let's say you're writing about diving. You might start with
your fear, at age five, of jumping from the diving board, then remark
how ten years later you performed a perfect jackknife from a thirty-
foot cliff into the pool of the LeGault stone quarry outside Sher-
brooke, Quebec.

The rest of the piece might consist of what happened to you
physically, intellectually, spiritually, and emotionally between
those two events—not necessarily in chronological order. You

might want the freedom to jump back and forth often in time, comparing your coach's encouragement in high school with your mother's when she taught you to splash in a plastic pool in the backyard. Then leap ahead seven years to your first meet and how the captain of the opposing team laughed at your short arms. This free-flowing time travel allows you to connect events that are distant in time but close in meaning.

If you find yourself in a this-happened-then-this-then-this pattern, stop. Ask yourself, "Is this the best form for my story or am I trapped in chronology? Do I need to break free?" You're trapped if you feel anxious to get to an exciting scene but held back by having to record all that preceded it. Another clue is sensing that you may be telling too much. You're uncertain about what to skip, so you don't skip anything. If you've written a full draft in chronological order, ask yourself:

- Will the reader care about my beginning as it stands? Does it have tension?
- Does this piece have meaning?
- Is it shaped?
- Do I use what happened to support a point, or am I merely regurgitating events one after another?
- Is this the best form for what I want to express or just the most obvious?

If you decide to break out of chronology, do so with gusto and the conviction that yes, there are other ways to present these events and you will find them.

Try this

Take the scissors to your chronological draft, cutting apart the incidents. Lay the pieces out on a table and shuffle them. Using the shuffled draft as a guide, write a brief outline of what would come first, second, third, and so on. Let's say you were going to start with a description of trying to get to sleep that first night on the cruise ship. Then you might flash back to the death of your spouse, your loneliness, and how this trip was the first you'd ever taken alone.

Maybe you would describe how you resisted the idea six months ago when your sister-in-law suggested it.

Now choose a different incident to lead with, perhaps a conversation with another passenger and your discovery that she, too, is traveling alone. Your first reaction is to feel sorry for her; then you remember that you are in the same boat. Maybe you'll transition to your husband's funeral and the moment your grief subsided enough for you to feel the brunt of everyone's pity. You might describe how you resolved not to give in to self-pity, ever. Write a second brief outline based on this reshuffling.

Keep going. Try several new orders until you are struck by one that seems right.

Now return to your computer and put the pieces back together with a new time sequence—and, perhaps, a new focus.

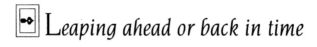

Leaping ahead or back in time

YOUR STORY BEGINS IN A CROWDED SUBWAY STATION, AND YOU DE-cide to flash back to a summary of all the times you've waited there. Make your transition fast: "For the past three years, I've waited at least five mornings and evenings a week at the Kenmore Square Station that stinks of urine, sweat, perfume, and cigar smoke while commuters have bumped and even shoved me aside." You might continue to describe the sensations that repeat—the sounds, your anxiety, feeling faint, late trains. Then return to the body of your story—the now, on-this-particular-afternoon—quickly: "Today at the station . . ." or "As I watched the train doors slide open for the five-hundred-thousandth time . . ." This will show readers where and when the scene takes place.

Move back and forth between background and the immediate scene as often as you like, so long as you let readers know where they are in time and place. You can leap ahead: "Three years later in Chicago . . ." or "Within six months I'd be out of Boston, for good, milking cows in Vermont."

You don't have to explain the lapsed time. You don't have to show Julia as she puts on her coat and red gloves, holds out her right hand, and bids good-bye. If the point of your scene is to reveal her as drunk and sloppy, show her gesturing like a bad actress in a bad play, knocking her wine glass, spilling burgundy on the white plush rug of her publicist's Manhattan apartment.

Then leave it. Move on. "Three days later, I saw her on Park Avenue." Or insert a space break and start right in on the next episode.

Michael Lowenthal in "Saying Kaddish for Peter" (page 259) travels gracefully through time in this sentence that follows a space break: "Then at this year's seder, the tenth Passover since my grandfather's death, I learned that in his final months, Papa Eric had recorded a cassette of his memories."

Sometimes background information takes the form of a scene, sometimes a time stretch or summary, sometimes straightforward presentation of facts. One sentence might be all the background you need: "For three years, every Sunday supper over macaroni and cheese we argued just like this." Whatever the scope of your background, be sure it moves your story forward. Avoid the memory or detail that interests only you. Tell or show readers what they need to know when they need to know it.

You need to include background if, without it, your story would seem superficial. Flashbacks and background can move a story to a deeper level of meaning.

At the beginning of a flashback, if your main story is in past tense, use the word *had* two or three times. This alerts readers to the time shift. If your flashback is many pages long, after another page or two you may want to throw in another couple of *hads* as reminders.

If your immediate scene is present tense, as in Pat Parnell's "Visitation" (page 275), alert readers to a flashback with a shift to the simple past. Pat describes a surprise visit from her dead mother in which the mother shares her bed and body. "When I look in the mirror, I see her face with mine, her blue eyes staring at me with their hawk stare" (present tense). A few lines later, Pat transitions to a flashback: "When I was very young, I shared her bed sometimes, when we took our naps together in the big mahogany four-poster" (past tense).

Readers notice the tense changes and follow Pat's transition. Be clear, always, about where you are in time and place. Before you lead readers into a long flashback, leave the present scene at a memorable moment with one or two strong details you can return to after the flashback is over. One of our students opened her story by saying a real estate agent had just knocked on her door. The agent had a client with her, and the writer hated to have to sell the place. She described the agent's aggressive sales pitch and mentioned that the woman wore a dozen thin silver bracelets. As the agent gestured, the bracelets would fall, clinking, first toward her elbow, then toward her wrist.

She then started a new paragraph with information about what the house had meant to her for ten years and why she had to sell it. She returned to the opening scene with the agent slapping her palm flat on the pink bricks of the fireplace four times to emphasize the solidness of the construction. The silver bracelets clanked against the brick. And readers knew precisely where this scene was in time and place.

Your leaps ahead and back should be guided by your theme, your focus, your sense of tension, and what the reader needs to know when. You can leave a restaurant scene where you and Ty argued by saying: "We never did move to Kansas City, and the boutique idea shriveled quickly. Six months after we had fought in Jenny's House of Pasta and Seafood, we opened a marina in the Florida Keys and in addition to being business partners we became man and wife. But at the restaurant that night, eating spaghetti, we fought, hard and loud over who would be president and who vice-president of our venture."

Try this

1. Revisit a book or essay or article or story where the writer uses background information, flashbacks, and flash-forwards. Read the page before the flashback or flash-forward. Mark the transition. Pay attention to the words and phrases that keep readers on track.

2. In the section titled "Their Voices," read Sandell Morse's "Canning Jars," Hillary Nelson's "Mildred's Snowdrops," or Pat Parnell's "Visitation." Note how the time patterns vary from essay to essay, from many quick moves back and forth to staying with one scene for the bulk of the essay, shifting for a paragraph or two, and then returning to the main scene. Would one of these patterns work in a piece of yours? Try it.

⊡ Stringing a subject along: a way to look at structure

WHEN YOU THINK ABOUT SHAPING YOUR PIECE, YOU MIGHT IMAGINE an outline, a list of ideas, a puzzle, a collage, a mosaic, or a frame like the studding of a house that holds up the roof and separates one room from another.

Certainly when your piece is finished it will have a recognizable structure. Readers will see how ideas and details connect. They will see how the information is organized, how you moved through time, how you used scenes or didn't, included dialogue or didn't, cited experts or didn't. They may see, for example, that the ending echoes the beginning but more forcefully. They may notice that you've hinged your argument on three anecdotes and each presents a fresh angle including several pertinent statistics. They may notice you listed five strengths of the novel you're reviewing, switched to five weaknesses, and ended with a quotation from the novelist. If you are skillful, readers may not notice the structure at all. They'll read what you've written, feel the impact—intellectually and emotionally—and say something like "Wow!"

One useful way to think about *creating* a structure is to imagine your subject as a maze of caves and tunnels. At the beginning of the process, you enter the cave closest to the surface, taking care to tie one end of a long ball of string to a tree just outside so you won't get lost. This string will link all you find within. Then you wander. You creep and slide and crawl and slither and explore—unwinding the string as you go. Is the string *intuition* or *theme* or *resonance* or *momentum*? Call it what you like, but don't let go. Sometimes you hit a wall and must backtrack. Sometimes you come to the edge of a precipice and get scared. You must decide whether to jump in, scoot around, or leap across. Generally, we recommend jumping in.

Writing that evolves from this kind of exploration is often surprising, especially to the writer. We don't know if Hillary Nelson imagined herself stringing through a cave when she wrote "Mildred's Snowdrops" (page 267), but as we read it after the fact we see evidence of an active, open, inquisitive mind at work. She ties her string to something solid right away. The essay begins: "Mildred's snowdrops are in bloom down on Shaker Road; they light up the leaf-matted earth like pools of warm spring sunlight, though the cold April sky is still spitting rain and snow." The string is secured to those snowdrops and she will return to them in the end. Nelson also orients readers. She names a place (Shaker Road); a time (April); a mood (cold sky still spitting rain and snow).

These flowers belong to Mildred, she tells us, even before we know who Mildred is. Turns out, she's Hillary's mother-in-law, who'd been telling Hillary about the snowdrops for years. "She always promised to show them to me one day, but last April was the first I spent in Canterbury, and Mildred died two months before the snowdrops bloomed, so I had no one to remind me to go look at them, to see the proof of spring."

From "proof of spring," the writer steps into another chamber—her baby. It's a natural connection: baby/new/spring/renewal. Another connection: "Oliver was born ten days after his grandmother died, on a snowy night in the heart of February. . . ."

Not the *middle* of February, but the *heart* of February, another connection, because this essay explores love and family and respect. It is not about Mildred or snowdrops or even the writer. It's about a relationship, the place at which Mildred's and Hillary's lives intersect. That place happens to be the garden—the garden Mildred planted and nurtured; the garden Hillary took over. So the string leads us into the garden: Hillary culling, Mildred defending the overgrowth and undergrowth. We see them weeding. We smell Mildred's welcoming bouquets. We ache as Hillary wrenches out "an enormous bed of bearded iris, matted with witch grass and plagued with iris borers," then relents and replants a few to please Mildred, who "greeted them like old friends when they bloomed the next summer."

At any point a less skillful writer might have taken a wrong turn and refused to backtrack. For example, Hillary could have gone into detail about her father-in-law's illness, or his divorce from Mildred, or Oliver's first year, or even technical information on iris borers or the best varieties of peony for central New Hampshire. She may have included some of those things in earlier drafts, but in the final draft she knew which caves to enter and which pits were full of meaning.

She stays with the garden, the flowers, growth, blooming, color, and the passage of time. And, always, she returns to Mildred—the things Mildred said and did that most affected the writer. Mildred's love of life shines through: "Just look at those crocuses, the way the sun comes through the petals, like stained glass." Mildred calls Hillary an optimist, and it's clear to readers that optimism runs deep in both women.

This essay comes full circle. Hillary explored, kept tight hold of the string, and returned to the place of entry: Mildred's snowdrops. She lets readers see the snowdrops in the first paragraph, but on the last page or so we see them again, in greater detail and, now, having been to the garden and back, we understand why they are significant and something of their meaning: "mounds and mounds and great sweeps of snowdrops, hundreds and thousands of them, blooming furiously, unseen, unaware that the hands which had planted them had long since returned to dust, that the garden which had once contained them had been replaced by choking bittersweet—that Mildred hadn't been there that spring to welcome them."

This meaning is not forced or imposed. It emerges naturally from a full, spiraling, open-minded, open-hearted exploration. Paraphrase won't do it justice, but here are some words we think speak feebly to what Hillary Nelson is getting at: *renewal, beauty, hope, mortality, love, loss, continuance.*

Try this

1. Think of an activity you love but you're not sure why. For Hillary Nelson gardening is a joy and a challenge, and not just because she likes fresh tomatoes and getting dirt under her fingernails. What is

it that draws you to watching suspense movies, burning brush, vacuuming, making teddy bears, playing golf, climbing mountains, refinishing furniture, volunteering at the soup kitchen, baking pies? If you can figure out the appeal, you will figure out meaning, and you'll have an essay.

Begin by picturing yourself engaged in the activity. Write down exactly what you do and how and what you're thinking, how it feels. Tie the string to some solid detail: snowdrops; your favorite ski course; Hitchcock's *Vertigo*; the motorcycle you bought for $500 and restored. Once the string is tied, explore. What are your associations with this activity? Memories? Bad experiences and good? Mistakes? Triumphs? People? One particularly influential person? How does this activity tie in with other aspects of your life?

Once you've explored as much as you'd like and generated lots of material, circle back to the beginning. You may have the shape and substance of an essay. If not, you'll have plenty of material to work with as you draft.

2. Think of a person important to your life. This may be someone you've known for years, or someone you knew for a short time who left a lasting impression. Rather than try to write directly about the person, think of something you had in common or an experience you shared. Maybe you and your high school drama teacher shared a love of Sondheim and you were cast in the part of the witch in *Into the Woods*. Then you got sick the day before showtime and . . . ? Or that summer you and your dad fixed up the Mustang—maybe working on that car you fought with him more than you ever had, and felt closer to him, too. By writing about a specific shared interest or experience, you may discover and reveal much about the person, yourself, the relationship.

3. Think and write about a time you were at odds with someone important to your life. What did you disagree about? What did you do about it? How was the problem resolved? Looking back, do you understand the other person's point of view any better? Do you still think she was *all* wrong and you were *all* right? How is your perspective different now? What would you do differently now?

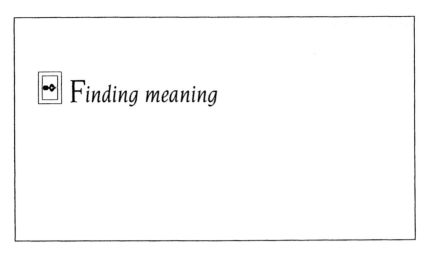

Finding meaning

IF YOU TELL A FRIEND A STORY ABOUT YOUR CANOE TRIP IN THE Rangely Lakes, he won't, after you finish, say, "So what? What's the real meaning of the trip beyond the facts you told me?" He's your friend. He's glad you had a great trip. He enjoyed your story.

When you write for a wider audience, assume no one knows you. Your readers have no reason to care that you camped on Turtle Island and toasted hot dogs over an open fire. Readers want payback. They want a compelling surface story—what happened—as well as a sense that what happened mattered, affected you in some way, perhaps even changed your thinking or led you to a fresh perspective, insight. They want to know why you choose to preserve the story on the page. Why should they be interested in the fact that you ate hot dogs cooked over an open fire unless, say, you'd always been afraid of being alone in the wilderness. By building a fire, cooking, staying overnight, you proved to yourself you could survive, overcome fear. So the meaning has to do with self-reliance. Meaning stems from the events of the story, but it is larger than the story and has everything to do with the writer's perspective—how he or she sees the story

Some people use the word *theme* when they discuss meaning. The theme of fear in the Rangely Lake story might arise from details like the darkness; the cold, frightening sounds; memories of other times when the writer was nervous, anxious, afraid; the skittering of a small animal in the leaves, perhaps running from a larger animal. As you write about the experience, you pay particular attention to details that connect to themes of fear, self-sufficiency, personal growth.

Novelist Theodore Weesner said, "Theme is what the hell it is you're really trying to say." Grace Paley has said, "Every story is two stories." Stories are convergences, perhaps between a surface story —I paddled across the lake and camped on an island—and the underlying story or theme of overcoming fear. Meaning comes from a writer's exploration of theme—what he makes of it; how he shows or explains the effect of this experience on his thinking, his life.

When you have discovered your theme, address it all the way through. In music, theme is presented early, then enlarged, altered, enriched. Same thing with writing. Every fact, incident, and comment should connect to theme and advance your story as you move toward meaning. Five different campers might explore the theme of fear in five different essays—and each would have different meaning, because each camper has lived a unique life and has a unique perspective.

In "A Father's Eyes" (page 278), Stephen Schultz, a medical intern, draws meaning from a moment he spent with a couple whose infant has severe brain damage. He structures his piece simply. In present tense he tells readers that he's been called to a hospital room; he's not sure why except that he's the intern on duty. He is sleep deprived. He wants to lie down. When he arrives at the room, the mother is rocking the baby and trying to breast-feed. She tells Schultz that, yes, they had called for him because they thought the baby was worse, but he seems better now. The father is asleep on a cot, turned away from the doctor. Schultz notices the soles of his Birkenstocks—a humanizing detail that makes readers see the father as an individual.

The father wakes. He says, "What happened?" and, later, "I don't understand."

The doctor excuses himself. He leaves the room crying, later sobbing.

End of story.

Not much of a story, really, even with details that put us in that hospital room and let us see the parents and infant: "floppy, grotesquely swollen . . . perhaps 6 weeks old. He has a tube coming out of one nostril, and an IV in one hand." What gives Schultz's essay power, and it is a deeply moving piece, is the way he traces theme throughout and comments, offers his perspective, makes meaning by connecting his life to the lives of these devastated parents, by examining his feelings and coming to understand them.

Of the hundreds of details he could have chosen, he consistently picks thematically resonant ones: the woman is rocking the child (a universal image of mother love and comfort); she is breast-feeding him, or trying to (giving him nourishment to make him strong—but the doctor knows this baby will never be strong, may not survive); she guides her breast to his mouth, but he doesn't move. Later, Schultz thinks of his own son; again the details suggest theme. In contrast to the sick child, Schultz's son had "sweet breast-milk breath as a baby." He was a "mischievous," active toddler—"tricycle rides, the snowball fights, the ice cream cones, the love." Like the mother, Schultz held his son protectively in his arms. Like these parents, Schultz loves his son "fiercely."

Themes of love, family, protection, mortality, possibilities, vulnerabilities bubble throughout. Schultz makes sense of these themes when he looks into the father's eyes and understands, as perhaps only this writer at this moment could, that when the father asks "What happened?" he's really asking, "Oh, Sweet Jesus, please, what has happened to my son?" Schultz goes on to try to understand his own intense reaction: What is it in *him* that responded so ferociously—with tears, later sobs, and uncontrollable purging of emotion? What triggered his response? Through writing, Schultz figures this out and shares his insight with readers. Through looking closely at the details of the experience and the themes they suggest, he discovers and expresses meaning.

Some pathways to theme and meaning

Ask "so what?"
Ask, "What do I stand to discover as I write on this subject? What do I want to see in a new way or ways? Am I writing to understand?" Then, as you write, try to learn.

Of course, for many subjects you will have little or no idea from the beginning where the learning might occur, yet you have an inkling that there's more to the subject that you know. This is enough to go on. Judy O'Donoghue had no sense of wanting to learn one specific thing, no notion of meaning when she began "The Nursing Home" (page 110). Had she forced herself to pose and answer a question, to work with a theme from line one, she probably wouldn't have started the story at all. But she knew and trusted her sense that the old women and her grandmother frightened and fascinated her. She trusted that fascination indicates meaning or theme, somewhere. And drafting was her way to find that place. If a subject draws you in, assume that meaning will come, maybe not in your first draft but in your third or fifth.

Just write your story, alert to clues and insights that may be thematic. You remember and choose to record certain details and scene *because* they struck a chord. Once that chord has sounded four or five times in a draft, you'll recognize theme, and once theme is established, meaning follows.

After a first draft, many of us face the terrible question "So what?" After her second or third draft, Judy asked herself, "What did that visit with Grandmother mean? Why did it have such an impact on me?" Many of her details had to do with aging, mortality. She began to see the meaning as her growing awareness that those she loved were marked for death, as we all are. In later drafts, she emphasized the parts of her story that spoke most strongly to that theme.

Comment

Reflect on your material and record those reflections on the page. These comments may be as short as a phrase or go on for paragraphs. An accumulation of insights can lead to theme and wisdom.

Resist the urge to hoard insights, to save them for your ending when all is revealed. Chances are if you think you know the insight that will conclude your paper, it probably isn't very insightful. When you have an insight, write it down. In fact, write everything you know about the situation, the people, the relationships, the issue, and the problem in the first pages of your first draft. These early insights form the foundation for deeper, less obvious ones in subsequent drafts.

The act of writing is an act of thinking. One good thought, insight, or comment will yield other even better ones. Trust this. Start commenting now. The comments may not be brilliant at first. They may even be foolish or obvious. Don't worry; they'll improve.

Examine your subject in a wider context

If your angle seems too narrow—not yielding enough meaning—
try backing away, looking at the subject in a wider context. One of
our students wrote about playing at the town dump. Her description of place and the other children was vivid, but the meaning was
unclear. When we asked why the dump had meant so much to her,
she said it was because of the fun she'd had there. That didn't help
with meaning, so we asked, "What was going on in your life at that
time that might have made the dump experiences special to you?
Or what went on earlier or later in your life that might have made
the experiences special?" These questions can lead to meaning
and, in this case, they did.

This student's larger context was that she lived in a town where
parents enrolled their children in many lessons and activities: piano, dance, scouts, gymnastics, French. After school and on weekends, she was shunted from one appointment to another. But on
Sunday, after church, the adults would gather at someone's house
for Bloody Marys and let the kids alone. They stripped out of their
Sunday clothes, put on ratty jeans, and met at the town dump, bliss-
fully unsupervised. It was at the dump, she realized, that she learned
about getting along with people. She realized the importance of in-
venting games and having time to explore and learn independently.
She vowed at the end never to over-lesson her children.

Explore then and now

When writing of a past event, it's easy to return to the same frame of
mind you were in at the time the event occurred. Yet the advantage
to looking back is the added perspective of the time that has passed.
When you fought with Andrea, you may have felt furious with her.
Now, looking back, perhaps you see her vulnerability in ways you
couldn't *then*. Perhaps you see *now* that she couldn't help herself *then*.
Maybe you, too, were vulnerable or unreasonable. When you work
with *then* and *now* on the page, meaning will emerge. Through revision, you may be able to separate what you thought and felt at the
time from how you regard the event *now*. This is revision in its truest
incarnation, reseeing.

In "To Paris, Please" (page 250), Sybille Goldberg writes about her
six years as a foster child in Paris. As a child, she felt loved. She
supports the feeling with the details of her life that led to it. Nanou

welcomed her into the kitchen, called her a "treasure," cooked delicious meals for her, kept her clean and neat. *Now*, as Sybille writes, she realizes: "There is something about regularity and routine that acts as a fertilizer of human bonds." She could never have thought this as a child. The meaning here arises from looking back, reflecting, reseeing.

In "Two Years in Deep Whiteness," student Chandra Edwards writes about being black in a mostly white university and, after saying to her parents, "I'm living in Whiteville U.S.A. . . . You know, home of the ignorant and backward," she reflects on what she's been told about this school:

> Yes, I had known what I was getting myself into before I returned my acceptance form. I had heard all the misconceptions (which held some truth) that people had about New Hampshire: the first national Ku Klux Klan meeting took place in a little town there and, yeah, the natives didn't appreciate the idea that Martin Luther King deserved a holiday in their state. My best friend, Sheree, during my senior year said it best. "New Hampshire is the last place on earth where white people outnumber the trees. And there are a LOT of trees in New Hampshire."

Chandra goes on to discuss what she liked about UNH: the prestigious English/Journalism program; its *low* tuition; its location, which was close enough for her to drive to see her parents on weekends but far enough away to prevent "surprise visits." Now, as she writes, she speculates about why she finally chose this school:

> Perhaps it was the changing colors of the leaves on Main Street or the lack of students walking around during my orientation that lulled my apprehension and allowed me to fall in love with the physical beauty of the campus. Who wouldn't love a thousand chipmunks and squirrels running around on freshly cut, manicured lawns in front of regal, red brick buildings? Even though I had that statistic of 99% white implanted in my skull and tattooed to my recruitment forms, I knew as I drove back to diverse Boston, Massachusetts, that this was the university for me.

You, too, can compare your thoughts now as you write to how you regarded an event earlier. Begin with a short comparison or comment here, another later in the piece. You'll find yourself returning to earlier remarks, adding to them as your understanding broadens. You'll surprise yourself with the depth of your insights.

So what if your first comments seem shallow. They get you started and lead to deeper insights.

Read nonfiction writers who comment frequently and with wisdom such as Maya Angelou, James Baldwin, Wendell Berry, Joan Didion, Annie Dillard, Carlos Fuentes, Donald Hall, Maxine Hong Kingston, Richard Rodriguez, Susan Sontag, and John Edgar Wideman.

Ask questions and speculate on the page

Chandra Edwards speculated, "Perhaps it was the changing colors of the leaves on Main Street. . . ." That thought led her to another and another as she analyzed her motives. These words and phrases lead writers and readers into speculation: *perhaps; maybe; I wonder if; sometimes I think X, other times Y; what if; I used to believe X, later Y, still later Z, but now it seems to me that* . . . This language can free your thinking, get the ideas flowing, open your mind to possibilities.

Student Corrine Lin questioned her major, her goals, her identity all through an essay. She writes, on page one:

> For the last five or six years, I have lived my life based on "the perfect plan." Five years ago, at 14 years of age, I felt positive about what it was I wanted. I decided to become an aeronautical engineer. First I would major in mechanical engineering as an undergraduate, and then go on to graduate school to receive a doctorate degree in aeronautical engineering. My goal was to end up working for NASA or Boeing. . . . As for having a family or where I would live, I figured those things would take care of themselves.
>
> I was so sure of my goals, I defined myself by them. This was who I was, who I would be, not just career-wise, but also in my character and personality. . . . But now that this plan is starting to become a reality, I question it and who I thought I was. . . .

Corrine looks back on her high school years and carefully, intelligently, compares what she once thought to what she is beginning to think now about her goals, identity, and life plan. She asks questions—the whole essay is a question—and speculates. She examines her passion for music, the appeal of different fields, and concludes:

> Maybe in the end . . . I will be an aeronautical engineer working for NASA or, on the other hand, maybe a pianist in the Boston Symphony, or a teacher or a doctor. Whatever the case, when the time

comes, I want to know that I will have experienced all that I could have, and been the best person possible. . . . I want to know that whatever I end up making out of my life will be for me and not for anyone else. . . . After going through a period of doubt and uncertainty, I can now accept that the future is not written in stone . . . it's not written at all. That is what terrified me so much—not knowing. Not knowing what classes to take, what major to declare, what profession to be in, or where I fit in this world. But I realize now . . . this is where I fit. This is my time to explore and to discover myself. . . .

I'm still searching, but I'm okay with that now. This is where I am in life. This is me. I know if I keep my mind open and follow my heart, one day, I'll get there . . . wherever that may be.

It's fascinating to watch a writer or narrator in the process of questioning and speculating, piecing thoughts together, moving toward conclusion or, perhaps, another question. When you tackle a complex subject, questions will be whirring in your head anyway. Why not examine them on the page and let your readers take the intellectual journey with you?

 ## Try this

1. Pose a question. A real question—one you don't know the answer to but want to explore. You might question your goals, your marriage, your former friend's life choices, your religion, how to survive in a hostile neighborhood. You may want to examine more fully an event that left you wondering or with feelings you'd like to clarify. Tackle the question on the page. Speculate, comment, discover.

2. Think of a person you feel strongly about, someone about whom your thoughts and feelings have changed over time. For instance, children change their views of parents drastically from babyhood through adolescence and maturity. No matter where you are on this child-looking-at-parent spectrum, you will see changes in your perceptions. If you have a parent about whom you are or have been conflicted, write about your relationship using this model: Once I thought X, later I thought Y, and now looking back I think Z.

You may find yourself speculating that maybe the parent acts this way because . . . or perhaps it's because . . . . Try using words like *maybe, I wonder if, it could be that,* or *might be.* You can also use phrases like "Sometimes I think this way, other times that way."

Any person, place, event, or position you have strong and changing feelings about will yield interesting material if you write to learn more—to move closer to understanding, though not necessarily to conclusion.

3. Look up two of the writers listed on page 135. Study their use of questioning and speculation so that you can apply these techniques to your own work.

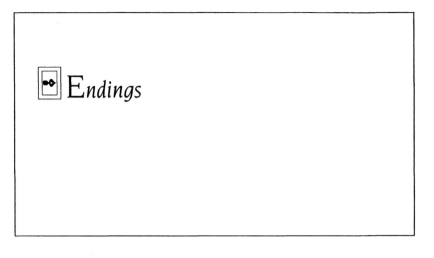

Endings

AN ENDING IS NOT A BORING REHASH OF EVERYTHING THAT'S GONE before. An ending gathers together the threads of a piece in order to arrive at a new insight or perspective. It pushes your meaning ahead. Be sure you keep thinking and making discoveries right through the last sentence.

Look again at the last three paragraphs of Judy O'Donoghue's "The Nursing Home" (page 110). If she had simply summarized, her last paragraph might read, "The old people in the hall of the nursing home as well as my grandmother frightened me because of their ages and decrepit looks and behaviors, and I wished my father would take me home." Instead, Judy advances her story's meaning; she keeps thinking on the page. She notices that her father's and grandmother's noses are alike; the skin under her father's chin is beginning to sag. She describes lacing her fingers through her father's. Then comes the insight, the knot that ties all the threads: "I wanted to tell him I loved him and wished he'd never get old."

Judy's ending, like all good ones, emerges from the main focus and theme of her story, which she has refined over many drafts. Beware the ending that flies in like a spaceship from another galaxy. Young children, unconcerned with logic, will write, "And then they all died. The end," but more mature writers can't get away with it.

Beware, also, of overshooting your ending, going on and on trying to explain what is already clear. Trust your readers' intelligence. Check the last several paragraphs. Are they needed? Is something new and substantial introduced? Often writers cut their last paragraph, or two or three.

Some endings refer to the first paragraphs. Some are logical and closed. Others are emotional and open. Some writers end with a scene or detail, continuing the action. Some, like Judy O'Donoghue, add brief comments to the final scenes. Others, like Sandell Morse in "Canning Jars," end with a longer commentary that seems to rise above the story. After she describes the owner of the thrift shop telling her he hates "a woman Jew," she draws connections between that last insult and a time earlier when she had heard cows being shot in Wyoming; then she connects these two memories to Polish Jews in World War II being slaughtered. In the final paragraph, she comments:

> I think I must be nuts, linking a man in a thrift shop in rural Virginia to slaughtered cows on a ranch in Wyoming to dead Jews in a Polish forest, all so distant in place and time. But in my heart, I know I'm not. In fertile soil, misunderstanding takes root, grows and flowers into hate. Best to dig up those roots and dry them out in the glittering sunlight of a nearly perfect autumn day.

Don't worry about your ending until the final draft. As we have said before, if you preplan a piece right up to and including the end, you'll put it in a corset and make it stiff. If the ending eludes you after several drafts, chances are the problem is caused by something off kilter earlier in the piece: you've lost focus; evaded a difficult truth; haven't grasped the larger meaning of your subject; you've relied on generalities without the specifics needed to earn them; you've been careless with words. Go back to the beginning and edit, word by word. If you write one honest, true, accurate sentence after another, the ending usually reveals itself.

Try this

1. Read the endings of your favorite essays. Do they end in commentary? Long or short ones? Do the commentaries seem to rise above the stories? Or do the stories end in actions, specific details, or scenes? Be sure you notice how each ending pushes the story ahead—how none of them is a mere rehash.

2. Revisit one of your pieces where the ending feels inadequate. Edit word by word and see if an ending emerges. Is there a paragraph or passage in the body of your piece that might work as an ending because the idea is so central or the image so unifying? Move it to the end. What else would you need to do to the piece to make this fresh ending work?

Writing about people

PEOPLE ON THE PAGE NEED TO BE AS DISTINCTIVE AS IN LIFE. EVEN someone who appears briefly should have one or two memorable characteristics. If you write "She had brown hair and brown eyes" you're describing about half the female population. Provide memorable information, unique physical and personality traits. Create what writer Donald Murray calls a "dominant impression" that reveals as much about what's going on inside the person as outside. You might describe a kind person's big, gentle hands and the way they rest lightly on his knees when he sits. You might mention how a suspicious person nearly closes his eyes when he speaks, but a glint says he's watching your every quiver. Physical description should reveal personality. The following description from Toni Morrison's *Song of Solomon* not only paints a physical picture but suggests eccentricity:

> [She was] on the front steps sitting wide-legged in a long-sleeved, long-skirted black dress. Her hair was wrapped in black too, and from a distance, all they could see beneath her face was the bright orange she was peeling. She was all angles, he remembered later, knees, mostly, and elbows. One foot pointed east and one pointed west.

To write about someone you feel strongly about, tap into your feelings about her. Reflect on her actions, manner, quirks, needs, desires. Wonder about her, and try to learn more as you write. When she is firmly planted in your mind, decide on your strongest impression of her. Begin with that. Perhaps a physical description like "She was all angles. . . ." Or a scene, a quotation, a series of revealing details or incidents. Student Shannon Mullen wrote this about a friend who decided to forego college:

> Jamie Mary Margaret McLaughlin runs a homeless shelter in San Antonio, Texas. She lives on a weekly salary of one hundred dollars in a little apartment with a girl whose name I do not remember. She lights candles and puts them on the floor and dances around until people tell her she is losing her mind. She likes to dance in the street when the rain floods over the sidewalks and into the gutters. She likes to eat tacos, the real tacos with jalepenos and chilies and salsa and cheese that a lanky gringo sells by the corner. She likes to drink margaritas in the desert with her friends and watch the cars go by on the highway. She likes to go to work barefoot and in dresses with no waistline. She wears her hair down and says accurately that she is an American Native American Mexican woman. She is my best friend.

Shannon's specifics reveal character.

Another student, Jeffrey Meulenbrock, creates a dominant impression of his father in this paragraph from the essay "My Father Moves Stones."

> He builds walls of stones. Blending the natural landscape with a livable environment around his home. . . . He has been doing it for years. Fitting stones together. Lugging them down the railroad tie and stone steps he built himself from a van or truck he had loaded by hand. He placed stones and meticulously built retaining walls. Stone walls lead you along the winding path to the water. They are carefully laid out. Orderly. Tight fitting . . .

Already we know something of the father and Jeffrey, too, because what a writer notices reflects on him, reveals his way of seeing the world. Now Jeffrey poses a question: Why does my father move stones?

> I could never understand what drove him to work so tirelessly at moving stones. I knew it was healthy, invigorating, honest work, which has its own merits, but so did the work he did at his flower shop. I couldn't see why he enjoyed the solitude of bearing rocks. I . . . could only picture it as a task fit for Sisyphus. I saw . . . the futile labor of carrying stones from a truck down steps and then carefully re-stacking them in neat walls.

Jeffrey's puzzlement drives this essay. He had helped his father lift and place stones, had sensed why the father did this, but he didn't *know* why, couldn't articulate why—so he wrote to find out. This wanting to know gave him purpose. It added tension and provided the impetus for the discovery in the ending:

> There was a soothing rhythm in finding an order from the stones. I was carefully constructing a cairn, marking a new understanding with my father. The work was calming and it was rewarding to find how stones fit together. There was a Zen enlightenment attainable through pondering each stone, and their relationship to one another as the stack grew. I realized my father had been on to something for years. . . . They were only stones, and were heavy, but there was a magic to their careful placement. I now understood why he would run away to work. . . . The air and strain on the muscles was recharging to the body, while the rhythm of the stones soothed the mind.

Comment as you write. Make connections. Seek insight. Sybille Goldberg comments frequently in "To Paris, Please" (page 250). Nanou cared for Sybille as though she were her "fourth and youngest daughter." Describing Nanou, Sybille learns about her and their relationship. She also makes discoveries about her own upbringing, her values, and who she is now. Here's an excerpt in which Sybille mixes specifics and commentary:

> . . . every day, after my nap, I would find her sitting in the kitchen, drinking her coffee. When she saw me, she would invariably welcome me enthusiastically, calling me her treasure, her chick, her morning rose, and then proceed by giving me a small cookie.
>
> There is something about regularity and routine that acts as a fertilizer of human bonds. I think of Saint-Exupery's "The Little Prince." Didn't the fox advise the little prince to come every day at the same time, so he could relish in the anticipation of his visit? . . . I think Nanou tamed me that way, with her routines, all centered around me, keeping me clean, fed, and healthy. Every day, much time was spent on those routines, and I got to learn that I was worthy of such energy and seriousness. Nanou didn't just clean, cook and wash. She did it in such a way that discern those who merely exist from those who know how to live well, . . . who use those small details of life to assert that they are worth this attention. . . . This is why she cooked and still cooks two meals a day, with an appetizer, followed by meat and vegetables, a starch, salad, cheese, fruit, yogurt and coffee; she never fried with butter, she said it's bad for your liver. She never ate more than three eggs a week . . .

Sybille uses details, incidents, anecdotes, and commentary to express her discoveries, to make her way to insight.

Some writers stand back and make long, extraordinarily wise statements about their characters. Toni Morrison in *Song of Solomon* describes and comments on Pilate, born with no navel. In the town where Pilate lived during Prohibition, she made and sold liquor; the people were superstitious. Morrison comments on Pilate's position in the community.

> [Her lack of a navel] isolated her. Already without family, she was further isolated from her people for, except for the relative bliss on the island, every other resource was denied her: partnership in marriage, confessional friendship, and communal religion. Men frowned, women whispered and shoved their children behind them. Even a traveling side show would have rejected her, since her freak quality lacked that important ingredient—the grotesque. There was really nothing to see. Her defect, frightening and exotic as it was, was also a theatrical failure.
>
> Finally Pilate began to take offense.

Morrison tells readers that Pilate decided to abandon what she had learned about her world and considered:

> . . . how she wanted to live and what was valuable to her. When am I happy and when am I sad and what is the difference? What do I need to know to stay alive? What is true in the world? Her mind traveled crooked streets and aimless goat paths, arriving sometimes at profundity, other times at the revelations of a three-year-old.

This commentary continues for more than two pages. Read *Song of Solomon*, especially these pages about Pilate's place in the world. As you read, you may think: I couldn't possibly write this. It's far too profound. I'm not up to it.

We disagree. We can't all write like Morrison, but writers at all levels are capable of drafting their way to insights. Let's say you are writing about a foster mother as Sybille did. You have just described the foster mother, and the description leads to a comment about her. You write it down. Just one comment. You keep writing; maybe you remember another incident. Two hours later, you leave your desk and walk to the library. You begin to think about your childhood some more, and another insight occurs, one that pushes the first comment a little further. Write this down quickly or you may lose it. The second insight leads to another. Next day, next draft, still another.

Brilliant insights don't always flash like lightning. Some may, but usually you will layer your insights one after another, over time, eventually generating long, intelligent statements you didn't realize you could write.

Key: Ask questions and speculate on the page. Play psychological detective and work your way to understanding.

Why does your friend slam doors? Why does he throw books on the floor? Yell? Is it because he saw his father shout and bang doors? Does he think punching holes in the walls is manly? Or is he just a spoiled brat who doesn't think at all or try to control his impulses?

Posing questions and then trying to answer them on the page will bring you closer to the truth than merely turning the questions over in your mind. And readers will want to keep reading to find out how you make sense of your subject.

Try this

1. Think of a person you feel strongly about. This could be someone you love or hate—perhaps (best of all) both; someone you're jealous of; someone you're competitive with; someone you worry about; someone who's hurt you; someone you've hurt; someone you miss or admire.

Write and, at some point, reveal the person physically. Show him in action. Include incidents, anecdotes, scenes that reveal personality. Explore your subject's spirit, psyche, soul. Ask questions. Speculate. As you write and revise, you will comment and add to your comments. Prepare to be startled by how small insights accumulate and what you are able to figure out about your subject and yourself.

2. In your notebook, write a letter to someone who bothers you, gets you riled. Use the person's name: "Dear Jody." Do not show this to anyone, ever (tear it up when you're through). Write for five minutes, as fast as you can, without regard for logic, full sentences, grammar, punctuation. Tell this person every single thing you've ever wanted to say. Now look over what you've written. We're betting it's full of energy and voice. Why? Because it's honest. Now write

about this person honestly. Show him in action. Return to your subject the next day. Comment about the person. Comment again. On the third day, see if you can add to the comments—even just a phrase or a sentence. Return to this subject for at least five days in a row. Then wait a few weeks. Reread what you've written. See what happens.

3. Read a physical description of a person in a book you have loved. Read again a whole essay or short story with one person at its center. How did the writer reveal character? Where has she commented on the subject's life? Apply these techniques to your own writing.

⬅ Writing about places

DISTINGUISH EACH ROOM, ISLAND, NEWSSTAND, TRUCK, LOBBY from every other. Use memorable details.

Don't cram a room with people and furniture. If Grandfather sits at the head of the long rectangular dining table, there's no need to say Betsy sits to his right, Great Aunt Stofie on his left, Jacob next to Stofie, etc. Just say eleven sat down to Thanksgiving dinner. If Grandfather and Stofie start pounding the table, tell readers they're side by side.

Create a dominant impression. If the room has a broken window held together by electrical tape, wobbly folding chairs, a table set with paper cups and red plastic plates, readers will guess the nature of this place. No need to describe the curtains, rugs, baseboard heater, salt-and-pepper shakers. Similarly, if you note that a crystal chandelier hangs over the polished cherry table, which is adorned with a bouquet of white calla lilies in a blue bowl, there's no need to go on and on about the imported wine glasses unless Grandfather, raising one hand in an outburst, sends red wine swooshing across the hand-embroidered tablecloth, splattering the monumental bosom, encased in yellow silk, of Great Aunt Stofie.

Generally, the more important a room is to your story—or the more important an encounter in the room—the more clearly readers need to see it. Let readers see how place influences people and events.

Student Bob Solomon, describing the death of his mother, began with these details about the most important item in the hospital room, the oxygen tank.

> The transparent plastic tube swooped gracefully down from the green oxygen cylinder almost touching the speckled tile floor before arching up again to fork onto two nose plugs which fed her a steady stream of air. There were two small circular meters on the air tank. One dial reflected the amount of oxygen within. The other recorded the air pressure and was controlled by a nozzle on the side of the cylinder. The higher the air pressure, the more oxygen flowed through the tube to the patient. For the past few days the arrow on the pressure dial had swung upward and the burden of breathing became more difficult. Gradually, the chore fell from patient to machine.

Bob goes on to describe the room and finally the bed and his mother.

> Across from the base of the bed and a little to its left stood a bureau. Its drawers were empty except for the nightgown she had been wearing when rushed to the hospital by ambulance two nights before. The reflection from a vase of roses with a get-well card dangling from its side by a string shone from the mirror hanging above the bureau. Except for the roses and the white linen cloth spread across the bureau, the mirror was filled only with the drab, white stare of the wall from the opposite side of the room.

> To the right of the bed, overlooking the hospital parking lot, and pelted by a late October rain, were crank-out windows. . . . A vase of yellow chrysanthemums and a pot of white azaleas sat on top of the gray metal heater which buzzed softly above the downpour outside. On the right of the bed, rooted to the floor with metal braces like a tree, a pole rose upward and branched out into two arms. A bottle dangled from either side spouting out plastic tubes inserted into the patient's left wrist for intravenous feeding.

The detail of the get-well card, dangling by a string, distinguishes this hospital room from every other. All the details show the room, and they reflect Bob's feelings. When you are sad, what you notice and how you describe it will be different from when you are happy, angry, confused, or nervous. Describing place is a way for all of us to hold up a mirror: Our perceptions of what's outside reveal what's going on inside.

Historian and essayist Ronald Jager focuses primarily on place in his nonfiction book *Last House on the Road*. He writes about restoring an old farmhouse and, in the process, informs readers about the history of the region as well as his life and how place has shaped it;

he reveals, too, his philosophy, his way of seeing, and his sense of humor:

> We began to scout New Hampshire backroads looking for rural property, for we had the implausible idea that we might again find a creaky old farmhouse, perhaps lost in the woods and pleading for rescue before it collapsed. Most of the backroads in central New Hampshire are flanked by woodlands that were meadows and farmyards a century and a half ago, and the land under those trees is pitted and pocked with cellar holes, scars from thousands of farmsteads now reverted to forest. Some of these residual stone structures are seven-foot walls and chimney foundations masterfully constructed without mortar of quarter-ton granite boulders up to two hundred years ago. They remain rigidly intact to this day, as if buildings had never stood upon them, though they surely did.
>
> We spent little time with real-estate agents, rightly believing we couldn't afford most of what they would offer. We needed a bargain: more than a cellar hole but less than a colonial, something in between that wasn't leaning too far the wrong way.

Though Jager's surface task here is describing place—what it's like along those back roads, what kind of place he seeks—what that description reflects and reveals is a person, himself, as a thoughtful man full of admiration for those things that last, one who's willing to rescue "a bargain" that's not "leaning too far the wrong way." It isn't the quaintness of the New Hampshire countryside that provides the charm of *Last House on the Road*; it's the author's spirit and perspective. This is a man with "a touch of the vandal in his soul":

> I blasted away at the openings in the ceiling, pounding and yanking and tearing away at the lath and the ancient plaster. A prodigiously dirty and dusty business it was, but I scarcely stopped or looked until the entire ceiling was hacked to pieces and dragged to the floor: an appalling mess of splintered hemlock and plaster, wallpaper, snake skins, squirrel nests, nut shells, bat residue, old sawdust, rusty nails, a mousetrap, ages and ages worth of dried rat droppings and bushels of mouse turds. Down it all came, cascades of grime and litter, trailing clouds of noxious dust.

Jager's details put us in the middle of the mess, especially those bushels of mouse turds (and anyone who's worked on an old house knows this is no exaggeration). But what makes this scene

149

memorable is his reaction, which says so much about the kind of man he is: "The wreckage was so extravagant," he writes, "that I retreated into another room and shut the door and read a book."

Try this

1. Think of a place you love, long for—or one you fear or dread, wish was yours, or wish you'd never seen. Limit size: Choose a rock in the desert rather than Death Valley. Choose a room, a deli, a porch, the attic, a bridge, a tree swing, the principal's office—a place that will yield a dominant impression. Establish this place firmly in your mind. Start with a fact, a detail. It could be a sight, smell, taste, touch, or sound. Describe the place using as many of the five senses as reasonable.

This may turn into a longer piece where you describe something important that happened here. You may recount a frightening or funny incident, or use the place as a jumping-off point for a series of incidents. Or you may want to stick with a simple but complete description.

After a draft, notice the best of your details. Substitute memorable details for generic ones.

2. Think of a place where you once spent a lot of time, and maybe still do: under a bridge, on a street corner, in a tree house, at a pool hall, in a dance studio. Describe it. Try to loop out into incidents that happened there. Do you associate a certain person with this place? Who? Did you have a memorable encounter with this person? What?

3. Think of a place where something wonderful, amazing, or terrible happened. Describe the place and just keep writing.

❖ Exploring with metaphor

BY METAPHOR WE MEAN A COMPARISON THAT REVEALS, AN ANGLE that leads into the thick of a subject and out the other side with new understanding. Titia Bozuwa uses dance to illuminate her relationship with her husband, Gijs:

> On the dance floor Gijs did one of his fancy passes in which he made me step beside him, backwards, while he moved forward with sure strides. Then he switched me around. Now I strode forward, and he took the steps backwards. It felt elegant and easy to execute. His feeling for rhythm was uncanny. As I twirled in his arms I couldn't help think that he'd done this to me in more ways than one. He'd taken me to America, and it had felt like being backed into the unknown. After twelve years I'd switched around. I was moving forward. The new world had become familiar. . . . While I went forward, with the seventies stretching before me like a rich promise, I felt hesitation in Gijs while he stepped backwards. The emigration had been an adventure. Was it time for something else? A whole new adventure . . . ?

Titia recognizes that the way she and Gijs dance reflects the way they live. And readers recognize this, too.

In "Visitation" (page 275), Pat Parnell builds on a metaphor introduced in the first line, "I wear my mother's skin, snug across my shoulders." Later, she extends the metaphor to grotesque extremes:

> The skin of her arms covers my arms, warmly, snugly, her hands hanging above my hands like ruffles coming out of a sleeve. She is wrapped around my ribs; her heavy breasts sag swinging from my chest. My buttocks fit neatly into hers, her thighs grip mine. Her feet flop over my feet like fringed shoe-flaps.

Note her use of comparisons within the comparison. She *feels like* she is wearing her mother's skin, and the skin itself *seems like* "ruffles coming out of a sleeve," and feet flopping over feet "like fringed shoe-flaps." It's as if she's asking, "How far can I go with this? And what will I discover?"

An extended metaphor gives you permission to discover. It gives you room to discover.

As the essay continues, Parnell wears her mother's skin through her day—first swimming and then to the mall. In the swimming scene, she plays with the image of a swimmer in two skins, fully imagining what that might be like: "Her fingers and mine play paddycakes in the water; her feet and mine flip, frog-kicking."

At the mall, she imagines others wearing skins, and here the meaning begins to surface. We all wear somebody's skin. We are all affected by those who raised us, praised us, criticized us, exerted their influence over us when we were young or vulnerable.

Using italics, she inserts a few literary allusions, describing Hercules in a lion skin, Jesus carrying a rescued lamb across his shoulders. Probably when she first thought of writing about her relationship with her mother, these historic figures did not spring to mind. Metaphor led her to them and they work—they illuminate.

Later readers learn that just as Parnell experienced a visitation, so was her mother visited—by her own mother's ghost. The essay turns, at this point, quite naturally, from a mother-daughter piece, to a mother-daughter-granddaughter piece. It's not about two generations, but three, maybe all the generations—skins being passed from one strong personality to another.

A less skilled writer might have yielded to the temptation to write more about the grandmother, or give many examples of the grandmother's influence on the mother, or the mother's influence on the child. Perhaps in earlier drafts she did write about cooking with Grandma or the time Mother threw Parnell's stylish dress in the garbage because it wasn't "decent." Instead, a few examples suggest many; a couple of scenes represent three lifetimes.

No doubt, the metaphor helped her stay focused. She comes back to it in almost every paragraph. She keeps it front and center, never strays far, and the meaning that emerges is equally striking, an ending that ties all the threads together with a fresh new image and insight.

Warning: Don't sweat over metaphors. If one emerges naturally, wonderful. Use it, but resist pushing it too far. A metaphor works only if it is as true as the rest of your story—and as believable.

Try this

Go through your lists of subject possibilities developed in other chapters. Choose one or two and try an extended metaphor for a sentence, a paragraph, or a page.

Using your life as you write about reading

OFTEN WRITERS USE READING TO JUMP-START THEIR WORK. THEY may be inspired by an image in a poem, an insight in a political analysis, a situation in a novel that reminds them of something from their own experience. Reading provokes ideas and reactions. It expands our world beyond what we experience physically. What you read in newspapers, magazines, books, on the Internet, the bulletin board at work, the bumper of the car ahead feeds your writing; it is an endless source.

Sometimes, especially in school, you will be assigned to respond to reading or include excerpts, or information gained from reading in a report, essay, or research project. This happens out of school, too—every time a professional writes a scholarly article or quotes another writer in an editorial or feature. Becky was recruited to write a column for a magazine. It would appear in an ongoing department, "West-Running Brook," after the Robert Frost poem. The editor said to use the poem for inspiration, though the essay didn't have to be *about* the poem. In early drafts, Becky connected lines from the poem with her experiences. After several attempts, she found a line that resonated. It concerned *contraries* and how one brook runs west, all the others east. This got her thinking about the stereotype of the contrary Yankee:

> Yankees may seem reserved, even cool—but there's tolerance in them, in us; it runs deep and allows for all kinds of contraries and differences. Companion to this tolerance is an ingrained patience that not only accepts the stones that make the soil hard to work, but welcomes them.

The word *differences* brought to mind times when she felt different, was different, including:

> In 1972 when I went off to school at UNH, folks were concerned. My first time home, their concerns seemed justified: I was talking funny, different.
>
> What was I, putting on airs?
>
> To this day, with family or when reading my stories to audiences, my accent thickens. When I'm teaching, it thins. I don't mind being different—writers are—but sometimes I don't want to be *too* different. Wouldn't want Uncle Junior to think I'm putting on airs. Don't want my students distracted.

Articulating the fact that writers are different, or perceived to be so, led to family associations, the surprise (she hadn't thought of it quite this way before) of a family culture that tolerated difference, even admired it—though not uncritically. She remembered family phrases, used again and again—*different* and *well enough*.

> "He's different," my Yankee grandmother would say about a boyfriend some cousin imported to try out on the family. "It's different," an aunt might say about the new purple-rose paint on the walls. Neither praise nor condemnation, "different" left room for developments. Same with "well enough."
>
> "Do you like him?"
>
> "I like him well enough."
>
> "Is there too much celery salt in the potato salad?"
>
> "I like it well enough."

She recognized the freedom such phrases provide to be critical without being mean-spirited or close-minded. Maybe this family attitude had something to do with her choice to become a writer. Certainly, her work is closely connected to the home place and home people.

> I learned young to respect New Hampshire's rocky landscape. Our house was wedged between a side hill and Corn Hill Road. To add on, we had to dig. I say "we," but it was mostly my dad.
>
> Miserable digging, hard pan, until he struck a boulder. Then it got worse. Progress halted. This was not unexpected. Our family credo,

applied not just to digging but most things: "It'll go along like this for awhile, then it'll get worse."

Dad used a hammer and wedges to find the fault that split the stone. Rocks don't want to split. They don't want to move or be moved. Like natives, they want to stay put.

He said since you couldn't out wait a rock, you had to finesse it. That was one of his favorite sayings. Also, "Life's too short." Which I think is pretty much the same thing.

Though she didn't say so directly, Becky realized that writing about a tough subject is much like trying to split a rock—it takes patience, strength, time, and a good deal of finessing. She and her Dad had this in common; she had discovered parallels of experience and attitudes toward work.

I grew up to be a writer of stories that stick close to what might very well be. I write about rock-like obstacles I've stumbled over, herniated myself trying to persuade, been caught between, nearly crushed by, climbed over, and—occasionally—fallen from and landed on my head. Rocks substantial enough to make a difference—roundish ones for walls; flattish ones for foot paths—but not so heavy I can't move them on my own: these are my favorites.

One rock leads to another, echoing Frost's attention to the stones in the brook, diverting the water, contraries within the contrary. She concludes with an anecdote, an attempt to pull all the threads together, including the unwritten thread of "West-Running Brook," the poem that got her started.

Here's a family story: Near the Barker homestead—a one-room cottage (two if you count the attached outhouse)—sits a boulder twenty feet high and forty feet through if it's an inch. Years ago, when a visitor wondered how such a rock came to be in this place, my Irish grandmother pleaded ignorance. "I don't know," she brogued, "t'was here when I arrived."

My stories record the truth, near as I can figure, about people as stubbornly committed to this place as the tree sprouted from the fissure in my Irish grandmother's mysterious boulder. These stories, too, were here when I arrived. Like rocks rising in the garden, it seems a shame to leave them lay.

Through several drafts, she explored various incarnations of contrariness, the value of being different, how writers are almost always different, and how one difference between writers and others may be that they are able to see the potential in rising rocks, see subjects where others do not, and—stubbornly—refuse to leave them lay.

In the end, her column didn't mention the Frost poem at all, though the editor included a quote from it at the top of the page. She and the editor believed that readers would sense the connection between the column and the poem.

When a teacher or an editor assigns you to respond to reading, he'll usually give guidelines. Sometimes you'll be asked to write on a subject inspired by the reading as Becky did. Sometimes you'll be asked to seek out a theme in the text and explain it. Or simply to note your thoughts as you read. You may be assigned to incorporate a number of readings with your own ideas and experiences, perhaps interviews as well, in a research project, report, argument, or feature article.

Student Emily Jacobs chose anorexia nervosa as the topic for her research project. She combined her harrowing personal experience with what she learned from reading.

> Anorexia nervosa is an ugly disease. A loss of up to 60% of starting body weight leaves the anorexic emaciated. The eyes become sunken; the face takes on a grayish hue. The hair becomes coarse and dull. Fingernails become ridged due to vitamin deficiency. The smile disappears, due to lack of energy and depression. The gaunt, delicate anorexic is only a phantom of who she once was.

The 60 percent statistic probably came from her reading. The details of physical deterioration probably came from her reading about typical symptoms and her personal experience.

Emily combines italicized passages that read like journal entries, personal insights, with medical research.

> *Walking through the halls of my junior high school, I honestly feel like I am trudging—like a tired, old brown work horse. To anyone passing by I probably look more like I am floating, like a pale yellow moth or a snowflake. I am too thin to be able to plod like this, but they don't know how heavy I feel inside. To them, I am just skinny and delicate and feminine, like china on a mantle. Don't touch me; I may break.*

This is Emily's self-perception. Later, she cites the effects on the body as described by doctors, complete with references so readers can check out her sources:

> Anorexia is debilitating, as the starvation progresses. As far as physiological strength, it wreaks havoc on the major systems of the body. Metabolic and electrolytic imbalances occur as a result of dehydration. Cardiac complications are the most common cause of death due to muscular weakness. Pseudoatrophy of the brain occurs, as well as seizures. Anemia, acute and chronic renal failure, and cessation of menstruation are not uncommon among anorexics. The digestive system gets damaged, with irritable bowel syndrome and constipation being the most common offenders. The immunological system is weakened, and anorexics are especially susceptible to bacterial infections, such as staphylococcal and tuberculosis (Beumont et al.). The body is pushed to its limits, tested, and pushed even further.

Emily's research project became a personal quest for understanding. She used her experience as a foundation for information gained through reading and research. Instead of a generic anorexic, readers came to know—and care about—a particular anorexic with the courage not only to heal herself but to write about it.

Emily's paper relies heavily on anecdote and is written in first person. Her assignment was open enough to allow her to experiment with form and the mix of scientific fact and personal narrative. Sometimes assignments are more restrictive. For example, a teacher or an editor might forbid use of first person. No I's allowed. This is a style preference and need not constrict your writing or stifle the exploration of your subject. Instead of I, many writers—especially journalists—will say "this writer," or "one," or "some people." Check out any daily newspaper and you'll notice a variety of substitutions for I, including use of the passive voice: "The question *was* asked," rather than "I asked him the question." You'll also see "an onlooker suggested . . ." Usually that onlooker is, guess who, the reporter, a.k.a. I.

Assignments, rules to work from and within, almost always make tasks easier. Being told what to do is far less challenging than having to figure out what to do. Have fun with assignments; test the limits of your guidelines without flouting them. Whenever you write about reading, you reap the benefit of using what you read as a model for your own writing in the future, especially if the author is skilled.

If you know you'll be using readings in a piece, keep notes from the beginning. Mark up the text. Use a highlighter, dog-ear pages, star key sentences. Organize notes on cards or mark references with Post-its. If you know you'll need extensive detail on contents—say for a formal presentation or an in-depth analysis—keep a running list of page numbers and key words to help you remember why that page was important and what it contained. Often this means reading through once or twice, but thoroughly and all the time thinking about the writing task ahead. Or read through once, then reread the more significant chapters or passages. By the time you've finished a careful reading, you will probably have discovered your lead and have a sense of the general direction you want to take.

In a prose writing class, Stephen Small received an assignment to respond to a book of his choice by discussing content and analyzing the writing techniques. He chose the anthology *Hometowns: Gay Men Write About Where They Belong*, and he began his response on a light note: "I hope my interest in this book is obvious, but in case it's not—I too am from a hometown . . . and I'm gay." He goes on to compare the work of two of the authors, John Preston and Harlan Green. He also compares their growing-up-gay experiences with his own. "I've spent a lot of my life being silent about this issue," Stephen writes, "so I don't like to pass up an opportunity to educate people when it presents itself."

Stephen notices that the authors "captured very different aspects of growing up gay, but with the two pieces together you get a more complete picture of what it's like." He tells us that Preston relies heavily on the history of his hometown, Medfield, Massachusetts. "It starts back in 1649 and goes up to the American Revolution. Personally, I love history, but it immediately created an emotional distance that I didn't like. Usually, when we read history, it's from a factual basis and not an emotional one."

Yet, because Stephen was also raised in New England, much of what Preston wrote seemed familiar. "I clearly identified with this description of New England; and because I identified with him, it pulled me into the piece." One of Preston's themes was belonging, being part of the community. Stephen writes:

> I can remember feeling the same way about Newmarket. It amazed me that everyone didn't live in Newmarket. I thought, why would anyone not want to live here? . . . There's a cannon on Route 108 pointed toward Durham. It's directly aimed at every car entering Newmarket. The basic message being, we'll shoot you if we don't like you. Then, there's the green bridge you cross when you come into downtown Newmarket. My friends and I would spend hours underneath that bridge on the cat walk, knowing we shouldn't be there, spitting into the Lamprey River. There's a permanent fixture in downtown Newmarket called Marelli's Fruit and Real Estate. The joke in town has always gone like this, "Went to Marelli's today, bought an orange and an acre." These were the things I could count on. . .

From what's right about Medfield, Preston moves on to its problems, specifically the problems he faced in the community as a homosexual. Stephen uses Preston's observations about how he acted, was treated, and kept secrets to make a transition into some of his own observations:

> Kids can be cruel to one another, but I think it is more difficult for gay kids. Of course, I'm speaking from my own perspective, but what you have to remember is that gay kids have nowhere to turn when they are picked on. If you are black and kids make fun of you on the playground, you can go home to a black family who will understand and comfort you. If you are overweight, and kids make fun of you, you go home to Mom and Dad and they make you feel better. But for gay kids, they are not only a minority in life, they are a minority in their own homes.
>
> . . . Try to imagine if you can, being twelve years old and sitting at the kitchen table listening to your whole family making fun of gay people and you know you're gay. . . . You sit there sick to your stomach, trying not to turn red, and wondering if you should join in on the conversation because you CAN'T let anyone at the table know that they are talking about YOU.

The structure of Harlan Greene's essay "Charleston, South Carolina" struck Stephen as substantially different from Preston's, following the contours of "an emotional landscape" more than a "physical one." Greene, too, wraps his personal history in the history of the town, but less obviously. Stephen writes: "I loved the image of the ivy wrapping around the garden wall. Harlan Greene's visual image worked for me much better than John Preston's factual history."

Throughout his paper, Stephen quotes Preston and Greene often, usually following a quotation with an anecdote or observation from his own life. He discusses how themes of alienation, fear, belonging, secrets, identity played out in his own life. Both essays end sadly, Stephen writes. He ends his own with a challenge to readers:

> If you had a choice to either live your adult life as a sexual being or living in your hometown, which would you pick? Because that is what is expected of gay people. Picture being married and living with your husband or wife and when you go downtown someone asks if you're married and you have to say no. You can't mention your spouse to your friends, your family, your co-workers or anyone in town. You have to pretend that the person you are building your life with does not exist. You must pretend that you are single for the rest of your life because it upsets people when you talk about them. And this is not just about sex. It's about the person you want to spend the rest of your life with. What would you pick? Would you stay in town, or would you move somewhere that will accept you as a sexual being? I hope that gives you a better understanding of why these men feel they have to move away.

Among the strengths of Small's reading response, strengths to emulate in your own work, are his careful attention to the text, wise selection of quotations to tie the writers' ideas and experiences to his own, and, especially, his stark honesty.

Try this

Keep a reading journal. The left-hand page should remain blank at first. As you read, jot impressions on the right-hand page. Later, add comments on the left. You might revise an earlier comment. You may want to note a relevant experience. The ending of a poem may change your impression of the beginning. In this way, using left and right columns, perhaps even different inks, you spiral into the material. You respond to your responses. You think about your thoughts. You dig deeper into the ideas and their implications, connections to your life. This process often yields ideas for writing.

Passion on the page

AND WE DON'T MEAN SEX SCENES.

Much writing develops slowly, over days, weeks, years. You have an inkling there's a great subject lurking, somewhere. Gradually, you intuit connections between ideas, experiences, imaginings, feelings. The connections are fragile at first, strengthening through the drafts, until at last you find meaning and express it to your satisfaction and, you hope, the reader's.

Sometimes, though, an essay will bubble out nearly intact. All you need to do is catch it before it dissolves or bursts or settles into the grass and disappears. You produce a first draft in a couple of hours. In a burst of passion, the essay is born remarkably whole and coherent—because you have something to say and you know pretty much what it is and how you want to say it. Not only that, but you have to say it right now before you explode.

You are crushed to learn that the classical radio station is going contemporary. A swastika has appeared on the stone wall in front of a synagogue. Someone steals your three-year-old's tricycle and you wonder what the world is coming to. Fifty families, including yours, will be evicted from an apartment building to be renovated, the rent raised. They took half the nuts out of your favorite candy bar, reduced its size, and raised the price. Police dogs sniffed lockers and backpacks at the high school searching for drugs.

You are moved to write a highly focused, personal, topical, timely essay. It can't wait until next week: By then the passion may have faded, the situation changed. The essay will probably be short and get to the point fast. It may even call for political, social, institutional, or individual action:

- Don't support this candidate.
- Boycott Nuttybutty bars.
- Make the school gymnasium more accessible to the community.

Some readers will agree. Others will disagree so passionately they may be moved to respond with essays of their own. Either way, your writing will elicit response—passion breeds passion—and that's what you want, readers paying attention. You want to evoke and provoke. You want action.

Editorials, opinion or op-ed pieces, magazine and newspaper columns, letters to the editor, letters to your senator or school principal, sometimes even personal letters fall into this category. You write with an immediate, up-front purpose. Your message is not soft or subtle, but it's not ranting either. To be persuasive, you must gain readers' trust and respect. They must believe you are a reasonable person with a sensible outlook and a valid point to make— even if, in the end, they disagree with the point itself. Otherwise, they'll label you extremist, radical, hysterical, or just-trying-to-make-trouble. Worse yet, they'll dismiss your ideas. Controlled passion can engage readers; out-of-control passion will disengage or enrage them.

Recently in a small New Hampshire town, controversy erupted over the high school basketball coach's decision to take away a high school senior's position as captain of her team, remove her from the starting lineup, and make her sit out several games. She had been invited to attend the presidential inauguration as part of a youth leadership group. She went, but missed a game and a couple of practices.

Steve Varnum wrote a column about the situation for the *Concord Monitor*:

> She dreams of a career in United Nations, but [this young athlete] is already learning some hard lessons about leadership. . . . As a result of her once-in-a-lifetime trip to Washington, [she] was stripped of her team captaincy and her spot in the starting lineup.

She had been honored as one of the nation's exemplary young leaders. Now she was told she wasn't enough of a leader for her high school basketball team.

Varnum praised the school's basketball program and the coach. The team had a strong record, undefeated this season, back-to-back state titles in the course of sixty-two straight wins.

> That kind of prolonged success requires at least two things: great coaching and a group of talented and dedicated athletes. [This school] has both. [The coach] is emotional and notoriously volatile; many parents object to his in-your-face sideline style. But few question his dedication . . . or his bedrock loyalty and love for his kids.

Nevertheless, Varnum concluded his essay by criticizing the policy that made a trip to the inauguration and team leadership mutually exclusive.

> Maybe this is a simple case of competing interests. [The player] did what she thought was right for her. [The coach] did what he thought was right for the team.
>
> Maybe it's the overheated atmosphere of a state championship bid producing overheated reactions.
>
> One thing is clear. . . . [The player] shouldn't have felt like she had to choose between loyalty to her team and going to Washington. There should be room in a student-athlete's life for both.

The story was picked up by the wire services, reprinted in papers across the country. It turned up on the radio and local television, and inspired a number of letters to the editor, letters to the school administration, several editorials. The first wave of response was critical of the coach. His priorities were mixed up. He showed lack of vision. This is high school, not the NBA. His actions were inexcusable, without compassion or common sense. He should apologize. He should be benched.

The second wave criticized the critics and the player, praised the coach as a man who encouraged excellence, commitment, hard work, discipline. He was dedicated. He went beyond the call of duty. He was just implementing school policy. The player, on the other hand, should have let the coach know she'd miss a game more than three weeks in advance. She didn't deserve to be captain because she'd let her team down. She wasn't committed. She should learn to accept the consequences of her actions. Basketball, for her, wasn't enough of a priority.

The debate lasted for weeks and warmed the cold New England winter. The controversy broadened. It transcended the individuals involved and their particular situation. Across the state—in diners, at games, at board meetings—people talked about priorities, balancing athletics and academics, school policies. Gary Myers wrote one of the more thought-provoking responses and published it as a letter to the editor.

> *Tension raised right away: what is the price of excellence? The curse of versatility.*

> *Inclusive you may refer to reader, all talented students.*

> *Strong verb*

> *Inclusive, common ground, since we all have gifts as well as career/family conflicts.*

. . . So now it begins for you—the price of excellence, the curse of versatility. The recognition of your singular abilities has come into conflict with your responsibilities to your team. Consequences flow. You are stripped of your captaincy. You sit on the bench out of uniform. You know there are those who see you as selfish. You comport yourself with dignity; you do not run, you do not hide.

Your individual achievements, acknowledged in Washington, are demeaned in one of the few places that matters to you—your school. What to do? What to think?

First, the only reason for your turmoil is that you achieved beyond those around you. Mediocrity could not beget your circumstance. The conflict between going to Washington and playing a high school basketball game could not have been experienced by your peers. It was not theirs to have.

Because you have many gifts and have worked hard to enhance them, much is required of you. The difficult decision you have just made will be repeated time and again in many and diverse forms. Some of these choices will be uniquely a woman's choice. Will you have marriage or children interrupt your career?

Along the way you will meet empire builders. Some will define their empires narrowly such as coaching a winning high school basketball team in a small town in a small New England state. Others will have more grandiose plans. All will have two things in common: they will need you to succeed and they will demean you when your horizons expand beyond their limits. You must either steel yourself to this reality or reject your own evolution into what you could be.

It appears that you truly have the potential to make meaningful contributions to our society. You are desperately needed. The bloodiest century in the history of mankind is coming to a close. Men led us through this carnage. Women need now to take the leadership roles to which you aspire.

Have confidence in your decisions, maintain your course. It would be a simple matter to emphasize the limitations of your coach. But he has done you a favor and in so doing you have moved beyond him. Keep going.

Empire builders in general broadens relevancy. This is about much more than one player, one coach, one empire.

SWISH! Three points. Myers shows what he thinks of the coach without name-calling.

Again, "demean"—condemnatory verb and who doesn't believe in expanding horizons except the small + narrow-minded

Here Myers pulls out all the stops. Does he go too far?

So... the coach is limited, but there are bigger issues here. Myers has redefined the situation. He speaks to all readers victimized by empire builders.

For Myers, the conflict between basketball and the inauguration, player and coach, team loyalty and individual development, goes beyond one player, one coach, one school. He's concerned about all empire builders who try to hold back those who make their empires possible. You can't have a winning team without talented

players. You can't have a successful business without talented workers. You can't be an effective governor without talented aides and
intelligent counsel. By speculating on and interpreting the motiva-
tions of the player and the coach, Myers describes a societal dynamic. By advising the player to have confidence, maintain her
course, keep going, he's expressing his vision of strength, success,
and leadership, and a firm opinion about how society works, and
how it ought to.

Tips for writing with passion

- If you're mad, get writing.

- Write an outrageous, no-holds-barred, rambling, wailing, rampaging draft to let off steam. Feel free to call names, be crude,
  rude, and offensive. Then throw the draft away.

- Once the steam has dissipated, write another draft in one sitting. Try to get all your points in, explore the whole subject,
  touch on many angles. Don't worry about structure, length,
  grammar, spelling, or even tone. Just get words on the page.

- Picture a reader who is reasonable, thoughtful, unbiased, open
  to new ideas—someone like you. This reader doesn't know the
  situation, so it's your job to explain it.

- Let the draft sit for a while. Return to it with a cooler head, a
  little distance. Read it as if you were new to the subject. Revise.
  This time do worry about structure, length, grammar, spelling,
  and especially tone.

- Control your tone. Even if you are angry or fearful, appalled or
  disappointed, you must not let emotion dominate. Show the
  emotion in strong verbs (*demeaned, stripped*) and nouns (*curse of
  versatility, mediocrity, conflict, gifts*).

- Avoid emotionalisms that don't add to the argument and may
  make you seem too involved or unreasonable. Don't say "I'm
  shocked" or "This is horrifying." Instead show what it is that has
  shocked you. Describe it. Name-calling is a kind of emotional-
  ism, too. Don't say, "The coach is an idiot." Instead, detail his
  actions so readers can draw their own conclusions.

- Avoid exclamation points! CAPITALIZING WHOLE WORDS! *Over-italicizing*! Too much **bold type. ESPECIALLY BOLD CAPITALS FOLLOWED BY LOTS OF PUNCTUATION !?!!** These typographical tricks make you appear HYSTERICAL!

- Structure with care. Move from the specific to the general (and perhaps back to the specific again). Start with the beautiful elm tree on the hill that the city wants to cut down because it's dying. Move to trees in general, the environment, open space, symbols of serenity in a hectic world—something broader, encompassing, and of interest even to people who've never seen your beloved elm. Then, maybe, go back to the elm. Reiterate your call to save it. End, perhaps, with a word picture of the dead elm as an ecosystem—with birds nesting, bugs digesting, a furry animal or two hibernating.

- Draw readers in with tension, a problem. "An elm tree, four feet through at the base, has stood on top of Munson Hill since George Washington was president. Now the city manager thinks it's stood there long enough—and has ordered it taken down."

- Find common ground with readers right away. If you know the community is split about the fire department budget, begin with the courage and dedication of the volunteer firefighters, maybe an example of how they helped you or someone you know. Get your readers nodding in agreement. "Yuh, that's a hard job. Those firefighters get called out in the middle of the night. And most of them are volunteers. . . ." Then bring up your more controversial points—how putting off the purchase of a new fire truck for just a year will give taxpayers time to recover from the last rate hike; or how leasing the truck now will save money in the end; how all the old truck really needs is new tires, which is about all folks can afford; or how the town needs a new truck now.

- Remember that shorter is better. Resist the urge to cover every angle, refute every argument. Focus on the points you feel most strongly about and can support most vigorously. Don't repeat yourself, although you may want to summarize or reiterate at the end.

Use short sentences and paragraphs to emphasize key ideas.

One-sentence paragraphs can be especially effective.

Especially if you don't overuse them.

List statistics or a series of related facts for concise presentation and easy reading.

- Maybe use bullets.
- Bullets look good.
- They show how organized you are.

• Most publications have maximum lengths for columns, op-eds, and letters to the editor. Make sure your submission fits; otherwise it may be rejected or cut. If you're writing a letter to a board, an agency, a committee, or an individual try your best to keep it to one page. Keeping your argument short shows your respect for readers and their time. Also, the fewer words you use to make the same point, the quicker and harder the impact. Fewer words, more punch.

• Be accurate. Your credibility depends on correct grammar, spelling, and keeping your facts straight. If you say the tax rate went down, and it didn't, readers will discredit everything else you say. If that elm tree is an oak, you're done for. If you say the player missed one game and two practices when she really missed two games and one practice, your critics will throw that misinformation in your face.

• Don't try to impress people with big words or complex maneuverings. Let your passion come through in your sincere, straightforward, well-meaning, logical, thoughtful assessment. And if there's a problem, be sure to suggest reasonable solutions.

• Don't whine. Avoid threats. Skip the breast-beating. Don't write anything that'll get you sued. Tell the truth.

↔ *Try this*

1. Next time something in the newspaper makes you mad, write about it: why you're mad, who you're mad at, what you think ought

to be done and by whom. Send your final draft to the paper as a letter to the editor.

2. Write another letter to the editor on the same topic but taking the opposite point of view. Don't send this one—unless, in the process of writing, you change your mind.

3. Think of a time when you or someone you care about was treated unfairly or unkindly. Describe the incident. Discuss why this specific instance represents or reflects a bigger social problem, like racial prejudice, sexism, homophobia, ageism, greed, environmental indifference, child abuse, political corruption.

4. Illustrate a large social problem without naming it. Show the problem without discussing it directly. For example, show a store clerk condescending to an eighty-year-old; or give the reader a tour of a laboratory where rabbits are used to test cosmetics; or let readers listen in on a conversation between two latchkey children.

5. What worries you, keeps you awake at night? Write about it. Try to figure out why you're troubled and what, if anything, you or others can do about it.

6. Is there a policy at work or at school or at home that you think should be changed? Write a proposal to administrators, student government, the school board, your wife (whoever is in charge) explaining why the policy is wrong or inadequate and how it should be changed.

7. Read columns in magazines or newspapers by writers with strong opinions and voices. These might be local columnists or syndicated ones. They might be columns about gardening, cooking, raising kids, education, sports, politics, history. Look at how the writer's passion comes through. Respond to a particular column or columnist with an essay of your own on a similar subject. Or imitate the columnist's style in an essay on any subject.

8. Write about a time you changed your mind. Explain the change. Explain why readers should agree with your new position.

ADVICE ABOUT PROCESS

▣ Take risks and fail: all writers belly flop

IF YOU HAVE A SUBJECT THAT'S IMPORTANT TO YOU BUT FEELS TOO complex, way too difficult to tackle, tackle it. Yes, you may belly flop, especially in early drafts. Anne Lamott in Bird by Bird says she consistently writes "shitty first drafts." We all do.

In fact, we've written such awful first, second, and third drafts that we've abandoned whole projects. Sometimes we never return, but more often we go back later and revise. The key is to recognize what you are ready to write about now. The subject that eludes you now might be perfect a year from now.

But you don't know until you try.

Why people expect writing to come out right the first time, we don't understand. Perhaps it's because in Grade 5 they had to write a report on polar bears. They didn't give a damn about polar bears; they just wanted to get the paper finished pronto so they could go play ball. They learned to produce fast, slick drafts; maybe they've been writing that way ever since.

We encourage a different kind of writing than the slapdash, get-it-done, turn-it-in variety. We encourage writing about ambitious, difficult subjects that gnaw at you, so you're willing to spend time thinking, evaluating, and researching—even if the research is in the library of your own memories. If you care enough, you'll be willing to rework a difficult subject until you've done it justice.

A skater learning a triple jump expects to fall often before he lands it. Actors would never expect to memorize a role and then walk through it on opening night without rehearsal. Anything worth doing requires practice and risk. Risk involves failure, sometimes much failure, before the skates hit the ice at just the right angle and speed and you glide away triumphant.

Children aren't afraid to fail; in fact, the concept rarely enters their heads. Children experiment. They play. We need to get back to the playfulness of children who, building a garage out of blocks, decide it would be better as a fort. With no sense of failure or why-couldn't-I-get-it-right-the-first-time, they knock down most of the garage and begin to build again.

In early drafts, return to that childhood attitude that allows play. Give yourself permission to fail. Give yourself permission to enjoy it.

◄► Writing habits: "one God damned word after another God damned word"

RUMOR: WRITERS WAIT FOR INSPIRATION.

Truth: Not so. Waiting for inspiration is like waiting for your numbers to come up in the lottery instead of going to work each morning.

Of course inspiration will strike now and then. We hope it's often and that you'll be thankful, but serious writers don't count on inspiration any more than serious gymnasts skip daily practices and count on inspiration to carry them through the Olympics. Inspiration tends to visit writers who've been sweating it out, day after day. They've tilled the earth and fertilized it; they are ready.

Writers write whether they feel like it or not. If you're lucky you'll look forward to sitting down at your desk. (We do.) But many writers say that while they enjoy finishing a piece, the actually doing is too hard, too uncertain to enjoy. We've heard of a writer who taped this over his desk: "One God damned word after another God damned word, day after God damned day."

Like opera singers and postal clerks, most writers keep regular hours. This is not to say you can't produce good work and hold down another job—like being a student, raising kids, running a restaurant, selling shoes, brokering stocks. The key is to set a schedule of hours you can reasonably devote to writing—and stick to it, just as you would stick to an exercise regimen or keep your evening appointment with your favorite television show. One poet, asked if she wrote every day, said writing was like eating breakfast. She didn't force herself to do it. It was something she just did.

Why keep regular writing hours? You'll find that if you start writing at, say, 7:00 each morning, five days a week, after a while you won't generate so many excuses to leave the room. When you keep regular hours, you can't help but mull over your writing project from time to time, consciously or unconsciously, perhaps even in your sleep. And when you walk into your workroom at 7:00 A.M., you'll be ready.

Excuses not to write are plentiful. Here are some we've used.

- My throat is sore. Maybe I'm getting a fever. Probably it's the flu. I can't possibly concentrate. I'll go to the drugstore for medicine.

- The writing's going nowhere. I may as well do a load of laundry or clean the carburetor.

- If I don't make the children's dentist appointment now, they probably won't get in for at least six months.

- The sale at Sears ends this week. I'd better get those snow tires or they'll be gone.

- I can think about my writing as I weed the tomato patch or walk to the newsstand or jog in the park.

- I can dream about my writing as I take a nap.

- Better deposit that paycheck before noon or I'll lose a day's interest.

- Well, I didn't write yesterday. What's one more morning?

- My brain is full. It needs to rest today.

When you start making excuses, pat yourself on the back for creativity and laugh at yourself. Then go into a room with paper, pen, computer—and stay there. Lock your front door. Order your roommates or housemates to stay away: No Matter What. Unplug the telephone. If, despite your request, friends or relatives keep interrupting, go to a library or even a restaurant where no one can find you. Write by hand; you can type what you've written when you get home.

Even if you're having a miserable writing day stay at your desk— at least for a while. As Flannery O'Connor said, you never know when an idea will pass by, and when it does, you need to be at your desk, ready for it. You can always write in your journal or brainstorm.

In general, you'll want to ease yourself into a schedule one toe at a time, rather than diving off the high board into ice water. If you were new to running, you wouldn't run ten miles the first day. You might run for ten or twenty minutes for a week, then work on longer times and distances. Let's say you decide you'll write Saturday and Sunday afternoons from 1:00 to 3:00. Tell yourself that some people play golf on Saturday and Sunday afternoons; you write. Or you might try writing on Monday, Wednesday, and Friday from 9:00 to 10:00 P.M. instead of reading or watching TV.

If you're the kind of person who tends to abandon schedules, tell yourself you'll write only ten minutes a day for two weeks. Or one week. Set a schedule that's realistic, but swear to yourself you'll stick to that schedule unless there's a wedding, funeral, fire, or earthquake at those very hours. At the end of your contract time, commit for another week, or two or three, and decide if you can extend the time by ten minutes or half an hour. Keep making contracts and extending the times until you've settled in.

After you've developed good writing habits, you'll find it's harder not to write at your appointed time than to write.

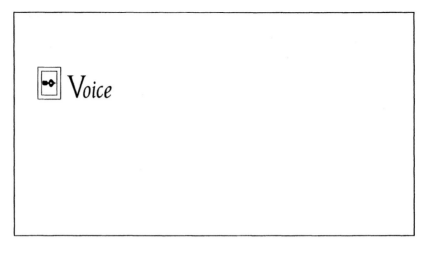

Voice

STRONG VOICE IN AN ESSAY OR STORY IS LIKE SEX APPEAL IN A person: You know it when you see it, but you probably can't explain it.

When a writer has a strong voice, a reader familiar with it will recognize work by that writer even if it's not labeled, just as a music lover hears three stanzas of her favorite pop star or opera singer and knows the artist.

Here are four distinctive voices:

You would never have known Herbie's place was a fish market unless you lived in Barrette's Landing all your life or your next of kin had left you a note. There wasn't any sign, just that old smell of rotten fish, decayed bait and lobster shells. Well, there used to be a sign there 'til Hurricane Diane blew through Maine a few years ago. Herbie wasn't in business to make money so much as he was to get ahead of a good tale, and to be with the old boys who hung around the fish market. It was thanks to Herbie's wife, Bertha, that the boys all ended up together.

"Yesterday's Fish Tomorrow," student writer, Nancy Greenlaw

I am sleeping, hard, when the telephone rings. It's my brother and he's calling to say he is now my sister. I feel something fry a little, deep behind my eyes. Knowing how sometimes dreams get mixed up with not-dreams, I decide to do a reality test at once. "Let me get a cigarette," I say, knowing that if I reach for a Marlboro and it turns into a trombone or a snake or anything else on the way to my lips that I'm still out in the large world of dreams.

The cigarette stays a cigarette. I light it. I ask my brother to run that stuff by me again.

Judy Ruiz, "Oranges and Sweet Sister Boy"

Even in this short passage, Ruiz's voice comes through: direct, honest, surprising, funny, cynical, exploratory, smart-ass, compassionate. She may or may not be all these things in life, but this is how she comes across on these pages. Big and real and resonant. The humorous tone here contributes to the shock effect, to her sharp voice. The spirit of the writer is caught on the page.

The voice in the next piece is formal, solemn. In her manuscript-in-progress, writer Titia Bozuwa describes the funeral of her daughter Joan in the Wakefield, New Hampshire, Congregational Church. Her son Paul steps up to the lectern:

> "Thank you all for coming," Paul said. "I would like to read an entry from Joan's diary, written in March of 1985," and he reached into the jacket of his linen suit that looked slightly rumpled from neglect.
>
> . . . Behind him the sun filtered through the stained-glass window, and blotchy shadows of maple leaves raked over its colored fragments of glass, back and forth, back and forth in gentle motion over a shepherd who held a lamb in his left arm and a staff in the other. The shepherd's hair was long and he had a beard, like the one Paul had sported the year before. He'd cut if off when Joan was in the Dana Faber Cancer Institute for a bone marrow transplant.

Finally, we include this Stephen Crane piece, "The Open Boat." It was originally published in a newspaper, a true story of the time he was shipwrecked and managed to survive with others on a lifeboat. This nonfiction account is frequently published as fiction in anthologies (which shows how fiction and nonfiction forms overlap). Like the Bozuwa piece, this is solemn; there is also, however, in the second paragraph, resentment: "These waves were most wrongfully and barbarously abrupt and tall":

> None of them knew the color of the sky. Their eyes glanced level and were fastened upon the waves that swept toward them. These waves were of the hue of slate, save for the tops, which were of foaming white, and all of the men knew the colors of the sea. The horizon narrowed and widened, and dipped and rose, and at all times its surface was jagged with waves that seemed thrust up in points like rocks.
>
> Many a man ought to have a bathtub larger than the boat which here rode upon the sea. These waves were most wrongfully and barbarously abrupt and tall, and each froth-top was a problem in small-boat navigation.

Imagine how Judy Ruiz might have recorded Crane's experience or how Nancy Greenlaw might have recorded Titia Bozuwa's, and you are imagining the differences among four strong voices.

These writers trusted their voices. You must work to trust your voice, too.

How does voice appear on the page? Not by intention, we think. Like most writers, we are not aware of voice as we write. When writers have strong ideas and feelings about their subjects or—even better—when they feel passionate about them; when they write with an abundance of information; when they find an angle, a way into the material that fascinates them; and when they have the skills to communicate these ideas and feelings with confidence and conviction, they can't keep their voices off the page.

If you feel your writing voice is bland, the problem may be your lack of fascination with the subject. Or perhaps you haven't yet found the right angle for it. Get an angle that excites you. Work with a strong attitude. Go ahead, give yourself permission to be eccentric, cynical, smart-ass, outrageous, envious, angry, or sad.

Often a "bad" attitude is good. For instance, if your view of the neighbors' child's fourth birthday is of pretty balloons and cake and ice cream with polite little children saying "please" and "thank you," you will come off sounding predictably sentimental and pleasant and bland. If you can't find an offbeat, surprising attitude, drop this subject.

But let's say your attitude toward this birthday party is cynical. You could show the competitive mother trying to better her neighbors in a competitive upper-middle-class neighborhood. The mother imports three professional clowns instead of the one other mothers have hired; she buys prizes for games from an expensive import shop; she has placed in the center of the table six baby chickens, which wobble and scratch and jerk about on narrow strips of green cellophane paper, contained by a small white picket fence. You can show one child shrieking in fright at the clowns, another running from the room, a third throwing up on the table after eating cake. Maybe one child, thinking the red, yellow, and orange whistle from Mexico is candy, tries to eat it and chokes; and maybe you, watching, have heard that pigeon feces can cause terrible diseases for anyone who touches them, and you wonder if this is true for chicken feces, which one child, right this moment, is pointing to on the table and shouting "chicken poo, chicken poo!" thus making the other children sing-song in unison "Chicky poo!"

And how is the mother behaving as the little bastards now bang their spoons on the table shouting to the point of hoarseness and hysteria, "Chicky poo! Chicky poo! Ickky dicky chicky poo!"? We'd love to see this scene from *your* point of view. Not from the point of view of the mother, who will tell her friends about the party at the neighborhood picnic the next afternoon, editing out the chicky poos; not from the point of view of the mother of the child who threw up, as she tries to assure the birthday boy's mom that really, her little darling had a lovely time.

Good writers have unusual ways of seeing their subjects. That's why you like them. Who wants to read the predictable cliché? If you have an offbeat attitude, wonderful. Nourish it. Let it out. But don't fake offbeat. Don't try, for instance, to pretend to see something in a sarcastic light if you truly believe it's sad. Readers will smell rats.

In your journal, write what you truly think and feel about specific people, experiences, and ideas versus what you have been taught you should or ought to think and feel. You may be frightened by what you've written, but if it's true, it's likely strong. It is the terrible "shoulds" that kill our voices. We've taught people who have said they have parents or even friends who are judgmental, righteous. You'll have to put up with your parents (or try to convert them, which is probably impossible), but get rid of friends who corset your true feelings and thoughts. Find new ones.

Becky and Sue rarely mention voice until near the end of a semester. It can make writers terribly self- or voice-conscious and kill their prose. A writer thinking about how she sounds on the page is as mincing and fake as an actress wondering how she looks to the audience as she crosses a stage. Voice has to do with energy and fascination and concentration and perseverance and a belief that your subject is worth writing about.

Voice comes from who you are. It springs from everything you've ever done and thought and seen and felt; from everything that's happened to you. Voice in a story springs from the writer being subject- and sentence-focused, not me-the-writer and how-I-sound focused.

Voice, finally, springs from the very center of your spirit. The wonderful thing about voice is the more you write honestly and with skill, the more you'll learn to have confidence in yourself; and the more confidence you have, the stronger your voice will become.

⊶ Try this

1. Free write. Write as fast as you can, without censure, without regard to spelling, full sentences, or grammar—anything that comes to mind even if it's "I'm almost out of toothpaste." Feel free to snarl, rage, snivel, be unfair, stupid, mean-spirited, goofy. If you do this for five minutes without stopping, every day for a week, you will hit core issues in your life, and you will discover attitudes you may not have known you had, or had as strongly. Better yet, do this every day for several weeks. Your voice may surprise you.

2. Choose three essays with distinctive voices. Type out a page of each. As you type you'll be experiencing the voices more deeply than if you merely read them. Then read what you typed aloud. And tell yourself that if these writers dared to let their strong voices show on the page, you dare, too.

3. In your journal write briefly—often a few lines will do—about something that happened in your past or someone you saw or encountered or an idea you do feel strongly about. You will not show this to anyone. Write a few lines, letting your thoughts and attitudes out without censure. Do this for a week.

List the "shoulds" of your life: what you were taught by parents, peers, the media about how you should regard specific situations and people, how you should behave. Then write how you actually feel or would like to behave.

4. Develop a bad attitude. Think of a subject that could be sentimental, predictable, a cliché such as the child's birthday party we mentioned. Here are some other examples: a week at summer camp, meeting an old friend, decorating a Christmas tree, making a Valentine's Day card, watching your child sing in a choir, walking your dog, buying a kitty, going to the beach, spending a week in Europe, watching the Northern Lights, looking at a famous painting at

an art museum. Now think of an approach to each subject that's irreverent, perhaps sarcastic, angry, perverse, or downright ghoulish. Write a few paragraphs expressing this attitude.

5. In your daily life, be alert to oddball, quirky ways you see things, people, happenings. Jot them down in your journal.

6. Have you ever been on a date or seen a movie or taken a vacation that was supposed to be fun but wasn't? Did you develop a bad attitude? Wonderful! Write about it. Think, also, of a family member or an acquaintance of whom most people approve, but you do not— or vice versa. Write about that person and your view of him or her.

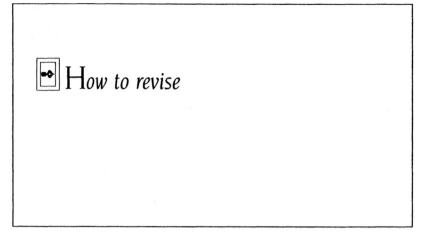

How to revise

REVISION ISN'T PUNISHMENT BECAUSE YOU DIDN'T GET IT RIGHT THE first time. It is your opportunity to look at a promising draft and vow, "I'm going to make this wonderful." If your subject has complexity, if it is meaningful to you and may be meaningful to readers, you'll need to revise to explore layers of meaning and possibility. By revision we don't mean diddling around with a comma or two or scanning the thesaurus for impressive words. We mean:

- Reseeing, revisiting, revamping, deconstructing, and reconstructing
- Looking at a draft through the eyes of readers, critics
- Recognizing what's actually on the page instead of what you intended to put there

Revision requires concentration and honesty, regardless of deadline, regardless of the fact that you're sick of it. You must carry on and make massive and small changes until a strong, clear-sighted inner self declares, "Now that's what I wanted to say, and that's how I wanted to say it."

Sometimes, if you're lucky, you get help from others: a writing group, a teacher, an editor, a friend who writes. This can speed the process. Seeing what's on your page is often easier for someone else. And if this someone is honest and articulate, her comments can be illuminating.

Alan DeCosta won a writing competition with his essay "Tracks" (page 248). The judge, though, suggested revision, including cutting the lead. At the same time, an editor who heard the essay read aloud as part of the awards ceremony recruited it for her magazine—with revision. It seemed to wander a little, she thought. It would have more impact if it were shorter and would fit better into the magazine format.

Al agreed to try a rewrite on speculation—meaning if the editor liked it, it would be published. Here's the lead to the first draft he submitted to the editor:

> A woman in town cross-country skis weekday mornings on the local golf course. I have never met her. But once, I happened to visit the course early enough to spy someone whom I thought might be *her* just finishing, lugging waxless skis and poles to her car. She trudged along, heavily clothed but purposeful, surrounded by steam, to the far side of the plowed-out parking lot. Was this the woman I had conjured stories about? I had followed someone's morning tracks through the snow on other days. There was something suggestive about this particular woman's walking stride across the parking lot. Her body shape, the length of her arms, her weight, the way her hips rotated with each short step—convinced me at that moment that I had insight into her truest nature.
>
> I imagine that this woman who precedes me in our common activity skis solo on the golf course in our town. Maybe she and her middle-aged husband (I'm quite confident she's a married lady) go away on weekends to large ski areas with machine-groomed and tracked cross-country trails. Possibly her husband and grown children also do downhill. She, of course, does not. I think she avoids logging roads and snowmobile trails, however—as I sometimes do not.
>
> Most of us tend to think in patterns . . .

The editor noted, in critiquing the revision, that the essay didn't seem to be about the woman, but the narrator—DeCosta himself. Speculation about the woman's life in the lead delayed introduction of the true subject—patterns, and DeCosta's experience with them, observations about them. She asked DeCosta to revise, getting more quickly to the tracks, the pattern, and his own skiing. And, by the way, cut extraneous words, references, images throughout. He did.

His next draft was shorter and more focused:

A woman in town cross-country skis weekday mornings on the local golf course. She has left clues there for me. I'm sure it is a woman, though I have never met her.

I imagine this woman who precedes me in our common activity skis solo weekday mornings. Maybe she and her middle-aged husband (I'm quite confident she is a married lady) go away on weekends to large ski areas which offer machine-groomed and tracked cross-country trails. Possibly her husband and grown children also do downhill. She, of course, does not. I think she avoids logging roads and snowmobile trails, however—as I sometimes do not.

Most of us tend to do things in patterns. Cross-country skiing on a golf course after a snowfall, the skier traces out physically in the form of tracks the route taken. Once around, it's easier to retrace that first pattern than to clamber off in other directions. The obsessive hill-runner and terrain hog—someone like myself—must instead forge beyond tracks, into wind-drifted depths. But I weary of being first into the wilderness some days. Then, I find myself following the morning woman's marks around the golf course.

In this version, DeCosta has ditched much of his speculation about the woman, including the striking image of her trudging along "heavily clothed but purposeful, surrounded by steam." He gave all this up to tighten his focus, to get to the point more quickly, to let the reader see his tracks on that first page. He introduces tension in the third paragraph, when he writes of being sometimes weary and "some days" changing his pattern—raising questions like, Why? What's the problem?

The middle of the essay explores patterns, habits, the reasons for them and for changing them. DeCosta describes himself as a "lone wolf," a competitive skier, a competitive person. He contrasts the woman's pattern with his own. She takes the easier route, goes slowly. She "eschews hills as she makes dull truck around the course perimeter." Yet, she has the harder task of going first.

DeCosta's pattern has changed over time, he realizes. A discovery! Now he rarely takes "random treks into storm-cradling ravines and forests alone. . . . It is not so much that my body has faltered—rather, a slow awareness of the tradeoffs I've made surfaces."

His thinking moves from the general to the specific, from the concept of patterns to the specific pattern of his own life and the changes of middle-age. "People once shouted 'Slow Down!' as I bounded past them. I would not. Checking my interval times from point to point, I focused on maximum effort. . . . Occasionally a pole broke. I had narrowed my vision, and lost sight of my life's more unclear tracks."

He continues: "I was in danger of discovering, and marrying, oblivion."

Part of this essay's power lies in the way Al seems to be discovering truths about himself as he writes and as he skis. This provides a sense of both intellectual and physical forward motion. Perhaps he did discover these truths in early drafts—and, wisely, maintained that sense of discovery in subsequent ones. The freshness of the ideas makes readers feel as though they can see into his mind as well as through his eyes. Readers understand how the change in perception at the heart of the essay evolves, because Al shows the evolution in a narrative of his thoughts. The woman's tracks act as catalyst. What the writer sees in them and comes to know through them is the essence of the essay.

In the next draft, Al boiled the paragraphs down even more—not just to make it fit the magazine (although that was part of it), but to make his points more crisply and comprehensibly, to emphasize theme and more clearly express meaning.

Suggestions to help you revise

Look at your draft through several critical lenses. Some writers work with one lens at a time, strengthening imagery in one draft, reordering ideas in another, expanding key points in another. Other writers tackle two or three revision tasks simultaneously, and edit along the way. Some see editing—spelling, punctuation, sentence length, phrasings, word choices—as separate from revision and concentrate on editing alone in a close-to-final draft. Here are six strategies useful in revision.

Fully imagine

Fully imagine scenes. Who's there? Where are they? What are they doing? What are they saying? What do they look like?

Fully imagine all the ramifications of an idea or argument. In "Tracks," DeCosta runs with the idea of patterns—patterns in the

snow, patterns of movement, patterns for living, patterns of his experience, changes in patterns. He didn't have all these ideas at
once. They developed through drafts.

Fully imagine territory. What is this really about? You may begin
with the subject of being the only girl in a family of boys, but as you
write focus shifts to the relationship between a mother and only
daughter. Maybe you decide to include other mother-daughter relationships, make assertions about how those relationships work,
or don't. What seems to be at the center of your essay in the first
draft may be peripheral in the final draft.

Select from many details

In arguing that nicotine is as addictive as heroin, you may choose
to include anecdotes, statistics, quotes from doctors or tobacco ex-
ecutives, your own experiences, testimonials from addicts. A detail
can be the color of the addict's eyes or the number of children who
become addicted to each drug in a single day. Whether you're writing from book research or life research or both, if you know your
subject, you will have many details to choose among. In revision
you decide whether to include details about your grandfather's last
days in the hospital dying of lung cancer. You decide whether to include statistics on the success of recovery programs for heroin addicts. You pick and choose, seeking the most powerful evidence to
support your point, details to create a mood, make an impression,
paint a picture, bring life and meaning to your subject.

Identify key points and expand on them

When you put too many mud worms in a can without enough soil
they ball up. Sometimes in early drafts your ideas get tangled together when you have a lot to say and it comes out in a rush. In revision, you pull one worm at a time from the tangle. For example, in
an early draft of "Tracks," DeCosta might have buried the line "habits
have their reasons" in a paragraph naming lots of habits. Maybe he
pulled that worm out. "Habits have their reasons": What does that
mean? What are the reasons behind my habits? What is the relationship between habit and passion and obsession? In my life? In
the woman's? In general? Maybe as he wrote on those questions, he
described himself as a lone wolf and that perception led him to the

idea that a "traveling spirit" sometimes "remembers a connection to community," his developing theme.

Identify themes and keep them bubbling

It's possible to write several drafts and not know, consciously, what you're writing about. Say you're writing the story of being cut from the eighth-grade basketball team. You ended up in band, playing fourth trumpet, miserable. So you describe the tryouts, coach, attitude, the blond kid with the stubby nose who tripped you and pretended he didn't mean to, but you knew he did. You saw him laughing with Jimmy—and you thought Jimmy was your friend. But he never had been much of a friend. Or had he?

Maybe when you started, you thought you were writing about how things turn out for the best, even if they're painful, because eventually you learned to love the trumpet and became a professional musician. But, in drafting, you can't find your way to the happy ending. The truth of your story is something else. The meaning evolves as you draft and you find yourself writing more and more about how condescending the coach was—and how you were sure she'd made up her mind about you before you set foot on the court. And how much Jimmy's laughter hurt. And how much your dad wanted you to be a jock because he'd been one.

You read through your most recent draft and notice details you've put in, almost unconsciously, about how when you jumped to make a shot your legs betrayed you by tangling; how the coach sat at the top of the bleachers during one-on-one like she was God—or, at least, some kind of judge. You remember the disappointment on your dad's face when he found out you had been cut. Even though he said it was all right, you knew it wasn't; you knew you'd come up short, again. You realize you're writing about judgments, judges, and betrayal. So you look for other chances to emphasize that theme. You explore connections: Jimmy judged you by laughing. He betrayed you, too. Your body betrayed you by not being what other people thought it out to be. You remember the coach saying, "By eighth grade, you either got it or you don't." Were your dad's expectations a judgment? Did he betray you? Did it feel like he did?

In subsequent drafts, you drop all pretense of a happy ending. You don't even mention the trumpet. You have discovered that the piece is about something else altogether. You lead with a scene between you and your dad in which he's saying one thing, but you know he means something else, and it hurts. The new direction, new theme, grew naturally from your details and insights. You trust them and revise accordingly.

Create illuminating comparisons

Once you've fully imagined your essay—the who, what, why, where, how—you will want to dig deeper into meaning. Comparisons are one way to do this. Call it simile, using *like* or *as* ("the sun was red as Celia's lips"), or metaphor, using the verb *to be* ("for some, leisure is not a dream but a nightmare"). Either way, you're comparing one something to another. An original comparison can express a lot and often implies even more. To make a comparison, you begin with the question: What is _____ like? Or how is _____ similar to _____?

Shape

Almost every essay can benefit from a healthy session of cut and paste. Cut your argument into paragraphs and play around with the order in which you present the supporting examples. Cut up your personal essay about a series of hospital stays that have made you distrust modern medicine. Play around with which experiences might be effective as the lead or ending. Which belong in the middle? Which could be left out altogether? Maybe in early drafts you wrote chronologically, from the time the doctor tried to take your tonsils out when you were five, to age sixty, when you were misdiagnosed and certain you had only days to live. In later drafts, you might want to arrange your examples from mild to severe, or from funny to tragic, or from most recent to earliest—to the time you saw the bright light at the end of the tunnel and Auntie Priddy reaching out to you with radiant hands.

Cutting and pasting, whether on the computer or with scissors and glue on the dining room table, can help you discover creative ways to organize material, stronger leads and endings, a tighter piece overall as you throw out whole passages because they don't fit your new, improved flow; as you add transitions to bridge an intriguing jump from one idea to another.

Even if the structure of your essay seems to work, it doesn't hurt to experiment. A change in order changes emphasis, and that changes everything.

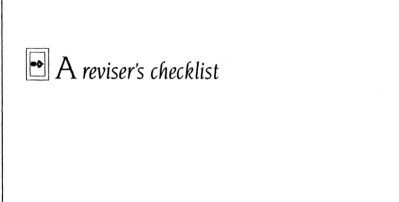

A reviser's checklist

HERE ARE QUESTIONS WRITERS OFTEN ASK THEMSELVES AFTER they've finished a first draft:

_____ Do I still care about my subject? Is that caring, involvement, fascination apparent on the page? Does the piece have energy and voice?

Some drafts feel flat-footed. Others soar. Readers sense if a writer is engaged by his subject; it shows in every line. If you don't care now and your writing reflects your disengagement, drop the topic and go on to something else. You may possibly decide to return to this one later, if your enthusiasm returns.

_____What interests me most about this subject *now*?

That *now* matters. Where is the energy? Where does the writing seem to work best? This can be a clue to where your interest lies. You may have, initially, decided to write about the family reunion last Thanksgiving, but now you're more interested in Great Uncle Henry. He appeared in only two paragraphs on page four of this draft, but those two paragraphs are juicy. Maybe you should focus on Henry, shift to a new angle. If so, you will be writing a new first draft, one that, nevertheless, you might not have been able to write without your original first draft. Nothing is wasted in revision: Even if just one line makes it to the next draft, that one line had to come from somewhere and you probably needed to write those six discarded pages to discover it.

_____Am I clear? Can readers understand me?

Reading aloud helps you hear what's actually on the page rather than what you wish were there. Reading aloud to someone else or to a group is even more helpful. Having someone read your piece back to you, without comment, can give you insight into what's clear and what's not. Just hearing a reader stumble over one of your lines can be a clue. And, of course, if you put the piece away for a bit, you'll be able to assess it more objectively than when it's hot out of the laser printer.

_____Is it honest? Have I faced this subject as honestly as I can or have I shied away from tough truths?

_____Is my subject ambitious or have I fallen into the trap of merely rehashing everything I knew before I wrote?

_____Is this focused?

Think purpose. What am I trying to say? Have I stuck to a central theme or veered into an area that really should be the subject of a whole new piece? If focus seems to be a problem, one solution is to try to articulate your main theme in a line. What is this supposed to be about? Once you come up with a clear, concise statement of focus, test each section of your draft against it. Does this paragraph fit my focus? Or this one. Or this one. Cut or revamp what doesn't fit. Expand or give more emphasis to what does.

_____Do I have something to say that will interest readers? Have I answered that rude and sometimes hurtful question, "So what?"

Back to focus, theme, meaning. A theme in writing is like a theme in music. It operates all through. It's fine to tell the story of how you and your ex-boyfriend went to a park and he stepped on a sharp piece of glass, was deeply cut, bled all over the grass, and you had to drive him to the emergency room, where he got twelve stitches and cried the whole time. Ask yourself, What does it mean? Why is this incident important? Was it a turning point in your relationship? Did you see something in him, in yourself, in your couplehood that you hadn't seen before? Why did you choose to write about this particular experience?

_____Do I comment? Do I make connections? Are there moments of insight here, places on the page where I made and expressed a discovery, saw and revealed something in a new light? Do I need to speculate or question on the page in order to make my meaning clearer? Did I learn something writing this? Does the reader understand that I learned something?

_____Is the focus too narrow? Do I need to add a whole new dimension? Another area of inquiry to deepen meaning? Do I need to see my subject in a larger context?

_____Is my subject broad enough to hold reader interest with possibilities, but not so broad that I'm skimming the surface without examining my subject in depth?

If you're writing about all your summers at Lake Toekey, for instance, you almost surely need to narrow your scope, perhaps to when you and your sister climbed Owl's Head Mountain and how, for the first time, you recognized how daring she was.

_____Have I emphasized the right material so readers will know what I'm trying to say? Is every sentence, every word, worth the space it occupies? Should I add a dramatic scene? Add details to a key section? Have I chosen the best evidence—incidents, quotes, details, facts—to illustrate my points? Have I placed the evidence prominently?

_____Have I cut out all unnecessary material? Have I rambled? Can entire sections or scenes go? Does each part, each paragraph advance the meaning, enhance the forward motion of my story enough to warrant its inclusion?

_____Have I organized this in a way that does justice to my theme and is mindful of my readers?

One way to *see* your organization is to jot down three or four words for each paragraph in a post-draft outline to check the order.

You may notice spots where it would make sense to move similar paragraphs closer together. You may notice that one seems out of place. Or that the fifth paragraph and the twenty-seventh say pretty much the same thing, so one can be cut, or the two merged.

Draw arrows to show where you want to move paragraphs. Or you can cut the outline into strips that can be rearranged until you find a perfect fit and flow.

_____Have I chosen the best possible lead? Does it hook the reader? Is there a conflict or tension or question explicit or implied that makes readers want to go on? Is it a true lead that points to the heart of my subject?

If you're not delighted with your lead, look further into the piece. Look at the second and third and fourth paragraphs. Maybe the fifth paragraph would make a stunning lead. Move it up. Or, cut everything that comes before it. Maybe the ending would make an effective beginning. See if some of the material on your last page might work better on your first.

_____Have I earned this ending? Does it pull the threads through, gather them, and push my meaning to a new level? Is something fresh emerging in that last paragraph and last line, or have I just rehashed what went on before?

If you are mildly dissatisfied with your ending, you might try rewording for more oomph. Maybe you're ending in the right place, with the right ideas or specifics, but your language is not precise enough to create a *the end* impact on readers.

If you are deeply unhappy with your ending, the fault may not lie in the ending but in what has come before. You can't tie up threads that aren't there. If you've woven in too many threads, that can be a problem, too. Maybe you're trying to do too much and you have two pieces going instead of one. Maybe they need to be split.

If your threads are strong, colorful, integral, the ending will present itself to you.

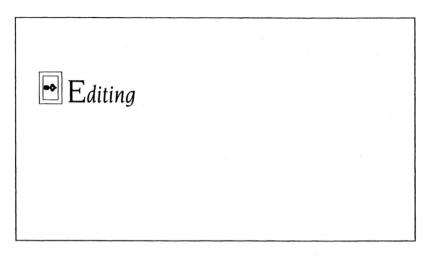

Editing

UNEDITED WRITING IS LIKE A CLUTTERED DESK: YOU CAN'T appreciate the grain and design when it's littered with papers, coffee mugs, and books. Professional writers edit obsessively and, often, in spurts of intense concentration. They cut words, phrases, whole sections, move passages around, change words and punctuation, add details, sentences, paragraphs. They type the change on the computer, leave the work alone for a few days, and return with renewed vigor to edit the same pages again. And again and again.

A well-edited piece, like a skilled gymnast, works efficiently. When the gymnast moves along the balance beam, her feet and legs don't flap. Her wrists aren't wobbly. Her head doesn't roll as she flips through the air. Every muscle is directed, every movement purposeful. So it is in writing. Each word counts. Each word pushes the subject ahead. Extra words, wrong words, clichés, awkward phrases, poor punctuation or spelling weaken the final effect.

In the next two chapters we describe several editing strategies. In addition to these chapters, you'll need a thorough grammar and usage text on your desk at all times, as well as a dictionary and a thesaurus. And you'll need to consult them regularly until you've learned every nuance of language, every comma and semicolon rule, every frequently misused word, every preferred spelling. Which means you'll need to consult them from now on.

Radical surgery

WE DIVIDE EDITING INTO RADICAL SURGERY AND FINE TUNING. IN this radical-surgery chapter, you go through your story like Grant through Richmond; and in our fine-tuning chapter, you tinker and polish and perfect.

1. Cut all the unnecessary words that you possibly can.

Get rid of lightweight words and phrases that take up more space than they're worth. For example: *thing, it, it is, it was, there is, there were, this is, a lot, quite, very, really, rather, awfully, sort of, kind of.* Especially *that.* A novelist we know, alerted to his overuse of *that,* eliminated, literally, hundreds of them in his final draft. Lightweight words don't evoke sight, sound, taste, touch, smell, or even concept. You can't picture *that* or *quite* or *thing* or *there.* Taken by themselves they don't mean much. Mostly, they connect or set up other, stronger words, and a simple restructuring can bring the stronger words into prominence.

When you spot a lightweight word, eliminate it or substitute something more substantial.

> Original: A quick temper is one of the things that gets me into quite a lot of trouble.

> Edit: My temper gets me into trouble.

Shorter sentences pack more punch. The phrase "one of the things that" fills space but doesn't add meaning. Let it go. Notice too, the difference between "quite a lot of trouble" and "trouble" seems negligible.

Original: It is well known that Shelties make good pets, but people considering adopting one need to know several things about their personalities. They can be affectionate but also tend to be skittish and snappy at times.

Edit 1: The affectionate nature of Shelties makes them lovable pets, but potential owners should realize this breed can be skittish and snappy.

Edit 2: Shelties make lovable pets, but before you adopt one you should know they can be skittish and snappy.

Two other lightweights to watch out for: *my* and *and.* For instance, you can say "Mother went to the office" instead of "My mother went to the office." You can say "The room was warm, stifling." That feels stronger than "The room was warm and stifling." The difference is subtle, but worth achieving.

2. Rely on strong, active verbs.

Generally an active verb carries more weight—meaning—than a passive one. The difference between active and passive is simple: the verb "to be" in any of its forms indicates the passive.

Use active: I ate the pie.

Avoid passive: The pie was eaten by me.

The verb *ate* is more concrete than the verb *was,* because *ate* evokes an image of a mouth in action more immediately and directly than *was eaten.* Sometimes in the passive, the subject gets left out altogether: The pie was eaten; papers were missing; lies were told.

Avoid "ings." They slow your story. *Not,* I was walking, *but,* I walked. Sometimes you'll want to slow a moment, such as watching a hawk soaring on a wind current. Then "ing" verbs work well.

3. Be plain, clear, direct. Simplify.

Original: As we were watching the clowns gyrating themselves into impossible positions, throwing pink sticks into the air—a feat that positively made us hold our breaths as you can well imagine—a collective gasp from the audience directed our otherwise riveted attention to one specific clown who, unlike the gyrating ones (he was the one with the biggest nose, a shiny lime green nose), was hanging upside down by his gigantic feet, which were red, from a high beam and he was lighting a cigar I swear was the size of a long stick of pepperoni and then throwing it; it proceeded to explode.

That sentence is a pretzel.

Edit: We watched the clowns twist and gyrate as they juggled pink sticks. Suddenly the audience gasped: the clown with the biggest nose, shiny and lime green, hung upside down by his huge red feet from a high beam. He lit a cigar the size of a pepperoni stick, then flung it into the air where it exploded.

4. Cut clunkers.

Clunkers do nothing. They contain no pertinent facts or important information. Often made up of lightweight words, they don't earn the space they occupy. Some clunkers: *on the other hand, when you consider the fact that, due to the fact that, it goes without saying, in my personal opinion, in a timely manner, as you already know, at this point in time, it is possible that.* Clunkers are the phrases you inserted when, assigned to write five pages, you could come up with only three. So you widened the margins, used the big font, and stretched your skimpy information with fat, flabby language. Redundancies are clunkers: *great huge trailer truck.* If it's huge, you don't need great. And if it's a trailer truck we already know it's huge. *Tuna fish.* Say tuna.

5. Be honest.

Don't say: I saw a field of pumpkins and they all were large and round as shiny beach balls sunning themselves in golden light.

Say: The sun shone on a field of pumpkins.

No one will believe *all* the pumpkins were large and round unless the setting is Oz. Some were lopsided. Many mud-splattered. And the pumpkins did not sun themselves. They lay in a field. The sun shone on them.

Don't say: I jumped out of bed.

Unless you are a kangaroo or a grasshopper.

Say: I got out of bed.

Don't say "Mother screamed at me" if she only raised her voice.

6. Check facts.

Call a forest ranger to be sure grizzlies hibernate in February and March. Don't describe daffodils blooming in July or geese flying north in October. Don't rely on an old statistic about the number of subway commuters during a work week in Denver five years ago. Go to a library. Ask a reference librarian for help. She's paid to steer you to information. Punch up key words on the Internet. Get the facts.

7. Avoid clichés.

For example: *light as a feather, red as a beet, sit up and take notice, packs a punch, makes you laugh and cry, fit as a fiddle, ready for action, slow as molasses, cool, awesome.*

A cliché is a too-familiar expression that once was clever and original but has lost its impact through overuse. *Mother Nature, Father Time, nature's bounty, rustic cabin, mighty oaks, majestic pines, bustling cities, sparkling eyes, darting eyes* (how do eyes dart, anyway? on wings? on tiny feet?); no *sweet little old ladies* or *crotchety old men*; no *excitable, arm-waving Italians* or *uptight, useless, overbred Wasps*; no *rhythmic African Americans*; no more *pounding, thumping,* or *drumming hearts* or *heart in my throat* or *sweaty palms* or *tingling spines* or *chills running up and down a spine.* For God's sake, avoid *heaving bosoms.* No psychological jargon: *open and honest relationship, hostile dependency, passive-aggressive, paranoid, toxic relationship*—unless you're writing an article for a professional journal. Don't say: I *couldn't believe my eyes* or *my eyes popped out of my head* or *her jaw dropped in astonishment.* No *single tear trickling down a pale cheek.* No *trembling lips.* No *breezes, waves,* or *wavelets kissing your hair, face, or toes.* Don't write: "She 'lost it'" thinking readers will forgive the cliché because it's in quotes. They won't. In fact, the quotes call attention to it.

Clichés often appear in early drafts before your thinking is clear and focused, before you've fully imagined. They should diminish as you continue to draft. Mark every cliché on your close-to-final draft. Sometimes, rarely, you'll decide the cliché makes your work sound informal and conversational, and you'll leave it, as we did with "packs more punch" in #1, here. Most of the time, you'll either eliminate the cliché altogether and let the sentence carry on without it, or you'll take the opportunity to substitute a more original, accurate image or idea. Consider clichés opportunities to tighten your prose and be creative. What could you use instead?

8. Cut vagaries. Be specific.

Take advantage of chances to add facts and details if they will advance meaning. Look for missed opportunities. Substitute specifics for vagaries and generalizations.

> *Vague:* We were all standing around speculating over what our old school friends were doing elsewhere.

If the speculation matters, specify it.

> *Specific:* We stood by the water cooler wondering if Nick was driving his father's mid-life-crisis Jaguar at ninety miles per hour down the I-95 or if Ann was studying for her pre-vet finals. Probably Saul was playing drums for some high school prom, but Jody could be doing anything: snow boarding in Montana, hammering shingles on shelters for the homeless, or holing up in her room, the phone unplugged, meditating in the Lotus position.

These friends are a diverse group. Some groups of friends might all be studying. Or partying. Or planning a drug run from South America. This speculation enlarges our understanding of the friends and of the "we" at the water cooler.

> *Original:* Whether she played soccer or some other sport or activity, she engaged in everything with skill and enthusiasm.

> *Edit:* She played soccer, tennis, climbed mountains, even did crossword puzzles with the enthusiasm and skill she brought to every task.

By choosing items to list, the writer gives readers an idea of the range of activities.

> *Original:* My Dad was a complainer. He would nag about every single thing we did or did not do.

This leaves readers out. What does the writer mean by "every single thing"? Edit to include readers.

> *Edit 1:* My dad would find fault with my clothes, the way I did my chores, my friends, my grades, and the way I didn't put things away.

Below, the added details give an even clearer idea of the extent of the father's complaints.

Edit 2: Dad complained relentlessly: my blue jeans were torn and greasy, my ball point pen was gummy so my history report looked sloppy. If I didn't get my hair cut by six p.m. tomorrow, he would cut it with the kitchen shears; my C- average wouldn't get me into a decent college, my bike blocked his car space in the garage. . . .

Vague labels like *people* should be specified. Ask yourself, who are these people? Potential dog owners? Disgruntled employees? Catholics? Sufferers of chronic ear infections? Prostitutes? Butterfly collectors? Students? Be as specific as possible. *Springer spaniel* is more specific and gives the reader a clearer picture than *dog*. *Brussel sprout* means more than *vegetable*, which means more than *food* or *material for human consumption*. A *wart* has more impact than a *blemish* or a *mark*.

Vagaries are bland and boring. Specifics energize your prose and your readers. They allow you to explore in depth rather than superficially.

9. Don't gush. No cheesy alliteration, no sentimentality.

Original: As I stood on the quaint rustic bridge, the breeze kissing my hair, the sun warming my soul, I noticed with a pang, a stately oak spreading its great arms outwards, outwards as if to shield the dainty spring florets growing in its shadow. I felt the earth shudder as though the very universe itself were speaking to me in sweet harmony. Below, so far and yet so near below, the lovely lithe lily pads floated fleetingly in untroubled waters while frogs frolicked, leaping lightly from lily to lily to lake.

This is ghastly. Readers will be embarrassed for you.

Edit: I stood on the old wooden bridge watching the frogs below jump from lily pads into the pond. On shore, purple and yellow crocuses grew in the grass under a substantial oak whose new leaves rustled in a light breeze.

Describing nature or love can bring out the violins in writers. We understand this. If you are profoundly moved by a sunset or a lake in the morning mist, you may want to communicate that feeling. So describe exactly what you see (smell, hear, etc.) and remember: When a subject is powerful—a fresh snowfall, a murder, sex, death or funerals, betrayal, loss, birth, love, lust, the bright lights of Vegas—understatement is more effective than overstatement. Choose your details with care, and try to be original.

The more dramatic the scene you're trying to re-create, the greater the temptation of melodrama. Don't get carried away with descriptors: "The poisonous snakes were hideously, murderously hanging onto the pitiful boy in the water and he lurched and lunged jerkily and obviously in horrible pain toward shore. He was clearly gasping close to his last feeble breath." Instead, write as John Yount does in *Trapper's Last Shot*, using precise nouns and verbs rather than pouring on the adjectives and adverbs: "When he got in waist deep water, they could see the snakes hanging on him, dozens of them, biting and holding on. He was already staggering and crying in a thin, wheezy voice and he brushed and slapped at the snakes trying to knock them off."

Cut exclamations like *horrible, horrific, gruesome, disgusting, terrifying, awesome.* Use a few, accurate details to create that feeling of horror.

10. *Swear sparingly.*

Yes, you may write "God dammit, you shit-faced motherfucking sonofabitch, will you for Christ's sake cut it the hell out, you flaming asshole," if there is just cause. By just cause, we mean if you're reporting the dialogue of someone who swears. Or if you used such words in rage.

Some people swear in nearly every sentence. In this case, give the person a few ripe obscenities to suggest excessive swearing, but don't report them all. An obscenity in writing is ten times stronger than one spoken aloud—so go easy.

Rarely, a writer will use an obscenity in the narration (as opposed to dialogue) to make a point. Nora Ephron does this effectively in the last paragraph of "A Few Words About Breasts: Growing Up Absurd." Of her friends who feel they should be pitied for having large breasts, while she complains of small ones, she writes: "I think they are full of shit."

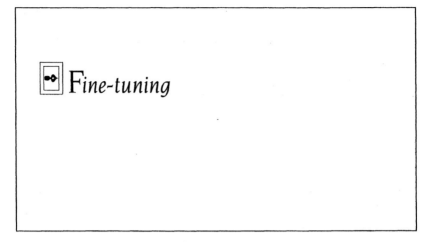

Fine-tuning

1. Use I with care.

I is a powerful word. Too many I's on the page stand out and make the writer seem self-involved. You can write about your experience and ideas without using I in every sentence. Here's an example of an I-cluttered paragraph, followed by an edit.

> *Original:* I speak with a New Hampshire accent. I've had some people say I sound like I'm from Maine, but I'm not. Strange thing, most of the kids I grew up with on Corn Hill Road don't talk like I do. They talk like television personalities, with inflections that don't sound like they come from any place I've ever been. I think this is too bad. I think that having no accent means you've lost something or pushed it away. (ten I's)

> *Edit:* I speak with a New Hampshire accent. Some think Maine—but it's not. Strange thing, most of the kids I grew up with on Corn Hill Road talk like television personalities, with inflections that evoke no place in particular. Which seems too bad, as though something has been lost or forgotten or pushed away. (two I's)

The edited paragraph focuses less on the writer and her experience, and more on the concept of regionalism, the true subject of the essay. Also, in the edit the sentences are shorter, tighter, denser.

2. Vary sentence structure.

Read a page of your work aloud. Listen for patterns, habits of construction, sentences that look and sound the same. Variety is the spice of prose—unless you are intentionally creating a parallel structure. For example, each of the numbered sections in this chapter begins with a command. We did that on purpose. At dramatic moments, writers often use many short sentences in a row to build tension.

Sometimes though, a writer will overuse a structure unintentionally. For example, if all your sentences are eight to ten words long, that's a problem. Same tune, same cadence, same emphasis. Or, if most of your sentences follow a single format such as subject-verb-object, the writing will seem choppy.

> *Original:* The squirrel saw the nut. He ran to the nut. He picked the nut up in his paws. The squirrel ate the nut.

Variety in sentence structure makes the prose more palatable.

> *Edit:* The squirrel saw the nut and ran to it. In his paws, he picked it up. Then . . . down the hatch.

Look and listen for patterns. Ask yourself, "Am I being lazy and falling back on what's comfortable? Or is this the best way to say what I want to say?"

3. Use the right word, not one that's almost right.

> *Not:* He was desperately unhappy.

> *But:* He was miserable.

4. Play with sentence placement.

The first and last sentence of each paragraph have the greatest impact. If you bury a strong sentence in the middle of a paragraph, it loses some of its power; the reader will not appreciate it as much. Consider moving it to the end of the paragraph. Or end the paragraph after your strong sentence; then start a new one with the next.

5. Play with word order.

The last word in each sentence carries the most weight. If you can place an evocative word like *love, heart, dying, grief, joy, misery, shame, exhilaration, pickle* at the end of a sentence do so, as long as the sentence doesn't become awkward as a result.

> *Original:* He is dying, I thought as I watched him.

> *Edit:* As I watched him, I thought, He is dying.

6. Don't clobber readers with adjectives.

Original: It was a stifling, hot, humid, sultry mid-to-late August early afternoon.

Readers can't remember all this. You need to choose.

Edit: It was a sultry August afternoon.

7. Check each adverb.

Adverbs are often redundant.
  "'Don't shoot!' he said excitedly." Obviously he is excited.
  Adverbs often tell readers something that ought to be shown. For instance:

Original: He looked at me furiously.

Edit: Leaning forward, he stared at me, frowning, his lips pulled back as though he might lunge and bite me.

8. Avoid cute.

Original: I trucked my little body off to the little girls' room.

Edit: I walked to the bathroom.

9. Stick to the conventions of punctuation and presentation.

It's easy to overuse dashes, parentheses, italics, capitals, exclamation points, ellipses, "etc.," slang, phonetic spelling, sentence fragments, very short paragraphs. All these techniques help vary sentence structure, get the reader's attention, emphasize important points. Short paragraphs—especially one-sentence paragraphs—highlight key ideas. But too many will stutter your prose. Sentence fragments can get a story moving, build tension. Too many can make your thoughts seem disjointed.

Dashes, parentheses, italics, ellipses, exclamation points can give an oral quality to your writing, help your reader *hear* what you're saying. Dashes can give the impression of stream-of-consciousness—thoughts that flow together—naturally—as if you're swimming in somebody's head. Overused, they make your thinking and prose seem sloppy or unfinished. Parentheses and italics can give readers the feeling they're being let in on a secret (as though you're whispering in their ears). Overused, they are self-conscious. Same with ellipses, capitals, underscores.

Don't be afraid to use these unconventional conventions—but treat them like hot pepper in the stew: A little goes a long way. Same with colloquialisms and slang.

10. *Substitute small words for long ones if they mean the same thing*:

Not: He exited the premises.

But: He left the bank.

Not: We conversed.

But: We talked.

11. *Be consistent.*

Not: I glanced at the statue for a long time.
Glanced and *a long time* don't go together.

Not: She sniffled violently.

Sniffled and *violent* aren't a match.

Not: A *student* who pays attention to *their grades* will do well.

A *student* is singular. *Their* is plural. The two halves of the sentence don't match.

Edit: A student who pays attention to his grades will do well.

Or: A student who pays attention to her grades will do well.

Or: A student who pays attention to grades will do well.

Or: Students who pay attention to their grades will do well.

If a bus driver is dazed in one paragraph and clear-headed in the next, without an explanation for the change, readers will be confused and distrustful. You don't want to show a woman in a green scarf entering the restaurant, but leaving with an orange one. Also confusing: Calling Mary-Louise by different names—Mary, Mary-Lou, Ma-Lou, my sister-in-law, my brother's wife. Readers will think you have six characters instead of one.

12. *Cut introductory or warm up words or phrases.*

Get to the point. Often you can strengthen sentences by cutting I *heard, I saw, I smelled, I remembered, I noticed, I figured out, I thought, I started to, I began to,* or worse: *In my opinion.* Worse still: *In my personal opinion.*

Original: Jane remembered the devastation caused by the hurricane of 1938 and shuddered at the memory.

Edit: The devastation caused by the hurricane of 1938 still made Jane shudder.

Original: I stood on top of Blue Hill. I looked across the valley and saw the sun setting behind Elephant Mountain.

Edit: I stood on top of Blue Hill. Across the valley, the sun was setting behind Elephant Mountain.

Original: I started to leave the room.

Everything has a beginning, so why say it?

Edit: I left the room.

Try this

1. Read the following aloud to experience the avalanche of unnecessary words, the clichés and redundancies. Then go through the piece with a machete. Our students enjoy doing this in pairs. They teach each other what to cut and what to keep.

SMOKERS AND SMOKING

When you stop and consider the fact that smoking is truly and profoundly hazardous to your health, it is astonishing to realize that so very many people still keep up their habits of smoking. I, for one, do not understand why they do. To be honest, it has always really bothered me, indeed worried me greatly, that my mother and my father are smokers, but it wasn't until I got into my high school that I was able to summon the bravery to communicate in a firm manner to my parents my extremely strong concerns for their physical well-being and what smoking was doing to their bodies, particularly their lungs. I cannot say enough bad things about cigarettes. It is my opinion that they are disgusting, foul smelling, stinking, filthy, and deadly. That's the fatal flaw in them. They are absolutely deadly. And I can't say enough bad things about the men and women who choose to work in tobacco companies or about the companies themselves. They are, as I see it, rotten to the core. And my parents go for cigarettes like there's no tomorrow. Please believe me that I am not trying to say that I think any the less of my mother or my father or that I don't love them greatly, for of course I do, but only that I am not happy at all about their continuing their terrible self-destructive, indeed, almost suicidal, I think, smoking habits. I am able to recognize that it is just a wee bit late on my part to be worrying about this matter but if by any chance their stopping smoking now would add even just one more precious 24-hour day to their lives that are so important to me, I would give just anything in the whole world for them to do so. The very thought of my losing either of them is one of my very most grave fears, and to think that it is possible that I might someday be faced with this terrible fact earlier than I ought to be faced with it because of the tremendous number of those dreadful cigarettes they consume—my father smokes four packs a day and my mother is smoking about two, maybe two and a half packs a day —anyway, it makes me extraordinarily worried, even at times I get kind of panicky, and worst of all, angry at them. It is conceivable, due to the age of my parents (early 50s) that they will not be able to summon whatever-it-takes to abandon their terrible habits no matter how hard they may actually try. Any group of addicts have trouble relinquishing their habits. I have been forced to face the hard truth that my parents are addicted to nicotine.

I just cannot believe the American people will continue to allow these destructive tobacco companies to continue making money hand over fist while being in the business of killing my parents—and maybe yours, too, not to mention millions upon millions of other innocent victims. Let us all rally round and do something about this perfectly shameful and wrongful situation before it is too late!

2. Edit a page of your own writing. Then give it to a friend to edit. If four of you work on the same page, you'll discover ways of editing you might never have thought of.

3. Choose a paragraph you love from a published writer. Rewrite it: Clobber it with adjectives, adverbs, clichés, passive verbs, and exaggeration. Then type the original and read both versions aloud to see, hear, and feel the differences.

ETHICS AND THE WRITER'S LIFE

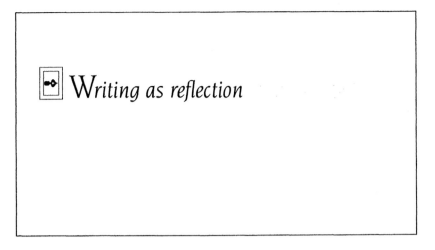

Writing as reflection

WRITERS DON'T JUST RECORD WHAT HAPPENED. THEY REFLECT ON the meaning of what happened. The process takes time.

A painter who uses watercolor works fast. It's one shot and she's done. The painting works or it does not. A painter who works in oils adds layer after layer over time. Colors and shapes change as she works to get the painting just right. Writing is like oil painting: many drafts, many changes, much thought, and often new direction and intention.

Tell the truth

TRUTH IS POWERFUL, MAGNETIC. PERHAPS TRUTH ON THE PAGE HAS such appeal because so often in life we feel forced into social lies. If a friend shows us a photograph of her new baby and says, "Isn't he adorable?" we can hardly answer, "You must be blind. The child is repulsive. His ears are pointy. He has no chin. His nose looks as though it has been struck by a spatula. How could you bear to bring him home from the hospital?"

Then there are the lies people tell themselves so they can go on. A young married woman who was an editor of a science magazine in New York moves to northern Vermont and writes to her worried mother:

> We're settled in our new house now! It certainly is a change from living in New York! Here I look out on miles and miles of flat farmland that stretches all the way to Canada. From the window by my desk I can see only one small stone farmhouse, so far away it looks about the height of a nail! Although of course I miss my editor pals and the excitement of the deadlines and the city, it's nice to have whole days without pressure. I've sanded the floors, wallpapered the dining room, and am now painting the corner bedroom yellow so it'll be ready next month when I return from the hospital with our newborn.

Understandably the young woman doesn't want to trouble her mother or admit to herself the bleakness of her new life, so bravely, she shades the truth. But she's not fooling anyone.

We hear too much polite social nonsense along with twisted promises from telemarketers and whopping lies from politicians who offer the moon and a tax cut if we'll only vote for them. Most of us are sick of it. Good writers tell the truth on the page. Readers appreciate it.

Ellen Gilchrist writes the truth about a businessman, Tom, in her story "Rich." When Tom messes up, he'll ask one of his bosses to lunch and solicit advice. As they talk:

> Tom would listen to whatever advice he was given as though it were the most intelligent thing he had ever heard in his life.
>
> Of course he would be thinking, "You stupid, impotent son of a bitch. You scrawny little frog bastard, I'll buy and sell you before it's over. I've got more brains in my balls than the whole snotty bunch of you."

Imagine if Gilchrist had glossed over the truth with narration like:

> Tom would listen attentively to the advice, but often he would be feeling somewhat superior to the person giving it. You can hardly blame him for that. After all, he had made a mistake and must have felt the need to bolster his own ego; besides, Tom was a businessman and couldn't very well insult his partners to their faces.

Writing the truth can be scary, but when you take the risk you'll gain energy, momentum, insight, and confidence—all of which will show in your writing.

Try this

Think of a person you can't stand, someone whose very presence disturbs, even riles you. Perhaps you love this person sometimes and despise her other times. Or he alternately amuses and offends you. Write a letter bursting with everything you've ever wanted to say to him or her. Use the person's name: Dear Gabriel or Dear Sally. Write fast for five minutes, telling the truth of how you feel right now as you write. Tell all.

When you've spilled as much as you can stand, read what you've written. The writing is probably vital, energetic, passionate, full of voice. Why? Because you dared to tell the truth. Now destroy the letter.

Imagine this same person has died. You have been elected by mutual acquaintances to write a letter to Jack's parents telling them how sorry you are. You'll have to come up with this man's admirable, even endearing qualities. You try to form an opening sentence in your head: "Jack was always so . . ." What? He was mean, nasty, self-absorbed, and a bully.

You try again. "Jack loved to . . ." What? Punch smaller kids in the school yard? Steal money from people's jackets? Belittle you whenever he got the chance? Gossip in order to get people mad at each other?

Whatever lie you come up with will be hollow, false. It's what happens when you don't find the courage to tell the truth.

◧ Finding the courage to tell the truth

NEW WRITERS SOMETIMES FEAR READERS WON'T RESPECT THEM IF they tell the truth about their fears, disloyalties, grade point averages. Not so. One of the traits most respected in writers is honesty.

Besides, who has not experienced basic emotions like love, hate, jealousy, joy, humiliation, and pride? Who has not failed, suffered shame, made a bad choice? Who has not felt regret? All of us have had thoughts or behaved in ways that, in retrospect, make us ashamed. By age five, we've experienced every emotion. Life thereafter is a repeat of those emotions with different intensities and new constellations of events.

When you write about a subject that's close to your heart, when you reveal secrets, your readers will not think, "What a mean-spirited, stupid, cowardly person." Instead, they will recognize themselves, their emotions, temptations, unwise acts. They will be grateful for your honesty and impressed by your courage. By writing the truth, you will have shed light on their lives, expanded their understanding of the human condition.

As you write about your life, remember that words represent only aspects of it, never the whole. *You* are not on the page. You are far too complex to be described, explained, or re-created on one page or a thousand. You reveal a sliver of yourself to make a point, or express a feeling, or explain a choice. If you got scared climbing Mount Washington, this doesn't mean you are a coward or will behave like one in another situation. There is much more to you than fear of heights. But because you must focus your story, you choose not to reveal your many admirable traits. You focus instead on the moment, and how, terrified of the height and slope of the head wall, you turned back and left your companion to go on alone. Trust that your readers understand this.

When writers need to distance themselves from painful memories, they sometimes use third person as Stephen Crane does in "The Open Boat" (excerpted on page 179). Instead of "I did this and thought that," they write, "She did this and thought that." After a draft or two, they may reinstate the first person, having realized what they felt and did was not inhuman, after all, but revealed them as very human indeed. In other cases, third person seems the best way to tell the story.

Our students and friends have written on subjects that caused them, at times, to sweat and worry what readers might think of them. Here are some topics they've tackled.

Being German in America

One student discussed American friends making fun of her heritage. Some used the word *Nazi* in a joking way. She does not know exactly why this should mortify her. After all, she was not alive during World War II. She moved to this country when she was ten. She is an American now. However, she feels angry, humiliated, and somehow accused. She needed to understand more. Writing helped.

Having alcoholic parents

A student wrote about coming home from school one day to find her mother passed out on the living room rug, a bottle of Popov Vodka, empty, beside her. She wrote about the years of her mother's drinking and of how, on this day, she, the daughter, decided there was nothing she could do to help or to change her mother's habits. She left the house, grabbed her field hockey stick and ball in the garage and went to her friend's house to play.

Caring for a seriously ill parent

John Colligan has the courage to face his ambivalence about having to bathe his father, who has multiple sclerosis. This is the lead to "George":

> Saturday was different from Monday through Friday. Saturday mornings I would wake to the dreaded call of my mother from downstairs: "John, are you going to give Daddy his shower soon?" It was the familiar question: we both knew the answer before it was asked. I was the only one who could give my father, George, his shower. My two

little brothers were not strong enough; my three older sisters were no longer at home. I was fifteen years old and the shower was a large undertaking. I hated it, and yet it made me proud. It was something important to Dad.

Stealing cars

A student spent a year in a juvenile detention center in high school. Three years later, he wrote about it in college. At first, he wanted his paper to be read only by the teacher. Later, he wanted it copied for the class, although he wished to remain anonymous. Then, halfway through the class discussion of the paper, when the student realized how much everyone admired his strong writing and honesty, he stated proudly that he had written it. No one shrank from him. He became one of the more respected writers in class.

Read Nancy Mairs' "On Being a Cripple" in her collection of essays, *Plain Text: Deciphering a Woman's Life.* In this essay she faces the truth about living with multiple sclerosis. She says that years ago she chose the word *cripple* rather than *handicapped* or *disabled* when she learned she had M.S. She was unaware of why she picked that word. Now, as she writes, she thinks *cripple* is ". . . a clean word, straightforward and precise." She also thinks ". . . people—crippled or not—wince at the word *cripple* as they do not at *handicapped* or *disabled.*" Then Mairs faces an unflattering, hard truth: "Perhaps I want them to wince."

Those who write with courage and honesty open the door to worlds we could not visit on our own. They show us people acting and thinking under stress, facing adversity, clearing the way through their own confusions. They teach us about life.

⊷ Try this

1. In your notebook, list two subjects that would demand courage and honesty to write about. Choose one. Write a few sentences about why this subject would be hard. In a few days, go back and see if you can write more. From time to time, add to this list of tough subjects.

2. Once a week, write one hard truth about yourself and/or someone you know well. This will encourage honesty and perhaps lead to a new subject.

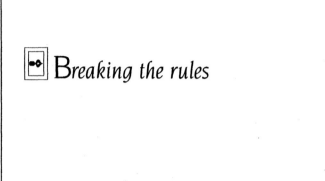

Breaking the rules

WRITING GUIDES—OURS AND YOUR TEACHERS'—ARE ONLY GUIDES. They've worked for writers for hundreds of years. They aren't formulas or rules. We hope they help. But if you have an idea you can't express in any way you've heard about, forget guides. Plunge headlong into your material. Start anywhere, but start.

Yes, it may be scary and awkward at first, but so what. Stagger and lurch about. Break into lists, poetry, free association, doggerel. Leave space breaks when you're stuck. Tackle the subject from another angle or perspective. Write backwards, write in the mirror, write in bats' blood if you have to, but write. Later, you'll figure out how to fix things.

We are not suggesting you abandon guides for the sake of abandoning them. We're saying that at some point many writers need to bust out. And if that time comes to you, DO IT.

Stretching the boundaries of nonfiction

IN HIS 1997 BESTSELLER, The Perfect Storm, SEBASTIAN JUNGER skillfully handles the problem of how to express the thoughts and experiences of people who aren't Sebastian Junger as though they were. That is, he gives the impression of seeing through somebody else's eyes, speaking with somebody else's voice, reading another person's thoughts, re-creating scenes as though he had been a witness, even a participant. This makes readers feel as though they might be witnesses or participants, too. Such scenes approach the sensuous, inside-out experience of fiction without actually fictionalizing.

When writing nonfiction, the more you reveal about the thoughts, actions, and feelings of people on the page, the more dramatic and emotional the impact on readers. Of course, in fiction you can make up the details, perceptions, and feelings of your characters. You imagine the thoughts of the captain when he realizes his ship will sink. *Oh God,* Captain Jim thought, *we're not going to make it. The next big wave . . . here it comes . . . Jesus, it's big as a mountain.* Then you make up what Captain Jim says and does, what his first mate thinks and says and does. You can even make up what the shark thinks as it takes a bite out of the captain's wooden leg.

But to maintain credibility in nonfiction you must dramatize without fictionalizing. You can't just make it up. Yet you want to bring readers as close to the heart of the material as you can—and the heart of any material is likely to be a human being's perception of it. Read Junger's book with a writer's eye and you'll see how he weaves library research with court transcripts, interviews, his own observations and experiences to inform and dramatize.

His subject is a storm that hit Georges Bank on October 29, 1991. It was called a "perfect" storm because the merging of a Nor'easter and a hurricane created extraordinarily ferocious weather. Junger's human-interest focus is a fishing boat, the *Andrea Gail*, out of Gloucester, Massachusetts. It sank with all hands. His details put readers on that boat as the men fight to survive. He tries to make us care by describing the men and their families, showing what kind of people they were, relating what they said and did and felt in the hours before they went to sea.

At the same time, he uses this one boat and these six lost men to illustrate the dangers of deep-sea fishing ("More people are killed on fishing boats, per capita, than in any other job in the United States"); and how diminishing catches and market pressure make the job increasingly dangerous. The possibility of big money leads fishermen to take big risks. And sometimes tragedy results.

He begins his story before the storm, introducing readers to the crew of the doomed *Andrea Gail*, one by one, sketching their lives and final days as accurately as he can based on the recollections of those who knew them and others who do the same work and have survived similar dangers. He asks and answers these questions: *What was it like?* and *What must (or might) it have been like?* The second question could easily push a writer into fiction—but Junger never crosses the line.

Here's how he does it.

In an introduction he lays out the rules of the book. Anything in quotes comes directly from an interview he conducted and recorded. So readers can trust that this is exactly what was said. Any other dialogue has been reported to him, "based on the recollection of people who are still alive." Unless Junger heard the conversation himself, the words appear in dialogue form, but without quotation marks. He assures readers: "No dialogue was made up."

What Junger shows is that you can create powerful scenes without fictionalizing. Here's how this might work in a research paper, researched article, essay, nonfiction book.

Say your topic is the work habits of a poet you admire. The poet is dead, but you interview her widower. You record the interview.

The widower says the poet, Rose, often wrote in the middle of the night on the porch overlooking the herb garden. When she felt restless and inspired on a hot summer night, she would slip out of bed, go naked to the porch, light three candles, and write longhand with her favorite fountain pen on parchment paper at the small oak table. She often talked to herself as she wrote. She would speak lines aloud. She would call herself names and berate herself when she was blocked.

"What exactly did she say?" you ask the widower.

"Well, it varied," he says.

"Can you remember any examples?"

"I remember hearing her say: 'Rose, where is your brain? Did you leave it in Vienna?' This was right after our trip to Europe in 1952. Or she'd say, 'Rose, you silly silly poet. What's the word, what's the word?' And she'd pace, I'd hear her pacing—the floor creaked on that old porch and she was never light-footed. I'd hear her pacing until she found the right word or gave up in frustration."

You have hours of tape like this, not only from the widower but from the poet's agent, from her high school English teacher (who happens to be your Uncle Saul, which is why you're interested in this poet in the first place), from her colleagues at the small college where she taught for thirty-six years, from her students, from her children, from her housekeeper.

You have read her work, visited her home, explored her herb garden, stayed late and sat on the porch at the table where she worked, inhaling the fragrances of a warm summer's night.

Now you have the material from which to create a realistic, dramatic scene that includes dialogue and sensuous details to make the poet come alive for readers, without fictionalizing. Something like:

> The wood of the round oak table was worn smooth from use and age. The table had belonged to Rose's father, and it was her favorite place to compose, especially late at night when the heat troubled her sleep. She would spend hours on the small porch pushed out into her herb garden—the lemony scent of balm, the pungency of mint mixed with the fragrances from the roses that climbed the bentwood arbor, and, perhaps, the damp of the river beyond. She wrote often of that river, and the flow of her poetry suggests that words, for her, moved as easily as water. But they didn't.

"Rose, where is your brain? Did you leave it in Vienna?" She searched for the right word, the perfect rhythm, and spoke her frustration out loud when the words didn't come as she paced ten paces one way, ten paces back, screen to screen on the creaky, uneven floor of that south-facing porch. On a clear night, she could see the moon over the water. The river reflected her favorite constellation, the Seven Sisters.

You combine information from many sources—your interviews; your reading of her poems; a biography; myths associated with constellations; your own experience with rivers, gardening, star-gazing, and writing poetry; your visit to the house; a book about herbs. You use bits and pieces from all this material to create a scene, perhaps several, to make readers feel close to your subject.

In *The Perfect Storm*, Sebastian Junger expresses what the lost fishermen might have felt at the moments of their deaths so effectively that readers will believe this is what they *must* have felt, or even what they *did* feel. His information probably comes from medical studies on the process of drowning, perhaps from the recollections of people who nearly drowned, perhaps from his own imagination or near-death experience. He begins the following passage factually, scientifically, and ends in the mind of a drowning victim. This might seem impossible to do without fictionalizing, but note how Junger pulls it off with detail and precise wording.

> The instinct not to breathe underwater is so strong that it overcomes the agony of running out of air. No matter how desperate the drowning person is, he doesn't inhale until he's on the verge of losing consciousness. At that point there's so much carbon dioxide in the blood and so little oxygen, that chemical sensors in the brain trigger an involuntary breath whether he's underwater or not. This is called the "break point" . . .
>
> . . . Lack of oxygen to the brain causes a sensation of darkness closing in from all sides, as in a camera aperture dropping down. The panic of a drowning person is mixed with an odd incredulity. . . . Having never done it before, the body—and the mind—do not know how to die gracefully. The process is filled with desperation and awkwardness. "So this is drowning," a drowning person might think. "So this is how my life finally ends."

Saying "a drowning person might think . . ." or "As Joe Cooke reached the break point he may have thought . . ." is very different from saying, "As Joe Cooke was drowning he thought . . ." The first two stay within the boundaries of nonfiction; the third oversteps them.

Observing that Rose the poet often said she felt unworthy of the title "poet" and in awe of her contemporaries, then suggesting that when she met John Greenleaf Whittier, she probably (or "very likely" or "perhaps" or "may have") said something self-deprecating like, "You're a poet, Mr. Whittier; I am merely a gardener who writes things down," holds the line of credible nonfiction. Imagining a conversation between Rose and John Greenleaf Whittier, presenting it as though it really happened, is stepping over the line. Writing a love scene between them that you've made up from beginning to end is fiction for sure.

The following phrases are useful in stretching the boundaries of nonfiction. Of course, there are many others, and you'll choose according to your own style and the voice of the piece you're writing. Still, these might come in handy: *may have thought; might have believed; is said to have visited; often mentioned; could have; was inclined to; may have been inclined to; had the type of personality that; if . . . then . . .* (as in: *if* he had played baseball, *then* he'd have wanted to pitch); *according to* (as in: *according to* her childhood friend, her shyness was all an act); *friends say; a persistent rumor was; in a letter, he said; perhaps; likely; logically; it would seem.*

Try this

1. Look at several essays, articles, or chapters from nonfiction books and mark phrases the writer uses to stay in the realm of nonfiction while incorporating elements of fiction like thoughts, feelings, and dialogue.

2. Find passages of dialogue in the same material. Where do you think the writer collected this dialogue? Is it from trial transcripts? Did he record it himself? Was it reported to him? Did he make it up? Do you think he made some of it up?

3. In a piece that effectively depicts a place (a bus stop, a room, the interior of a car speeding along a highway, a mountain top, a fishing boat), mark details that make the place seem real. How might the

writer have collected those details? Do you think he visited? Did he read about it? Did he look at photographs? Did he talk to people?

4. Try a few of Sebastian Junger's stretching techniques—using some of the phrases listed in this chapter—in a draft you think needs to be more dramatic.

◧ Revealing *other people's secrets*

MANY WRITERS FIND IT EASIER TO REVEAL UNPLEASANT OR alarming facts about themselves than about their families and friends. Yet these are the people you know best; they are your best subjects. Of course you will have to decide what you can live with; you will need to consider the repercussions if you use your sisters to illustrate sibling rivalry gone to extremes, especially the time one stole the other's diary and revealed her crush to the boy she liked. While the other, in retaliation, wiped her rival's term paper off the hard drive of their computer.

"What will these sisters do to me," you might wonder, "if I use their fight as an example—and they find out about it? Do I have the right to expose them in this light?"

Nevertheless, real-life examples make assertions believable, strengthen arguments, and, generally, make your writing more interesting and authoritative. Even when you change the names and some specifics, "hypothetical" scenes may remind people you know of actual events.

When you write about your life you *always* risk somebody in your life feeling offended or betrayed. And let's face it, all good writing is—in some way—connected to your life, your vision, and in turn the people around you.

On a radio talk show a man told how a published article about his wife's conversion to Judaism had infuriated her relatives. They had known about the conversion and raised no objections, but were embarrassed by the public revelation. In their eyes the woman had abandoned their traditions for her husband's. This, apparently, was something the relatives thought should be private, a family secret.

As a writer, you must be willing to tell the truth even if others think you should not. Few families are delighted to have a writer in their midst, aware of secrets, foibles, mistakes; listening at Thanksgiving dinner and taking mental notes. It is hard for nonwriters to understand that when you write about one aspect of a person's life or personality, you are not writing about the whole person. If you decide to write about your spouse's alcoholism, you are writing about one problem she faced—perhaps heroically, perhaps ineffectively. The piece is not about the spouse; it is about alcoholism. Or how someone else's dependency has affected you. Or a family dynamic created by one person's addiction. Or which treatments work and which don't.

You are not giving readers the full picture. You write snapshots. You catch moments. In the family album, the picture of the baby with a beer bottle on her high chair tray does not suggest much beyond what was going on in that moment—and perhaps the attitudes of the time and the photographer's sense of humor. Just as photographs reveal the photographer as much as the subject, so do essays reveal the writer as much or more than her subjects. Most readers understand this, just as they understand that when you write truthfully about yourself and your own life it's never the whole truth, the full picture.

Whoever or whatever your subject, don't flinch from the truth. Don't pretend a relationship or a person is better than it or she is. Or worse. Accuracy is the biggest service you can offer your readers and your subjects. The truth lies in the exact details—however painful.

Readers are tired of the polite little lies people tell each other. Those lies are not much fun to write either, because they offer no insight, no surprises. Good writing feeds our hunger for discovery and truth. As you begin to write about why your married children seldom visit or the irony of their criticism of *your* lifestyle, you may discover how deep the trouble goes. Or how your relationship with your children parallels the one you had with your own parents. If the process is working well, writing may lead to insights you'd rather not acknowledge. Yet insights that seem frightening or disturbing at first may, in the end, lose some of their negativity through the writing. A secret revealed may not seem as shameful or weighty as when it was kept hidden.

Of course, wondering and worrying about how others will react to what you reveal about them can paralyze you. If, as you write about your parents' divorce, you picture your mother's face, you may not be able to push past the platitudes.

> My parents divorced when I was eight. I was angry at the time. But I got over it. My mother has always tried to make me see that the divorce was for the best. She tried to make me stop idealizing our life before Dad moved out. She's been very supportive of me through a lot of ups and downs in my own relationships with girls.

Writing on the surface in this way won't get you far. On the other hand, if you can forget about your mother's reaction, you may begin to recollect and write down significant details and make meaning from them. Maybe Mother will read the piece; maybe she won't. Don't worry about who will read or what they might think until: (1) it's finished to your satisfaction, (2) you've found a publisher and the publication date is set.

While you are writing you *cannot* worry about others' reactions. Just write. Tell yourself you'll tear it up when you're done. Very likely, you'll change your mind, but this will get you going.

Write about overhearing your father tell your mother that if he *ever* caught her driving that fast with the kids in the car again, he'd report her to the police and have her license yanked. Write about how she replied that the only reason she drove like that was because he stayed out all night, making her crazy with worry, and she went out looking for him, hysterical. Write how you slipped out of bed to eavesdrop, the linoleum smooth and cold under your bare feet except where it was cracked and curled at the edges. How you crept to the door. How you could see your parents through the crack. How the light seemed too bright, their faces bloated. How they seemed like angry strangers. Write how the tears wet your face and filled your nose but you were afraid to sniff, afraid they'd notice you hiding there and turn their anger on you.

In our experience, family and friends, reading the truth as we see it and write it, even if it is unflattering to them, tend to accept it.

They may not admire it. They may not be entirely comfortable having a writer around, but they accept the work.

We're not suggesting cruelty. Or libel. Or betrayal. We're not suggesting gossip or mean-spirited criticism. But if there is a topic you are drawn to, and if writing about family or friends is crucial to exploring it, and if, in the writing, you discover and reveal secrets or unflattering truths, so be it.

Worry about consequences after the writing is finished and you're considering publishing or showing the piece to people involved. If you have to wait until Great Aunt Henrietta dies to expose the family gin mill, then wait. But the potential wrath of Great Aunt Henrietta should never interfere with the writing.

Forget her.

Just write.

◙ Bypassing writer's block

YOU SIT AT YOUR DESK AND THE PIECE YOU HALF-FINISHED LAST week seems stupid and boring. You start again. It still seems stupid and boring. Each new start, each new idea for a new piece sounds stupid and boring before you even get the words on the page. Next step: "I am stupid and boring. I can't write anymore. I'm a lousy writer." Writer's block.

If you feel as novelist John Yount once did, that he had a writer's block the size of Texas, remember that it's possible to drive through Texas and on to New Mexico. You can even drive *around* Texas, avoid it altogether. It'll take a while, but it can be done.

If you feel the juices draining out of a piece you're working on, it's important to know why. Ask yourself first, "Do I tend to quit easily?" If so, keep writing. But let's say you usually finish tasks, you know there's value to the piece you're working on, and you were excited about it earlier. Let the flame rekindle by leaving it alone for a bit. Work on another writing project for a day or two. Write a letter to the editor of the local newspaper. List possibilities for new subjects. Revisit that children's book you've been playing around with for years. Sort the slips of paper with random ideas you've been collecting in your shoe box. Review your journal. Write in your journal.

These activities lead most writers back to the piece they abandoned but with renewed commitment and vigor OR on to a new subject.

Free writing is another way to four-wheel out of the ditch. Free write for ten minutes nonstop, anything that comes into your head. Writers sometimes get stuck because something else is festering in their lives. Free writing brings the troubles to the surface. Then you can write about the festers.

Sara Davidson explored her discontent with the way she and other people were living in Venice, California, in her essay "Rolling into the 30's." She said that living there "is like living in a camp for semi-demented adults." She mentioned "the drifters, drug addicts, would-be movie makers, and aging hippies" who existed without purpose. She described the workaholics who lived by themselves, "longing in the silence before falling asleep, for connection." She listed her material possessions, which included a Mercedes, an outdoor Jacuzzi, and roller skates. Some time after writing this essay, she left Venice. You may need to write about your Venice, then move on.

For some people, writer's block comes not from serious problems but from just plain feeling stale. On the page and in life. If you suffer stagnation, make changes pronto. Try something you've always wanted to do. Sign up for acting or rock climbing or computer class. Learn a new language. Get to know one person you've always wanted to know better. Join a new group—bird watchers, bowlers, chess players, or line dancers. Volunteer to serve lunch to the homeless. Work Saturday mornings for Habitat and build houses. For an afternoon or a day each week—even for an hour—explore a part of your city or state you've never visited before. Tell your family or roommates you're taking off for three days. Throw a sleeping bag in the car and set out for someplace new. You may decide to head north and then choose as you go whether to take this or that road, destination unknown.

This is rather like exploring a fresh topic. You begin with a direction, it shifts, you go on; you discover what's around the bend.

Sometimes in order to go on, you have to clear the way. Clear everything off your desk, metaphorically or literally; clear the clutter out of your life, clear your mind. Maybe then you'll see the sign that says This Way to New Mexico.

When writer's block strikes, the temptation to quit can be tremendous: "Writing is so damned hard, and since I can't write anything good, I'll quit for today."

Don't. Whole days, months, years can go by.

We don't want to dismiss your insecurities, but we warn you not to take writer's block too seriously. Get some distance on the source of your frustration; humor yourself along. Tell yourself you're in a rough spot, but, "Every time I get about two thirds of the way through a piece, six weeks into the writing, the same thing happens. I hate it. I think it's stupid. I want to quit." Then look at the bright side. "I guess that means I'm two thirds through. Only a third to go. I can do that. I can sit down and write those last five pages RIGHT NOW.

Remember, also, that writing is *always* learning to write. Learning and relearning. You didn't learn to walk without falls and bumps. You didn't learn to knit without pulling stitches. Remind yourself that other writers hit dry periods, feel that everything they've written lately is bad. Some can shrug it off—"Lately, my work stinks"—but maintain underlying confidence that it will get better. Others work themselves into believing absolutely they are not and were never any good. In fact, they can't do anything well. They fall into a grotesque charade of exaggerating all their failures—with friends, jobs, school, even their choices of tropical fish and wallpaper.

If you begin to wallow in your role as the tragic failed writer, know that we all do it sometimes. It's okay to snivel. Go ahead: Snivel, groan, curse, cry. Do this brilliantly, flamboyantly. Call a writer friend and parade your griefs. Then cut it out and go to work.

Of course profound burnout does occur. Virginia Woolfe is said to have become depressed after she finished each book and unable to write for some time. Back then, writers lived through black despair. Now, we can seek counseling.

We have had three students who experienced deaths in their immediate families just weeks before their writing classes at the University of New Hampshire. One of the students wanted to write about the death of her brother. The others felt it was too soon, too painful to write about; yet the deaths were the only things on their minds. Everything else felt trivial. One student ended up writing feature articles about an acting group she belonged to. The other interviewed foreign students in her dorm to find out what being a foreigner meant at U.N.H. Then she interviewed a swimming coach, a professor doing research on growing melons, a fiction writer. She went on to interview a glassblower from nearby Portsmouth. A painter herself, she wrote an essay comparing the process of writing to the process of oil painting.

The point is that writers can overcome blocks by getting outside themselves and into the world. Or by trying a kind of writing they've never attempted before, such as poetry or a picture book for children.

Sometimes you can shrug off an attack of writer's block by saying, "Who doesn't get stalled? Bankers, cooks, carpenters, sailors, teachers all have days when they don't feel like working. They carry on. So can I."

Try this

1. Confess in your No-Critics-Allowed Notebook that you can't write. Indulge in self-pity and self-flagellation. Be mawkish. Then read your entry aloud. You'll see how unfair and absurd it is.

Now start a new page. List your writing strengths. Every one. Take one of your best pieces and list its strengths: details, a strong scene, an engaging stretch of dialogue, one perfect adjective. Then list every compliment anyone has ever paid you about your writing. Read the list aloud. Read it again.

2. If you've gone global with your criticism of your work and your spirit, if you are unhappy even with the way you browned the morning toast, list three positive things about yourself. You can include general attributes like loyal, attentive to detail, nice laugh, or you can list small actions like smiling at the tired store clerk last week, feeding the goldfish, flossing. Do this each day for two weeks. That's fourteen days. The list will be long. After a while, you'll find something to be pleased with.

3. Write an essay about writer's block. When did it strike? Where were you sitting? What did you think and do? What triggered it? What can you do to cure it?

4. List twenty-five subject possibilities. Don't spend a lot of time thinking about them. Start with ideas from when you were in kindergarten, then junior and senior high, on through adulthood. List your conflicts, past and present. List questions and issues you'd like to understand better.

5. Buy green or purple paper—some color you've never tried before. Buy several new pens, maybe an orange felt-tip marker. Go to a restaurant where no one knows you. Write there for an hour. (Be sure to order something.) You may decide to go back to that restaurant for a few days. You may want to try new places to write—even within your own home or yard—each day for a couple of weeks.

6. Try writing naked. Or wrapped in a blanket. Or while listening to music. Or not listening to music. Try writing with a cat on your lap. Or your laptop in your lap. Change the atmosphere to make the act of writing feel new.

7. Remind yourself, "It's only a temporary block. Like a kidney stone, it will pass."

8. Commit yourself to five minutes a day of freewriting in your journal. Do this for two weeks. Write as fast as you can, nonstop. Break into lists or gibberish, but keep writing. You'll find subjects to write about, eventually.

Writing workshops

A CONSTRUCTIVE WORKSHOP WILL IMPROVE YOUR WRITING. IT WILL provide a supportive community of fellow writers and sufferers. Most writing classes have workshops. Or you can form one with friends.

In a workshop, writers take turns handing out copies of their pieces to each member of the group. The pieces are read and discussed. The purpose of a workshop is to help every writer improve his or her work. In a successful workshop, everyone roots for each other and everyone benefits. The writer whose work is being critiqued learns how it's received, and how he can revise it. Each reader learns from the other writers' strengths and weaknesses.

The worst response for any writer is silence. The second worst is "I don't like it" or "I like it"—with no elaboration. Here are some of the ingredients of successful workshops.

Balance your comments

All-praise or all-fault-finding workshops hurt writers. The first is phony and misleading; the second is cruel. If you like combative, competitive workshops, get together with other gladiators. If you want a nurturing workshop, find one, or start one and establish constructive ground rules.

Be specific

Make many comments in the margin or on sticky notes as you read. Be specific: great detail; insight wonderful here; nice moment—expand a little?; consider moving this to page 1 paragraph 2; perfect

word; maybe cut this part down or out; good tension all through—
a page turner; slow start—begin page 3 last paragraph.

If a writer uses outstanding examples or details, mark them as
you read. Put lots of "goods" or "terrifics" in the margins. If the
writer is vague all through, it's probably best to mark four or five
vague places. With "specify this? give examples?" Then tell the
writer his work could be strengthened by specifics throughout.

Some readers underline sentences or words they especially admire, use wavy lines along sections that bother them, and use
straight lines along sections they love. In the margins they explain why. In your group, make sure everybody knows what the
symbols mean.

Write down your comments

After you've read the whole piece, write a letter to the writer. Summarize or list strengths and weaknesses. For each weakness, suggest a solution. Sign your name. Be honest. False praise leads writers astray. Don't play God. Professional critics often disagree. You
may be wrong.

Use the language of constructive criticism. Phrase your comments tactfully and realistically: "I think your beginning needs tension" is better than "Your beginning is boring." "I was confused here"
is better than "This passage is confusing." "You seem to me to slip
into sentimentality here—that's easy to do in wedding scenes" is
better than "This is sentimental slush." "I don't know what the
meaning is" is better than "This piece has no point."

Focus on your reading and avoid judgment. Pay attention to the
piece's interest level, honesty, ambition, sincerity, shape, and meaning as well as to the writer's craft, specific passages, words, and
punctuation.

Consider the draft

The writer should tell readers what draft they are looking at. Critics
should approach a final draft with tougher criticism than a first, raw
draft in which the writer is still trying to discover her subject. Don't
critique misuse of commas in a first draft unless they're so poorly
used they interfere with your understanding. The writer may say
what she'd like help with; she might be wondering if she should

expand a certain section. Or she may think it best not to prejudice readers ahead of time and prefer to say nothing.

Don't skimp on feedback

Give generous amounts of honest, constructive feedback. Some new writers and critics fear they'll say something wrong or stupid. Don't worry: You will. We all do. That's forgivable as long as you're trying to help. A reader may, later in a discussion, say, "I've changed my mind. Here's what I think now." Work hard to help other writers in workshops. It pays off. As you actively participate in critiquing, you'll improve just as you improve when you write. Don't worry that if you criticize a writer's exaggerations or vague passages, the writer will be psychologically damaged. You haven't got that kind of power. Yes, the writer hopes his work is good, but he knows it needs improvement.

In the workshop, readers should talk with—not at—the writer about the work. The writer may comment or ask questions at any point. Even if your written comments are thorough, don't hold back speaking to the writer. Everyone needs to hear what you think, and others may agree or disagree, in which case you can talk more about your reasoning.

Mention everything you like first. Writers often don't know their strengths. They need to know them, count on them, repeat them. They need confidence. Later, you may address the question: What does the writer need to do to make this better?

For each problem, the group can brainstorm solutions, which helps everyone since problem solving is important to the writing process. Often there will be more than one solution. Someone should take on the responsibility of leaving the writer with a quick review of his strengths. Don't worry, he'll remember the flaws.

As you talk point to specific parts of the paper. Don't say "Your examples of courage were strong" and leave it at that. Mention two or three examples and where they are on the page. Read one example aloud. It's helpful to everyone to hear good writing read aloud.

Avoid "but." For instance, "I like the lead but the second paragraph veers." "But" undermines praise. Just say, "I like the lead." Pause for several moments. Let the praise resonate. Then say, "For me, the second paragraph veers."

If you believe a piece is hopeless and should be abandoned, try to find one detail, one phrase, one point to admire. Say it out loud. Then, at some point in the discussion, you'll have to add, "For me, this piece has two major problems: It seems to lack meaning and I can't see how the subject can be expanded to make meaning. Maybe it can be expanded, though." Ask if anyone agrees with you. If so, can they help the writer see ways to expand the subject? You may need to tell a writer his piece confused you. You may want to mark each place where you were confused. But mention out loud only one, possibly two specific places. If no one comes up with a solution, you might tell the writer that sometimes it's helpful to leave a piece for a while. Perhaps later he might return to it and know what to do. In the meantime, he can count on X and Y strengths and bring them to a new subject. Don't drag out the discussion of a weak paper. Be merciful and get on to someone else's work.

Readers often disagree about writing. This is healthy as long as all readers try to get to what's best for a piece rather than to win an argument. Be prepared to back down if someone suggests a better solution to a problem. You haven't been diminished; you've learned something that will someday help you with your writing.

When your piece is the one discussed and you leave with conflicting comments, go home, read through the comments quickly, and put them away for a few days. The comments of those who seemed to understand what you were trying to do will stay with you. Use them and ignore the ones that seem wrong or off track.

If a group critiques your piece severely, go home and decide over the next few days if the criticisms are accurate. Ask yourself what is the spirit of your group: Were the critics assassins or were they trying to help? If the comments were well-intentioned and you see now that your paper was indeed weak, go ahead and cry; then get mad. There isn't a published writer in the world who has not written several profoundly rotten, hopeless, embarrassing pieces. Write in your notebook for a few days. Then start a new writing project.

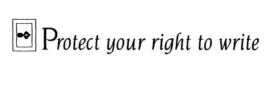# Protect your right to write

IF YOU CAN BE FIRM WITH PEOPLE WHO INTRUDE ON YOUR WRITING time, you're lucky, and strong. The same holds true if you're blessed with understanding friends and family. But some of you know people who don't respect your writing time. We're sorry if this is true for you, but this chapter should help.

If you're a repressed New Englander, thwarted by guilt and a heritage of politeness—like us—you're in for misery before you make intruders shape up. Take heart. If we can scrape up the courage to keep people away during our writing hours, anyone can.

Fine, we hear you say, but you're publishing; you've earned the right to say "I'm writing," and people respect that.

Sometimes. Not always. And long before we had published even one short newspaper article, we had certain family members and friends who were chronic interrupters. Here's our advice. Say to yourself and believe it: "I am a writer. I may not have published yet, but I am a writer. My writing time matters, and so do I." Repeat this like a mantra.

Then, never answer the telephone or doorbell during writing hours. Put the silencer on your phone. Lock your doors if friends might walk into the house. Be rigid until people are trained.

Some of us have loved ones who, if we were learning to figure skate, would never interrupt us on the ice. Yet these same people may feel it's fine to knock on our study door: "Can't you make the kids' doctor appointments now?" Or "I'm going by Tuttle's Farm. Want some fresh strawberries?" Or "Where are my underpants? I can't find my underpants." Or "Don't lock yourself up like this. It's not good for you. Come to the beach. Just this once?" Or—and this is the ice pick between the ribs—"You're no fun anymore."

Of course you are fun. You can balance your life. But when you start writing, your family and friends may feel deserted, think you're being temperamental, precious. They may believe writers sit down to write and words flow like a river. After all, when they write letters or business reports, they don't mind interrupting the flow to answer the phone or turn the stove on under the stew: What's wrong with YOU? Now, if you had taken up painting your house or making papier-mâché Easter eggs for a boutique; or if you'd decided to try weaving, repairing motorcycles, or playing the stock market—especially the stock market—they'd understand you needed quiet, and they'd see the results. But your passion is writing, so you must help them understand. Compare your need for quiet with their need to concentrate in order to create a budget or play tennis or chess. Or show them this chapter.

Here is one way to answer family when they say, "Jill's at the front door. Want to talk with her?" Answer: "Not now. I'm writing. Please don't interrupt me when I'm at my desk." You may feel foolish at first, but say it again. And again. After a while, drop the please. Throw in a dammit or two. You'll develop standing-up-for-yourself muscles, useful in many circumstances. Soon you'll speak with authority.

When you first decide to write and keep quiet hours, you must be consistent. Don't worry: You won't lose your friends. Here is a truth about human nature: Your family and real friends will, when they sense your determination, eventually come around. It's the wafflers who are hounded.

You may have to resort to out-and-out anger once or twice: "Listen. I know you don't understand my need to write and need for quiet. I'm sad and angry you don't, because it's important to me. I suspect in time you will understand. But you must respect this: I NEED quiet. Do not ever, ever interrupt me again."

When an infraction occurs after this, make sure the consequences are swift. Try words: "I can't believe you'd be so inconsiderate. You're supposed to be my FRIEND, for God's sake!"

Or: "So you can't find your underpants? Well, here they are!" And put said pants someplace the pant-deprived one is not likely to lose them again. Like on his head.

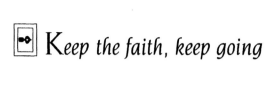

Keep the faith, keep going

MANY WRITERS CONFRONT A CRITICAL MOMENT IN THEIR WRITING lives. They may feel they haven't improved in six months and never will again. They may have been rejected by more than thirty publications in the last two years. They know how hard writing is: Is it worth it?

Some writers wonder if they should give up on a long essay or a forty-page research paper for school. They loved the subject at first, but now they're so sick of it they want to throw up. Should they quit while there's still time to start a new paper?

If you reach this critical juncture, don't give up without a struggle. First, tell yourself what writers have told each other for ages: "Oh stop it and get back to work." Or, "So don't write! Take up bridge or swimming." Often, this will get you going again. But if you are in deep despair, take a long walk by yourself in the woods or on a beach; or walk to a part of your city you've never visited before; or climb a mountain in the rain. After a while, think about John Gardner, who had four novels rejected before his fifth was published. Or Katherine Anne Porter, who started writing in her teens and didn't publish until her thirties. Ask yourself how much writing or your assigned paper really means to you.

We believe that if you've reached this moment of crisis—and it is a crisis of the spirit—the chances are excellent that you will keep writing. If you were not serious, you would likely have given up long ago and be studying law or perfecting your golf swing.

So, you decide, "I am a writer." Then you'd better keep writing. That's what writers do.

THEIR STORIES

The Painting Lesson
BY EMILE BIRCH

I'M IN THE FOURTH GRADE SITTING AT MY SMALL WOODEN DESK. IT IS
the sixth in the fifth row of ten. Each is bolted to a neatly polished
floor that reeks of shellac and lemon oil. Our teacher Sister Mary
Thomas has instructed us to take out our paint box. I am very excited. We have not been allowed to use these materials before today. I open the long enameled tin box, pick up the sleek red wood
handled brush and run the sable bristles across the palm of my out-
stretched hand, waiting anxiously for further instructions.

Sister Thomas, an abbreviation we were allowed to use since all
of the nuns at our school had Mary for their first name, stood in the
front of the class and held up an extra large sheet of manila paper.
Responding to a knowing nod from the good nun, two of the girls
who sat in the front of the room started passing out the unruly
bundle of organically fragrant yellow sheets. When my piece finally
arrived it filled my desk. There was hardly room for my paint box.
Wow! This was great, I thought. The only question? What do I paint?
A sail boat was my favorite. But, I like to paint horses and eagles,
and . . . "Class," Sister sweetly demanded. "Today for our art lesson,
we are going to paint a picture of irises." Irises!? No, not irises. I
gasped to myself. But before I knew it, like a magician producing a
rabbit from a hat, Sister Thomas produced a big purple bouquet of
irises. Irises were not my favorite thing to paint, as a matter of fact
I never even thought of painting irises.

"We will be using the colors purple, green, and yellow" was her
next instruction. My heart was sinking fast. I didn't like purple,

green, or yellow. My hand, as if it had a mind of its own, catapulted into the air. "Yes! Mister Birch?" the sister queried.

Standing erect next to my desk, I asked in my most polite voice, "Sister, do we have to paint irises?"

"Today's lesson sir, is to paint a picture of irises," was her emphatic response. In desperation my hand shot up again.

"Yes? Mister Birch!" she questioned.

"Sister, do they have to be purple, green, and yellow?"

"As you can plainly see Mister Birch, irises . . . are purple, green, and yellow."

She was right. They were purple, green, and yellow.

It was the next insipid direction that provoked my fledgling defiance. She held up cardboard cutouts of the flowers and leaves of an iris. Then told us to trace three flowers, one to the left and two to the right. The number of leaves was optional, though she suggested six. As the cardboard cutouts were making their way from student to student up the long rows of desks, I persistently brushed my quivering palm with fleeting images of sail boats in a rainbow of imaginary colors.

After tracing one iris to the left and two to the right, the big decision was how many leaves? My answer Why leaves? No leaves no green. No green sounds good to me. I quickly passed the patterns to the student behind me as my Dixie cup full of water was placed upon my desk by one of the front row girls.

"When you have your water," Sister Thomas announced, "thoroughly wet your brush and twirl it in the purple, allowing the color to absorb every bit of the water on your brush." Twirl, and Twirl, and Twirl I did, but these crusted pigments demanded more. I knew in my heart of hearts that it was going to take every drop of water from each little Dixie cup sitting on every little wooden desk to dissolve the insatiable crimson I was frantically churning.

"Now stay inside the lines" echoed incessantly from the good sister's lips as her habit swished and her rosary cross clanged up and down the even rows of desks masquerading as easels. It didn't take her long to notice that my flowers were not purple, or that my leaves did not exist.

With a choreographed gesture to protect her flowing robes she grasped my still liquid bouquet and crushed the non-compliant imagery.

"Don't you know that paper is expensive?" she bellowed, as my allotted Dixie cup danced wildly across the surface of the desk, then predictably spilled a torrent of scarlet across the shiny tapered surface and onto my chest and lap. I jumped. She said, "Sit there!"

I cried, "It's wet." Tears welled in my eyes and I began to sob.

The good sister barked orders to the front row girls to get the custodian. Then simultaneously she grabbed me by the ear and marched me on tippee toes across the front of the room, my chest and groin irrevocably stained in the vibrant hue of the sin I had just committed. A poignant lesson to all my classmates that there is only one way to paint an iris.

Tracks

BY ALAN DECOSTA

LIKE ME, A WOMAN CROSS-COUNTRY SKIS ON THE LOCAL GOLF course. I'm sure she is a woman, though we've never met. She skis solo weekday mornings. She avoids logging roads, snowmobile trails, the high frozen fairways—as I, sometimes, do not.

Many of us seek patterns. Skiing after a storm, the skier traces her pattern in the new snow. Once around, it's easier to retrace that trail than clamber off in other directions. The obsessive hill-runner and terrain hog—someone like me—forges beyond tracks into wind-drifted depths. But some days I weary of being first. Those days I follow the woman's trail. I set my skis down in her tracks and run where she has walked, complaining about some of her decisions. She eschews hills, making dull truck around the course perimeter. Her morning adventure lessens into my afternoon workout.

Habits have their reasons. For me, skiing is a passion, and I have sacrificed for it. Though I am no longer a ski bum, I still give it priority on good snow days. But I rarely trek along into storm-cradling ravines and forests, as I once did. It's not so much that my body has faltered—rather, an awareness of the tradeoffs has gradually surfaced. Some people need to get away to find their center. A lone wolf, however, must eventually return to his pack, or he won't survive a hard winter. Only when the traveling spirit remembers a connection to community does adventure provide resonance.

The woman ski-walking the golf course is not one for speed. The tracks of her poles tell me her pace varies little. She is a shuffler. When I taught skiing, it was easier to teach people how to get up after falling down than to inspire a shuffler to kick and glide. The woman stands rigid, knees locked, and places her poles straight down. I sense a slight hip-block in her stride. She is like an over-cautious driver whose brakelights burn out before the headlights. Her tracks, about two inches too narrow, straightline over gentle terrain. Hip-block or not, she knows where she's going, and where she's been.

Why do I follow her lead? Possibly because she's also a traveler. The detective in me longs to decipher the code of her movement. It isn't enough to picture her posture, build, and speed. I seek to enter the mind of this *other*, to gaze upon the world through her eyes. What is it like for her to pass a tall blue spruce holding overnight snow as the sun rises, as early morning mist rises over the frozen pond at the edge of her vision? Biting air, the scent of evergreens, frost on the scarf under the chin—the roughness under her skis smoothes with rising temperature to the texture of soap, easing her way. The honks of black-necked geese by the pond begin to sound like conversation. Troubles she has known seem less important. Rhythms of wind, tree, and bird seem timeless. I imagine all of this of her, the morning ski-walker I have never met.

People once shouted "Slow down!" as I bounded past them. I would not. Checking my interval times, I focused on maximum effort. Life was reduced to times, distances, snow conditions, altitude variation. My obstacles seemed to be lack of a proper training site, bad wax, poorly laid machine-made track settings, camber too stiff or soft for the conditions, no coach. Occasionally a pole broke. I had narrowed my vision and lost sight of my life's less defined tracks. A kind of forgetfulness had washed over me. I felt homeless. Even my name seemed strange. Rampaging over the snow, I did not become one with nature, I invaded it.

It has been many years since, and I have heard my body say that it wants to "Slow down!" My mind, which has always run too fast, wishes to walk along with ideas now instead of bounding ahead of them. My outraced spirit seeks a plodding, steadfast pace.

The woman of the morning has become my primary nature poet. In her tracks, I sense something essential, elemental. Her path holds secrets, so I trace her course with a hard-earned patience, a seeker bartering wonder for wisdom.

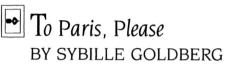

To Paris, Please
BY SYBILLE GOLDBERG

I

I love standing with both feet on the ground, like a tree, one-hundred years old, pressing all my weight on the soles of my feet. So little balance is required when you stand that way, your toes pointing slightly outward! And you can look at the sky and take a deep breath without any anxiety of falling.

But it is only in Paris that standing like that comes so easily. The sky looks different too: I sense a lightness, the sky seems bluer and wider than anywhere else. It pays to look at the sky, standing like that. But only in Paris.

I was born there, thirty-five years ago, in the hospital of the district of Boulogne Billancourt. My mother was twenty-three years old and single. She came to Paris from Austria for a year to give birth to me secretly. I was to be hidden away from her strict Catholic parents who, she was sure, wouldn't understand. I also lived in Paris during the first six years of my life with Nanou, my foster-mother. She took care of me as if I were her fourth and youngest daughter. In the meantime my mother went back to Austria, pretending nothing had happened.

When I go back to Paris to see Nanou, the first thing I do is plant my body in the ground, standing with my toes pointed outward, looking up to the sky. Then I go to the apartment I grew up in, where Nanou still lives and waits for me. Her apartment is the sanctuary of a world I lost a long time ago, a world small and safe, where I was loved.

There were no friends in this world, for only family seemed to matter, and so only aunts, uncles, grandmothers, grandfathers, and cousins came to visit. There was no money for family trips to theaters, movies, shows, or restaurants, just a visit to some castles or museums during our summer vacations in the Bretangne. But we were never bored. Kids were enough to keep ourselves entertained. Nanou was the center of our universe, our sun that kept us warm, fed us, and whose force kept everything in a harmonious rhythm, filled with routines and regularities. I felt loved. I still remember how every day, after my nap, I would find her sitting in the kitchen, drinking her coffee. When she saw me she would invariably welcome me enthusiastically, calling me her treasure, her chick, her morning rose, and then proceed by giving me a small cookie.

There is something about regularity and routine that acts as a fertilizer of human bonds. I think of Saint-Exupery's "The Little Prince." Didn't the fox advise the little prince to come every day at the same time, so he could relish in the anticipation of his visit? In any case, I think Nanou tamed me that way, with her routines, all centered around me, keeping me clean, fed, and healthy. Every day, much time was spent on those routines, and I got to learn that I was worthy of such energy and seriousness. Nanou didn't just clean, cook, and wash. She did it in such a way that discern those who merely exist from those who know how to live well (who have some "savoir vivre"), who use those small details of life to assert that they are worth this attention and it helps them becoming who they want to be. Cooking, cleaning, shopping, and washing were art forms to Nanou. This is why she cooked and still cooks two meals a day, with an appetizer, followed by meat and vegetables, a starch, salad, cheese, fruit, yogurt, and coffee; she never fried with butter, she said it's bad for your liver. She never ate more than three eggs a week; she always bought steak at Mr. Petit's butcher shop, but preferred to purchase chicken and rabbit at Mr. Lagrange's store, because it was better there; she always knew which cantaloupe to choose, and when not to eat fish; she washed, ironed, and knitted every day. In fact, I still miss the spotless, meticulously ironed laundry stacked up in perfectly straight white and colored columns, which would release their odor of lavender when I opened up the closet; Nanou changed the sheets once every two weeks and the bathroom towels every week; she knew what brand of undershirts not to buy, because it was made out of cheap cotton, and how to spot a sloppy sewing job. Our clothes were never dirty, our shoes always polished, our nails and ears, well even our belly buttons beyond reproach. We went to church occasionally, but always on the big holidays; she closed all the shutters at night and opened them in the morning.

That is why I'm always glad to visit Nanou and her world of details.

When I do I invariably walk through her apartment to see if it is as I remember it from my childhood. Each time, I remember it to be much larger than it really is. During my last visit two years ago I was surprised when I opened the bathroom door: the small square tub made out of massive gray granite was still there. In my mind it has always been enormous, reaching to my shoulders, but as I stood there it really was only as tall as the middle of my upper thighs. On the wall, I spotted the two sets of towels and washcloths hanging on a hook, one set for the upper, one set for the lower body, the way it used to be. Looking at this bathroom I remembered Nanou lifting cotton bed sheets out of the water, her arms stretched out as far as possible to the ceiling, and then submerging them in the water again, up and down, up and down. Nanou would then ring those sheets out with energetic circular movements. Her chin would protrude a little and her lips were firmly pressed together, which gave her an air of determination and authority. She would then hang the laundry to dry in the bathroom. We kids loved this room. We enjoyed playing hide-and-seek in this jungle of layers and layers of linens, and invariably Nanou would storm into the room and make us leave.

"Do you still wash yourself in this tub?" I asked Nanou. "You could kill yourself if you slipped."

"Yes," she said, "and I urged Yves many times to buy a shower stall, but he does not want to do it, arguing that the district administration will pay for it when they renovate the buildings. We're still waiting for them to show up."

"Do the Communists still run the district?"

"Yes, can you believe it? And they still come to collect."

Nanou had a lifelong affair with the French Communists. In this building she was the only one who did not support the communist cause, refusing to hand money to the volunteer who came knocking on our door once a month for more than thirty-five years. Who knows, maybe they wanted to wear her down. But they found their match in Nanou, who invariably would respond politely, but with an unmistakably firm tone in her voice: "No, thank you, but I do not give to the Communist Party." She would then inquire about the well-being of the visitor's family.

On a cold day in January in 1965, Nanou's sense of order and propriety was to be my downfall. My mother came to claim me, to bring me back with her to Austria. I barely knew about my mother: she was a friendly but rare visitor from far away. When I was told that I would have to leave with her, I could not believe it. It was, for sure, a mistake. Nanou would never let me go. I was her daughter. I was family. I was the one who was the reason for countless chores, the object of worry when I was sick, whose laundry Nanou had washed all those years and whose meals she had prepared according to the traditions of her family, of her country. How could she let me go?

I heard my mother and Nanou discuss the details of my departure. I saw Nanou pack stacks of laundry in a suitcase she had placed on the table, giving instructions to my mother. This is the way you fold that dress. Never mix colors with whites when you wash. Do you know how to wash wool? She doesn't eat liver, but she loves plain yogurt, with sugar.

No, it couldn't be true. Nanou would never let me go.

We stood on the platform of the train station. My mother was holding my hand. Nanou, her husband, Yves, and my three sisters were forming a half circle around me. Nanou kept a straight face. Yes, she was going to let me go. Something inside me froze up. I could keep a straight face too. Why should I show my emotions if it didn't matter?

It was only later, when I reached my twenties, that Nanou's oldest daughter Francoise explained to me what my departure had meant to Nanou and the family as a whole. For the first time, Nanou's sense of appropriateness had failed to guide her in making decisions she felt were right. She felt it was wrong for my mother to claim me back, after all those years, and it was clearly not in my interest. Besides, she considered me as her daughter, and loved me. Was that to be dismissed, too? However, my mother had a legal claim on her own child, it was not appropriate to fight her in that right. If Nanou was to show her feelings of distress about my leaving to me, wasn't she undermining my mother's position? Wasn't she fostering a sense of protest in me, thus making my inevitable departure harder?

After I had left, the family was in disarray. My mother had taken a member of their family away; it was a legal abduction no one could do anything about. The girls, especially Catherine, cried a lot. Nanou was in a dark mood for months, and she never again consented to taking in another child who needed long-term care. But she did manage to convince my mother to bring me back during the summers. So at the end of June, every year, I went home.

II

For a long time I thought my separation from Nanou had not left any scars: the emotional upheaval and the pain were replaced by a large black hole in my memory. I did not think much of it until I went to college and found that my inner compass had broken down, that I questioned everything including myself. I chose to measure myself relative to the abilities of people who stuck out for specific talents. I would look at Klaus for his perseverance and drive, which allowed him to sit twelve hours and more at this desk and study; Tamara and Stephan had the ability to give quick and brilliant answers in political discussions, no matter how large the auditorium; Martin's sense of humor mixed with his uninhibited anti-authoritarian behavior could make any pompous professor cry or leave the room in a fit of rage and was something I didn't even know how to emulate; Wolfgang studied only half as much as me and passed his tests with better grades; Willi's oratory abilities allowed him to stand in front of two hundred students and deliver long, improvised and interesting speeches. They all were friends, and I tried to reach the standards each of their talents set, never being quite on their level. I felt inferior. At times I didn't understand why they befriended me, I who had nothing extraordinary to offer, except the will to strive for those standards. I felt like a fraud who had succeeded in fooling everyone into believing I was part of the group. Secretly, I was living the life of a tightrope walker. Tightrope walkers have one thing in common: the way they see the world. We choose to walk on tightropes from one building to another, even though it would be easier to just walk across the street, and climb up the stairs of the very same building. Why do we do that? Because we have no sense of balance, which makes us determined to exercise it in every possible way. Hence, crossing the street is out. What makes you a good tightrope walker? You need a sense of goal; you need to set the highest standards to face your fear of falling. The goal isn't that important, but while you're on the rope, it is everything. Only the best tightrope walkers walk with somebody. Naturally, it is more difficult to balance when somebody is up there with you. So for the largest part, tightrope walking is a lonely business. There isn't that much room for love. But whether you're alone or with somebody, it confirms the walker's view that we're meant to be alone, and struggle alone. Looking at the sky is nice, but it's a luxury one can't afford when one is seeking balance.

Ever since I fell in love with Sam, tightrope walking is a skill I am trying to forget, often successfully. I live with Sam and our son, Ben, in the U.S. now. But sometimes I need to go back to Paris and see Nanou, whose compass has always been intact. Nanou's world and mine couldn't be more different. I'm uprooted; she is not. I cook every cuisine imaginable; she sticks to all things French. I don't believe in God; she is an active Catholic. I love books and ideas; she watches games on TV. I married a Jew; she has never seen one in her life. She doesn't understand how I live in America. I tell her I could live anywhere. However, these differences will never undo the bond we have. I will always be her daughter and she my first mother. I know it the minute she opens the door, dressed as usual in her simple skirt and white blouse. She calls me "my big one," as if I were a kid, and I feel five years old again. She greets me by kissing me on the right, the left, and the right cheek. I clean her refrigerator and carry her bags when she goes food shopping. She tells me she has missed me all her life. I give her the pearls I inherited from my mother, knowing I will never wear them. We peel potatoes and talk about husbands, children, and my mother. She makes my favorite dishes: stuffed tomatoes, breadpudding, and ratatouille. I ask for recipes. She shudders at the idea of some of the things I eat. I sew on buttons; she washes my laundry.

Sometimes when the world seems to have grown too large for me, I wish I could have stayed in Nanou's safe world forever. In those moments it seems to me that we can only feel safe in a small universe, and that as we choose to open ourselves to what is unknown we lose an element of security and belonging. I think of my son, Ben, who is the same age I was when my mother took me to Austria. Ben often complains that he does not see enough of his friends, of his cousins and grandparents in New Jersey, Pennsylvania, Florida, and New York. But even if I tried, I could not offer Ben the life Nanou had given me. It was a life where people did not move away, a life with many kids in the family to play with and a strong belonging to one place. A world in which you can contemplate the sky, your body firmly planted on the ground, and you know: whatever your fate is, you'll have the strength to embrace it.

Backstroke

BY DONNA J. KUETHE

ONE SUMMER EVENING, SWIMMING IN THE POOL AT MY condominium, I got to thinking about the elementary backstroke.

Though I spend hours swimming laps—at my condominium, at the health club—and see a ton of swimmers at varying levels of fitness and ability, I never see anyone propelling themselves up and down, lap after lap, on their backs recalling the words of past swimming instructors: "Up-out-together-GLIDE, 1-2-3."

And yet, what I remember most of umpteen years of American Red Cross swimming lessons at Camp Indian Run is the elementary backstroke. We spent an inordinate amount of time learning, practicing, and perfecting it. Thumbs to your armpits; then arms straight out; pull down; all perfectly coordinated with dropping your legs from the knees, rotating out; the arms ending at your side at the exact moment your legs finish the "whip" of the "whip" kick. Then, the most important part—"GLIDE, 1-2-3."

I was not alone there in Advanced Beginners. I suspect there are millions of us who have perfected the elementary backstroke. But who does it?

It is not an Olympic event. It isn't done in triathlon competitions. It's not "in" at health club pools.

So, I wonder why so much of my youth was spent on learning something so useless. I know the Red Cross' explanation. At least the one I used to give when, yes, I became a swimming instructor at Camp Indian Run. If you were ever swimming a very long distance and got tired, you could roll over on your back and do the elementary backstroke.

The truth is the elementary backstroke isn't any more lifesaving than, say, the sidestroke—which also didn't make it into the Olympic Games. Besides, the thing the American Red Cross hammered into me as a student and a teacher was never to swim beyond my capabilities; to always have a life jacket on in a boat so if I capsized out in the Bay of Fundy or the Bering Strait I wouldn't drown.

So, what good is the elementary backstroke? Maybe it's not good for anything besides itself. Maybe all those Advanced Beginners weren't learning the elementary backstroke for any other reason than as a way to propel themselves through water. It wasn't preparation for competitive swimming; it wasn't necessarily to save your life; it was just the elementary backstroke.

So one evening alone in a pool (and yes, the American Red Cross taught me never to swim alone), after I did a couple of laps of freestyle (we learned it as the crawl at Camp Indian Run) and breaststroke and the real backstroke, I brought my thumbs to my armpits and shot straight out with my arms in perfect coordination with my legs and the "whip" kick. I snapped it all together and glided 1-2-3.

I looked at a royal blue evening sky; an orange full moon. My arms pushed against the warm water. Glide. I learned well. I have a hell of a glide.

As I glided I couldn't help but think, if only the elementary backstroke had been an Olympic event, I might have been a gold medalist. My life might have been different—a Speedo contract, my face on a Wheaties box.

Then again, probably not. Maybe that's why I like it so much.

Maybe we need to learn more things like the elementary backstroke. More things that don't lead to something bigger, better, and faster. Things with a glide. More things you can perfect at ten years old at Camp Indian Run and know you learned it. Something you can still enjoy some thirty years later in the quiet solitude of a pool. There is no advanced elementary backstroke. No where else to go.

I pull and glide. I watch the sky. I just am, there in the pool. Not trying to set a world record; not even trying to improve my fitness level. Pulling and gliding. Me and the elementary backstroke. Just as we are.

Saying Kaddish for Peter
BY MICHAEL LOWENTHAL

THERE WAS AN ANGEL IN MY GRANDFATHER'S OBITUARY. HE WAS there, crouched between the lines of the *Boston Globe* clipping my father had sent, waiting for me to discover him.

Reading this utterly public recounting of my grandfather's life seemed a violation of his trust, when in the privacy of our home so little had ever been told. My father's father was a storyteller, but his tales were Talmudic, intellectual word games, never anything about his own life. He and my grandmother had escaped Hitler's Germany miraculously late, and they refused to speak about their lives before America.

Although almost all of the obituary's facts were news to me, most fit snugly within the image I had of my Papa Eric, a formidable, white-goateed rabbi with a severe accent. But one brief, chillingly matter-of-fact paragraph stunned me to a halt: "Rabbi Lowenthal and his wife, Suzanne (Moos), fled to New York in July 1939, escaping the Nazi purge of the Jews. However, a son, Peter, from an earlier marriage, was a victim of the Holocaust."

A son? Peter? Why had nobody ever told me about this man? The fact of the earlier marriage had been alluded to vaguely but never discussed, even when a daughter from that marriage visited one holiday. But nobody had ever mentioned Peter.

I was midway through my fifteenth year. Like most boys that age, I was struggling with raging hormones, but there was the confusing twist that my crushes were on other boys. Since my parents' divorce four years earlier I had been living with my mother and sister, a life nearly devoid of older male figures. I yearned for a big brother or uncle, someone I could trust with my secret.

Now, with a single line of the newspaper's cold black type, I was in one staggering instant granted and then deprived of an Uncle Peter.

I asked a few tentative questions about this mystery relative, but nobody in my family wanted to talk. The person who would know the most—even though Peter was not her son—was my grandmother. But her own father had been killed at Thereisenstadt, and I couldn't ask her to dredge up those painful memories.

So, knowing nothing more than the single sentence in the *Boston Globe*, I developed my own stories about Uncle Peter.

From the start I felt a strange, visceral connection to this gift of a relative. Sometimes a child will be born with red hair or green eyes, some trait exhibited by neither parent, and it will only be an uncle or cousin with the same features who proves that the new child is one of the tribe. Peter as I conjured him in the following years was precisely such a genetic match. Like identical twins separated at birth and then reunited as adults on "Unsolved Mysteries," a miraculously revived Peter and I would discover amazing similarities: we both drove 1978 Volkswagens, we were both jazz trumpet players, we parted our hair on the same side. In my most private moments I was sure that he, too, was gay.

I never told anybody about my feelings for Peter, embarrassed by what might be taken as desperate wish fulfillment. I distrusted the feelings myself; they seemed too easy, the convenient fantasies of a lonely teenager. But in synagogue, when we recited the mourner's Kaddish, I always said it for him. I would see him sitting on the edge of the bimah, dangling his legs awkwardly as if embarrassed that I would call his name.

Then at this year's seder, the tenth Passover since my grandfather's death, I learned that in his final months, Papa Eric had recorded a cassette of his memories. I asked for a copy of the tape, and when my grandmother gave me one on my next visit I rushed home to listen. I was eager to glean any details I could about my grandfather's sketchy biography. My secret, desperate hope was that he would say something about Peter.

I pressed play and suddenly the room was filled with the gravelly, cigar-stained sound that had haunted my dreams for a decade. In his painfully direct manner, still mixing Germanisms into his stiff

English after forty-five years in America, Papa Eric recounts his devout childhood and his studies at university. He explains his rejection of Orthodox Judaism, choosing to become a merchant instead of a rabbi like his father and grandfather before him.

Fifteen minutes into the monologue, I knew I was getting close. Papa Eric tells of marrying his first wife, then of going to Palestine during the depression of the 1920's. Finally, the payoff: "My former wife arrived . . . giving birth to our son Peter, born in Tel Aviv, February 17, 1924."

I moved to the tape recorder, slid the volume control up to high. There is a sentence about the baby boy's circumcision. Then, with no particular emotion: "On April 9, 1924, we returned to Berlin with our son Peter, who died in Bergen-Belsen concentration camp on March 14, 1945." Without so much as a pause, Papa Eric resumes his account of the Hebrew-character typewriters, flower-pot lamps, and mother-of-pearl jewelry he sold back in Germany.

This is all, I thought? A first-born son, reduced to a couple of dates?

I continued to listen to my grandfather's memories but with only half an ear, distracted by my disappointment. He recounts more of his merchant's life and eventually comes to the sudden death of his father, one of the most prominent Orthodox rabbis in Germany. Papa Eric says that he loved his father and knew it was the old man's "deep sorrow that I had alienated myself from the Jewish tradition."

He describes the large funeral and then sitting shivah, the traditional week-long mourning vigil in the dead man's house. "On about the fourth day," he says, "our son Peter led me into the study."

Subtracting dates in my head, I determined that Peter would have been only four years old. I pictured a tiny dark-haired boy in late 1920's European garb.

"On the huge table he had spread opened books from the bookshelves and told me, 'Study them!' That was like a voice from heaven. At that moment I decided to become a rabbi myself."

I stopped the tape, rewound, and listened again, memorizing instantly the cadence of the sentences and the sound of Papa Eric saying "heaven," a word he never once uttered in my presence.

My grandfather was probably the most anti-mystical person I've ever met. One of my clearest memories is of him at the head of the seder table, quizzing us grandkids on the Pythagorean theorem as if this geometric formula were the Eleventh Commandment. Yet here was his confession of a profound spiritual conversion—and the direct catalyst was Peter.

I have listened to Papa Eric's cassette over and over in the past few months. Strangely, each time I hear the story of Peter and the books—the only account I have of an actual event from his life— he becomes less and less real to me. Did a four-year-old's commandment really change the course of my grandfather's life? Did the actual Peter bear any resemblance to my fantasy uncle sitting before me in synagogue?

But Peter has never been about reality, he has been about possibility: The possibility of a merchant becoming a rabbi, the possibility of a confused gay teenager having somebody to turn to.

I am already three years older than Peter was ever allowed to be. Yet I still think of him as my protecting uncle, my benevolent guardian angel. I know that he waits for me in all the unexpected places.

"Saying Kaddish for Peter" first appeared in *Wrestling with the Angel: Faith and Religion in the Lives of Gay Men*, ed. Brian Bouldrey (New York: Riverhead, 1995).

◧ Canning Jars
BY SANDELL MORSE

THE OLD BLUE-GREEN CANNING JARS, OPAQUE AND BUBBLED, ARE the only things of beauty in this place. I lift them carefully and place them on a cardboard box where the light can shine through. The lids are that old silvery metal, dull and flaking. One of the jars is large, more than a quart. The others are pints, perfect for storing dried beans or lentils. Hanukkah gifts for my sons.

I approach an older man and an older woman sitting on wooden folding chairs in back of the shop—a thrift shop on a country road in rural Virginia.

I'm not the only person in this shop. I've come with a friend, an artist, and the stop is impulsive, a veering off on our way to Crabtree Falls. It's Sunday afternoon, late in November and we know the sun will not shine with such intensity much longer. It's been an unusually warm and sunny fall, and we intend to drive to the falls and bask in the sun's last warm rays.

Another customer talks with the owners, their voices rambling over and around counters and boxes, all stacked and overflowing with baseball caps, glass dishes, ceramic dishes, tottering in towers, glasses stored inside of glasses, old sneakers, old shoes (men's and women's), cotton skirts, woolen skirts, shirts and blouses, dresses and coats, hanging on and off of hangers, plastic bowls, all of it coated with dust or spotted with mildew and smelling musty.

The accent I hear is thick and Southern. The speech is rhythmic, soft and slow, and I'm taken with its lilting sounds. I catch words about sons and guns. "They ain't gonna take mine."

His sons or his guns, I wonder. "I'll take all four of these canning jars, if you give me a good price," I say to the woman.

"You go take a look," she says to the man. "I already marked them down, though. They come in with eight dollars each. More for the big one."

I follow behind the slight, small-boned man, weaving through the aisles. "You make me an offer. Go ahead, put a price on."

I look at the jars, their imperfect bubbles as tiny as pinpricks, as large as beads, all of them trapped inside those blue glass walls. I calculate. Not too low. Not too high. The man waits. It's a game we play. The stakes aren't high. I want the jars, not for myself, but to give as gifts. The total price is $25. I figure a twenty percent discount and offer eighteen, $2 less. I don't know why. Maybe it's the man's eyes, cold, gray and watching me.

He counters with twenty. I shake my head.

Instinctively, I know he'll cave. Won't lose a sale for $2. Now we wait. I walk away, lift a plate, turn it over, check for chips. In the center, pink roses fade and crack. I trace one with my finger, feeling grit. My friend feigns an interest in a mixing bowl. I set the dish back on the stack. "Ready?" I say.

Her head tilts toward the blue-green jars, still sitting on the cardboard box. "Aren't you going to buy them?" she says.

"Guess not."

Before I leave, I make my $18 offer one last time.

The man lifts his chin and looks at his wife who no longer sits in back of the store. She stands now, behind a counter, leaning an elbow on an old cash register. "Up to you," she says to her husband. "A bird in the hand . . ."

"What's the tax?" the man says.

The woman holds a small calculator and punches numbers. "Eighty-one cents," she says.

"Make it nineteen," the man says.

I smile, "Nineteen."

He looks at me, and I expect that he'll smile, too. After all, he's saved face. Nineteen. Less than the twenty, but more than the eighteen I'd offered, originally, so I'm not prepared for what he says, can't believe I'm hearing correctly. I lean in. His words slur. Understanding seeps, slowly, so slowly that he must repeat. "I hate a woman Jew," he says.

The blow is swift, rushing quickly into my stomach where revulsion and fear swirl in a vortex. I'm stunned; my friend is too, and in that instant our glances meet, I see her wince. She feels the blow as keenly as I do, for we are women; we are Jews. We know the same icy fear, bred into us for centuries—flee, but not too swiftly. She walks slowly toward the door, moving backwards. I want to move, but I can't. I feel rooted, rooted and mute, and I wonder: Does he see a telltale sign? Smell an odor?

Absently, I run my thumb over the worn leather and look down to see my brown wallet in my hand, and I know I'll never open it, never take out the bills, never give those beautiful bubbled jars to my sons, and I wonder if I've done something wrong—played the game incorrectly, been too cheap, should've gone up. And so I take whatever it is that is happening here in the room into my gut where it opens up old wounds—taunts on the playground, "dirty Jew," "Christ killer." And later, "jew you down," "Cheap Jew," words that make me into "the other."

I look the man in the eye. "You've just lost a sale, Mister."

In the car, my friend looks for ways to close the wound and scab it over one more time. "He'll look at those jars, and he'll know. They'll sit there. They'll haunt him," she says.

But, it's we who are haunted. All we can talk about is that man, the soft lilt of his speech, his deadpan face, and the way he drew us in. Was he joking? Didn't we get it? Would he have said those words if he knew? His words echo inside the car, woman, Jew, hate, as we try to figure out what went wrong.

We stop talking and drive along without words, lost for these moments in private thoughts. Perhaps like me, my friend looks out at the countryside and tries to recapture the pleasantness of the afternoon—blue sky, rolling hills, a long green valley where cows graze, and seeing those cows, my mind leaps back in time to a ranch in Wyoming. One morning, I awoke to the sorrowful mooing of a herd of cows. It wasn't a sound I'd heard before. Then I heard a series of pops. I knew the sound of the rifle shot, and I'd been warned that the ranch hands would be killing the herd. Too many head to winter over. Still, all that morning and afternoon, I felt sick. Couldn't eat. It was the cows and their awful mooing. I thought of their bulk, and the way they moved, lumbering almost side to side. I thought of their eyes and their moist pink muzzles. I thought of their bones holding up their hairy coats. Nobody else seemed to notice those missing cows.

At supper that night, a Jewish friend and I talked about those missing cows, and what I saw in my mind's eye was a long line of black-coated men walking slowly into a forest. I saw women in dresses clutching children. I saw the shiny boots of the S.S. These are images I carry like the bubbles trapped inside of blue-green glass.

"They told them they were going to another pasture," my friend joked about those cows.

I smiled. It is what Jews do; we laugh instead of cry.

The road narrows. It twists and curves, climbing the mountains, approaching the turnoff to the falls. Beside the road, a stream skims rocks and rushes past. Hawks circle and spiral up into the clear blue sky. Sunlight glitters and dapples the pavement as I drive, and I think I must be nuts, linking a man in a thrift shop in rural Virginia to slaughtered cows on a ranch in Wyoming to dead Jews in a Polish forest, all so distant in place and time. But in my heart, I know I'm not. In fertile soil, misunderstanding takes root, grows and flowers into hate. Best to dig up those roots and dry them out in the glittering sunlight of a nearly perfect autumn day.

Mildred's Snowdrops

BY HILLARY NELSON

MILDRED'S SNOWDROPS ARE IN BLOOM DOWN ON SHAKER ROAD; they light up the leaf-matted earth like pools of warm spring sunlight, though the cold April sky is still spitting rain and snow. This is the first year I've seen them, but Mildred had been telling me about them for years, and when I still lived in New York City she'd call especially every April to say they were up and winter was officially, finally over. I never really understood the tremor of excitement in her voice; the snowdrops didn't even belong to her, they bloomed on an abandoned lot down the road from her house. Besides, I could look out my window to daffodils and tulips, to newly leafed trees and a heavily budded lilac—my snowdrops had come and gone a month or more earlier, and I had forgotten how sweet the first flowers of spring taste to the spirit of a winter-hungry gardener. She always promised to show them to me one day, but last April was the first I spent in Canterbury, and Mildred died two months before the snowdrops bloomed, so I had no one to remind me to go look at them, to see the proof of spring.

And I had a new baby to distract me from the world outside my windows; Oliver was born ten days after his grandmother died, on a snowy night in the heart of February, and it seems as if it were May before I stuck my head out of the nest to smell the fresh air. I walked around the yard, holding the sleeping baby, clicking my tongue at the rampant celandine sprouting everywhere, a weed Mildred had loved as much for its tenacity as its yellow flowers and brilliant orange juice.

"It's a dye plant," she'd tell me over and over, when I cursed the yellow droplets it would leave on my clothes as I yanked it out of my flower beds, "It's very useful. Are you sure you want to get rid of all of it?", knowing full well *that* was a task worthy of Sisyphus.

She'd help me weed, watching me sidelong to see what I was pulling out, gently correcting me when she felt I was being too strict about what I would allow in the garden. Once she held a scallop-shaped leaf of what she called "Jill-over-the-hill," which I had just torn loose from the base of a peony, to my nose so I could admire its spicy scent.

"It does grow a little vigorously, but it makes an excellent under-planting for larger plants, you know, roses, baptisia. . . ."

"Peonies?" I asked, a little testily.

"Certainly, peonies, too," she answered, ignoring my snippiness.

Stinging nettles, she assured me, were delicious in soup and high in vitamin C, and the wildly prolific calendulas, which threat-ened to obliterate every effort I made at a flower border south of the house, she explained, had originated from just a few seeds she had brought back from France, and the people there had gotten them from India, and the petals made a marvelous salve or could be cooked with rice to turn it the most glorious saffron shade.

For several years after we bought the house, we still lived full time in New York City and only visited on odd weekends, and Mil-dred tended the garden in my absence. There was always a bouquet on the kitchen table when we arrived, great shaggy pink peonies with ants still skittering across their petals, or deliciously scented mock-orange, or, best of all, heaps of fragrant lilacs from the enor-mous mound in the backyard, which, Mildred had it from one of the Shaker sisters down the road, had been planted to separate the brothers' outhouse from the sisters' outhouse in the 1800s, when the North Family of Shakers lived here. Mildred always smashed the cut-end of the lilac branches with a stone on the granite steps of the house, before putting them in a vase she had made years before, glazed a lovely soft green, and heavy enough not to tip over under the weight of the blossoms, as they curved downward to touch the table top.

Mildred had lived in our house for over thirty years, before she sold it to us and went to care for my father-in-law, her ex-husband, who was slowly dying from Parkinson's disease, and so I understood when she maintained a certain proprietary feeling about the gar-den. Still, I was not kind. She had an enormous bed of bearded iris, matted with witch grass and plagued with iris borers, which I wrenched out and put in heavy duty trash bags to take to the dump. "I've been growing those since 1958," she told me at dinner that night, and would not respond when I protested they were diseased.

The next morning, I opened one of the bags and pulled out five or six of the healthiest clumps to replant. Mildred greeted them like old friends when they bloomed the next summer, pale lavender and softly fragrant, like old ladies' talcum powder, and grinned at me as if to say, "You see, there's a reason I grew them for twenty-five years."

In the end, I think she forgave me for all of it, the tinkering and cutting and pulling and editing I did in what was, after all, still *her* garden, because she could see I loved it almost as much as she did. And too, she had ways of getting even.

One October, a friend sent me a bushel of daffodil bulbs as a gift and, because we couldn't get up from the city to put them in, Mildred volunteered for the job. She had seen me spend many hours during the summer extricating daffodils and tulips from the middle of the flower beds where she had so carefully planted them long ago—"They get in the way of the perennials," I had explained, ignoring her baleful look—and so she knew that I wanted them placed somewhere their ripening foliage wouldn't interfere with the rest of the garden. "Don't worry," she said, "I know just the place!" The following spring they came up, lovely, nodding clumps of brilliant yellow—in the middle of the lawn. "Aren't they beautiful?" she asked, hands on her hips, beaming and proud. And indeed they were, though it was July before we could mow the lawn.

This spring, Oliver is old enough to entertain himself with ants and rocks, so I am back in the garden, paying attention. And every time I turn a corner, or rake away dead leaves from the flower beds, or glance out the window, I hear Mildred talking to me: "Just look at those crocuses, the way the sun comes through the petals, like stained glass. There are your anemones, Hillary; I said they wouldn't be hardy here. Lucky thing you're such an optimist. Jeezum, the peonies are peeking out already. That one there was given to me by a student in 1967. You might have replanted it a little too shallowly—we'll know if it doesn't bloom." I miss her.

The other day, I stumbled upon Mildred's snowdrops. I had gone out for a run on Shaker Road; it's all uphill for two miles, and when I turn around and run back, it seems it's all uphill in that direction, too, so I run slowly, and take time to look around as I go. In July I might see pink columbine growing among the roadside weeds, in August I keep a watch for wayward red efts to help cross the road as they return to their birth-waters to sleep away the winter. But in April, only the newly emerged tips of daylilies show green in the sandy road edge, there's still not much to see, and so I was day-dreaming when, attracted by a spot of white, I happened to glance through the tangle of underbrush on my left.

I stopped, amazed at what I saw, and walked off the road, pant-ing, to climb a ruined stone wall for a closer look. Here was the crumbling foundation of a house which had burned long ago, just as Mildred had so often described it, and all about it, mounds and mounds and great sweeps of snowdrops, hundreds and thousands of them, blooming furiously, unseen, unaware that the hands which had planted them had long since returned to dust, that the garden which had once contained them had been replaced by choking bit-tersweet—that Mildred hadn't been there that spring to welcome them. But I could hear her in my mind, just as clearly as if she had been standing next to me: "Gosh, they're something. Well, Hillary, it's spring. It's spring at last."

I stayed for awhile, long enough for my heart to stop pounding, then picked a few of the tiny blossoms and put them in the pocket of my sweatshirt and started for home.

On the way, I remembered that, for a long time, Mildred had tried to get me to dig up a white lilac that grew near that cellar hole, to plant in front of our house. I was vaguely shocked by the sugges-tion; my mother-in-law was a devout woman in her eighties and it seemed strange that she could contemplate larceny with such equanimity.

"We can't do that, Mildred!" I said, "That lilac doesn't belong to us!"

"Yes it does," she had insisted. "How can it belong so someone who never sees it bloom, who's letting it slowly die underneath the bittersweet? We ought to dig it up, Hillary, we really *ought* to."

But I was firm. I believe nothing I ever did disappointed Mildred as much as my refusal to rescue that lilac. I wondered, as I ran, if it were still there, if I could find it, where I would plant it if I did.

When I got home, I put the flowers into cold water in a sea-glass soft medicine bottle that Mildred had once dug up from deep in our garden. While I was showing my daughter the place where bright green hearts hide under a snowdrop's petals, my husband came in.

"Where'd you get those?" he asked.

"From your Mom," I said, and he smiled. He knew exactly what I meant.

Visitation
BY PAT PARNELL

I WEAR MY MOTHER'S SKIN, SNUG ACROSS MY SHOULDERS.

In this surprise visit, she shares my bed and my body. Her head nestles against my neck, cuddling to my left ear. Her silver hair is soft, comforting, like a toddler's favorite blanket. I sleep on my right side so I won't crush her against my pillow. When I look in the mirror, I see her face with mine, her blue eyes staring at me with their hawk stare.

The skin of her arms covers my arms, warmly, snugly, her hands hanging above my hands like ruffles coming out of a sleeve. She is wrapped around my ribs; her heavy breasts sag swinging from my chest. My buttocks fit neatly into hers, her thighs grip mine. Her feet flop over my feet like fringed shoe-flaps.

When I was very young, I shared her bed sometimes, when we took our naps together in the big mahogany four-poster. Her broad, smooth back was toward me, her skin gleaming opalescent in the shaded room. Then I would nestle up to her, secure and comforted in her warmth, like one silver teaspoon to another. Her body had its own faintly earthy smell, a smell that clung to her clothes, years after she had worn them. When we emptied her bureau drawers, I put on her cardigan sweater and held a blouse up to my body, breathing the trace of her.

She loved to swim, and now we swim together in the warm, chlorine-scented pool in the old town she loved so well. Her body hugs mine beneath the bathing suit; her skin moves with mine. Her fingers and mine play paddycakes in the water; her feet and mine flip, frog-kicking.

After our swim, I take her to the mall. Everywhere, people crowding the bright promenade wear at least one skin besides their own. Some have two or three heads bobbing along beside their own, eyes rolling sideways or straight up to the sky.

People don't have to be dead to have someone wear their skins.

Do the wearers even know the skins are there? Do the owners know someone is wearing their skin?

Hercules wears a lion skin, hide of his adversary, the Nemean terror. The great head hangs behind him, mouth open in a final fierce roar, eyes still staring.

My mother is not my adversary. Once past the skirmishes of my adolescence, years ago, we made our peace, friends as well as family. She did for me what she could not do for herself for all her education and experience. Throughout her ninety-plus years, she judged herself by what she felt was her mother's judgment of her, always finding herself lacking.

My grandmother died when my mother was about forty. In the final illness at home, mother, my aunt, and a nurse cared for Grandmother. After her death, while my aunt and the nurse accompanied the hearse into town, my mother stayed behind to clear out Grandmother's bedroom. She was down on her hands and knees, in the closet, sweeping out the corners carefully, just as her mother had taught her. Suddenly, she told me, she felt her mother present, standing in the doorway to the bedroom. Mother froze, suspended, back in her girlhood again. Her only thought was, "What have I done wrong now?" Her mind was blank, awaiting condemnation; she didn't know how long the moment lasted.

Then her mother was gone. "I thought later," Mother said, "that she had come back to tell me good-bye." But the visit brought no peace.

Mother was a social worker; she knew about carrying the dead weight of the past. "He can't get his father off his back," Mother would say of a client. Or of another, "She needs to get her mother off her back." She just couldn't heal herself. One of the last memories she let go, as her mind went on ahead of her, was the coal in her Christmas stocking the year she was seven. Her mother had decided she was selfish and greedy.

But negative images do not fit this visit. My mother is not weighing me down, trying to run my life. She has not been a monkey on my back. Not a succubus straddling my shoulders and cracking her whip, making me stumble, panting, a two-legged pony in the race of life.

Jesus the Good Shepherd carries the rescued lamb to the sheepfold, carries it home across his shoulders. Saint Christopher carries the child Jesus on his back across the raging river, carries the child who becomes heavier and heavier at every step with the weight of all the sins of the earth. And Aeneas carries his father, old Anchises, safely out of burning Troy.

This visit feels like love. Why has she come, across the miles and the years? I study her face in my mirror, looking for answers. But the hawk eyes stare beyond me, blue as the vistas she is seeing, ahead on her long journey.

Now, as suddenly as it began, the visit has ended. She is gone, as quickly and quietly as she came. She has flicked me easily out of the pod of her skin. Flicked me with one thumb as though she were shelling peas on a June afternoon, sitting in the sagging basket-weave of the old green rocker on the screened back porch. Freshly shelled, I glisten in my new birth.

First published in the *New Hampshire College Journal*, Spring 1996, vol. 14, no. 1.

A Father's Eyes
BY STEPHEN SCHULTZ

IT IS INTERNSHIP. AUTUMN. SHORTER DAYS, LONGER NIGHTS. I AM doing pediatrics. It is 3:30 A.M. I am answering a page to talk with parents on the infant floor. I have not yet been to bed, and my eyes have begun to burn. I want to lie down. I want to sleep. I enter the room. A young woman with long frizzy red hair sits just inside the door, facing away from me. She is rocking in a rocker, in short, clipped strokes that seem odd, almost frenetic. A man is sleeping on a cot, turned away from me. He is wearing Birkenstocks; the soles face me.

"Excuse me . . ." I trail off softly. It has been more than half an hour since I was called. I hope the question has answered itself. She looks up. I see now she's holding a baby.

"I'm Dr. Schultz, the resident on call. Did you need to see me?"

"Oh, yes, Doctor. I'm glad you're here. I thought Daniel was looking a little bit more swollen, but I think he's better now. He's starting to breast-feed a bit again, see there?"

I look down at a floppy, grotesquely swollen infant, perhaps 6 weeks old. He has a tube coming out of one nostril, and an IV in one hand. A nipple is being brushed across his lips as his mother persistently guides her breast into his mouth, but he is not making any movement at all. His eyes are swollen shut. My God, this kid looks bad. I am suddenly, painfully aware that in my haste to get to sleep I have neglected to check the chart, or even to locate the name on the sign-out sheet to find out the principal diagnosis. What an idiot. A slow sensation of mild panic begins, similar to when I have to introduce someone whose name I should definitely know but cannot remember. This woman continues to talk, almost to herself. I am suddenly reminded of a crazy woman in *King of Hearts*, clutching a blanket she thinks is her baby. This kid is as interactive as a blanket.

Suddenly I know. This is the infant presented at morning report two days ago. Had a low-grade temp for two days, then spiked high. They took him to their doctor the third day, after he became lethargic. An LP was done. Sheets of polys, sheets of gram-positive cocci. Decreasing mental status. Transferred here. CT scan showed cerebral edema. NG tube placed secondary to inability to feed. Difficulty with fluid balance. Grim prognosis, unlikely to recover neurologically. Toasted squash.

"What do you think, Doctor?" I look down. Mom is looking up at me. I don't know what the question is. What am I doing here?

"What happened?" I turn around. Dad has woken up and is sitting on the edge of the bed. His hair is rumpled. He is hunched forward, his arms straight down at his sides, his hands clutching the sides of the cot.

I don't understand. "What?"

He straightens, looks up, and our eyes lock. "What happened?" he repeats softly, but more clearly.

I only have to look into those eyes for a second to know what he is asking. I realize he's not asking what happened to make this doctor come into this room at this hour. Three days later this man is still trying to sort out what happened to his son, what happened to the baby he already loved more fiercely than he thought it was possible to love. Will he live? Will he breast-feed again? Will he walk? Will he ever laugh with me? Oh, Sweet Jesus, please, what has happened to my son?

He looks away, and shakes his head. "I don't understand," he mumbles.

I stand in the center of the room. I don't know what to say, and very quickly I am unable to say anything. It is all I can do to suppress the ball of grief that is growing in my chest. Images of my own son fill my mind: the toothless grins and sweet breast-milk breath as a baby, the squeals of laughter of a mischievous toddler, the warmth of his sleeping body nestled in my protecting arms, the innocent questions that challenge me, make me pause, make me smile. The tricycle rides, the snowball fights, the ice cream cones, the love. And through it all, the fierce desire to protect him, to allow him to explore, but to shelter him from all harm. The love.

The rocker squeaks faintly, rhythmically.

Grief rises into my throat. "I . . . excuse me," is all I can say, and before I can even get out the door the tears start. I walk quickly past the nurses station, and the sobs begin, like the vomiting spell that can be suppressed only so long, and once started cannot be controlled. A runner from transport walks by, staring. I duck into an unlit conference room, lean against the wall, and surrender to it, purge myself. It is the discordance of those father's eyes and the cynicism of "toasted squash," of sleep deprivation, of the insecurity of internship, of the fears of my own son's mortality. I cry for a long time.

My beeper goes off. I wipe my face, blow my nose. I don't go back into the room, and I don't leave a note.

I never see them again.

First published in the *Journal of the American Medical Association,* April 20, 1994, vol. 271, no. 15.

Rabbit Doll
BY PAT WILSON

I FOUND HER AT THE STRATHAM MEMORIAL SCHOOL CRAFT FAIR last Saturday. Around one booth huddled children and parents touching an array of doll-size dresses in blues, greens, reds and yellows, plaids and prints. Amid the array of dresses sat cotton rabbit dolls. There I knelt, a 43-year-old single career woman with no children, looking for a doll I did not need.

Each rabbit doll looked basically the same: long floppy ears with ribbon ties. Each was the size of a small cat. It was the placement of the button eyes that created variations of expression. I became choosy about dress, expression, and the way the doll felt. I replaced each doll carefully, as though she would remember my hands. Then, I saw her.

She sat on the second shelf, stooped because it was too short a space for her. She wore a lavender and pink print dress. She balanced well on my thigh, her legs dangling over the side of mine. Her eyes seemed bright; her expression content. She smelled of clean, fresh cotton.

"What will I do with you?" I asked myself. My nieces are grown, my nephews won't appreciate you. I already have gifts for my sister and my mother. There was no answer. There was no putting her back either. "I guess you are for me."

I paid the clerk $19.00 and would not let her put the doll in a bag. She nestled comfortably in the crook of my arm, resting against my side as I finished wandering and left to go home. Outside, the November light made her cheeks seem rosier as though the cold wind had invigorated her as it did me. As I placed her in the seat of my car, I grinned. She looked so comfortable against the light gray up-holstery that I buckled her in. We drove home listening to Yanni's "Keys to Imagination."

I did not want to put her away when I arrived home. I carried her as I heated water for tea and put away the other gifts I had bought. She sat with me as I drank Plantation Mint and scanned the news-paper. I carried her as I straightened my desk. She sat in a chair in my office as I typed.

Finally, I took her upstairs to see how she would look on the blue-green quilt of my bed. I stood in the center of that light and airy room and gave her a little toss toward the ceiling. She appeared momentarily suspended as images of children washed through me. Children I taught. The neighbor's children, my nieces, my nephews. None of them my own. None would be mine; I'd decided years ago not to have children. Though I know the decision was the right one, and though largely at peace, tears blurred my sight. I caught the rabbit doll in a lavender dress. I held her close, and let myself dream of the daughter I would not have.

Recommended Reading

WRITERS LEARN A GREAT DEAL FROM OTHER WRITERS. SCRUTINIZE their techniques as if looking through a magnifying glass and adapt them to your purposes. Pay attention to voice, style, form, and subject matter. Reread favorite passages, often, and type whole pages, take in words, figure out how an essay is built.

A good place to start is with an anthology. Find one that interests you at a bookstore. University bookstores often have a good selection. There are two ways to approach an anthology: Read each piece in it even if you don't like it; in this way, you'll expose yourself to many writers' subjects and styles. Try to learn from each. The second way is to commit yourself only to reading the first page or two of each piece. The theory is, if a writer doesn't interest you, you won't learn as much as if you love his work; you'll find many writers to admire; why waste time on those you don't.

If, in any anthology, you discover a writer who fascinates you, look up more of her work in the library.

Philip Lopate's *The Art of the Essay* includes works by contemporary and long-dead writers. His introduction is a clear, intelligent discussion of what an essay is. It also reviews the history of essay writing.

If you've found *True Stories* helpful (and we hope you did), you may want to check out other how-to books, including our first, *Creating the Story: Guides for Writers*. Donald Murray has written inspiring and practical how-tos, including *A Writer Teaches Writing* and *Write to Learn*. Anne Lamott's *Bird by Bird* and Natalie Goldberg's *Writing Down the Bones* are bestsellers beloved by many writers. Barry Lane and Bruce

Ballenger teach writing through exercises in *Discovering the Writer Within*. Lane devotes an entire book to the art of revision in *After the End*. A classic writing manual is William Zinsser's *On Writing Well*. For the basics of punctuation, grammar, and common sense, try another classic, *Elements of Style* by Stunk and White (E.B. White, that is—one of the finest nonfiction writers of this century).

For stories of writers' early lives, try A *Child's Christmas in Wales* by Dylan Thomas, Doris Kearns Goodwin's *Wait 'Til Next Year*, Frank McCourt's *Angela's Ashes*, Maya Angelou's *I Know Why the Caged Bird Sings*, Eudora Welty's *One Writer's Beginnings*, or Elizabeth Yates' *Spanning Time*.

We've mentioned many writers we admire throughout this book. More complete references to their work follow in the selected bibliography, but here are some of our favorites, by category:

- *Humor*: Bailey White, S. J. Perleman, James Thurber, E. B. White, Dave Barry, Nora Ephron

- *Aging*: May Sarton, M.F.K. Fisher, Helen Nearing

- *Nature*: Aldo Leopold, Loren Eiseley, Annie Dillard, David Carroll

- *Spirituality*: Peter Mattieson, Thomas Merton

- *Medicine*: Richard Selzer, Lewis Thomas

- *Short stories* (the essay and short story forms sometimes blur): Ann Charter's anthology *The Story and Its Writer*; also *Best American Short Stories* (published annually). Among our favorite short story writers: Eudora Welty, Thomas Williams, Alice Munro, Ursula Hegi, Raymond Carver, Ethan Canin, Tim O'Brien, Grace Paley. Read *Best American Essays*, published annually.

One of the joys of writing is discovering colleagues and learning from them. Ask your friends, teachers, librarians, bookstore managers for recommendations. Find writers who write somewhat like you and others who are very different from you but whom you admire. Read commercial magazines to see what others are up to. Try *Atlantic Monthly*, *Harpers*, *The New Yorker*. Read literary magazines such as *The North American Review*, *Sewanee Review*, *The Paris Review*, *Ploughshares*. Find the literary magazines published in your region—often they are sponsored by colleges or cultural organizations.

Read poetry. Buy an anthology. Learn from poets how to pay particular attention to every nuance of language. Among our favorites: Wesley McNair, Charles Simic, Mekeel McBride, Donald Hall, Maxine Kumin, Marie Harris, and Maya Angelou.

A *selected bibliography of books mentioned in* True Stories

Ballenger, Bruce and Lane, Barry, *Discovering the Writer Within* (Writer's Digest Books, 1989).

Carroll, David, *The Year of the Turtle: A Natural History* (Camden House, 1991).

Charters, Ann, ed., *The Story and Its Writer* (St. Martin's, 1991).

Garcia Marquez, Gabriel, *Chronicle of a Death Foretold* (Random House, 1982).

Goodwin, Doris Kearns, *Wait 'Til Next Year* (Simon & Schuster, 1997)

Griffin, Pat, ed., "Diamonds, Dykes and Double Plays" from A *Whole Other Ball Game: Women's Literature on Women's Sport*, Joli Sandoz, ed. (Noonday Press of Farrar Straus Girous, 1997).

Gutkind, Lee, ed., *The Essayist at Work, Profiles of Creative Nonfiction Writers* (Heinemann, 1998).

Gutkind, Lee, *Surviving Crisis* (Tarcher Putnam, 1997).

Goldberg, Natalie, *Writing Down The Bones* (Shambhala, 1986).

Jager, Ronald, *Last House on the Road* (Beacon, 1994).

Kelly, James Patrick, *Think Like a Dinosaur and Other Stories* (Golden Gryphon Press, 1997).

Junger, Sebastian, *The Perfect Storm* (Norton, 1997).

Lamott, Anne, *Bird By Bird* (Anchor Books, 1994).

Lane, Barry, *After the End* (Heinemann, 1993).

Lopate, Philip, *The Art of The Personal Essay* (Anchor Books, 1994).

Lowenthal, Michael, "Saying Kaddish for Peter" from *Wrestling With the Angel: Faith and Religion in the Lives of Gay Men*, Brian Bouldrey, ed. (Riverhead, 1995).

Recommended Reading

McCloskey, Robert, *One Morning in Maine* (Viking, 1980).

Paley, Grace, *The Collected Stories* (Farrar Straus Giroux, 1994).

Murray, Donald, *Write to Learn* (Holt Rinehart Winston, 1987).

Murray, Donald, *Shoptalk: Learning to Write with Writers* (Boynton Cook/ Heinemann, 1990).

Shepard, Robert and Thomas, James, eds., *Sudden Fiction* (Norton, 1996).

White, Bailey, *Mama Makes Up Her Mind and Other Dangers of Southern Living* (Vintage Books of Random House, 1994).

Williams, Thomas, *Leah, New Hampshire* (Morrow, 1992).

Yates, Elizabeth, *Spanning Time* (Cobblestone, 1996).